ALSO BY JOHN M. GOTTMAN

The Heart of Parenting:
Raising an Emotionally Intelligent Child

Why Marriages Succeed or Fail . . . And How You
Can Make Yours Last

When Men Batter Women

New Insights into Ending Abusive Relationships

Neil S. Jacobson, Ph.D.

John M. Gottman, Ph.D.

SIMON & SCHUSTER

Simon & Schuster
1230 Avenue of the Americas
New York, NY 10020

First Simon & Schuster trade paperback edition January 2007

SIMON & SCHUSTER and colophon are registered trademarks of Simon & Schuster, Inc.

Designed by

Manufactured in the United States of America

10 9 8 7 6 5 4 3 2 1

Library of Congress Cataloging-in-Publication Data

ISBN-13: 978-1-4165-5133-1
ISBN-10:   1-4165-5133-6

For information about special discounts for bulk purchases, please contact Simon & Schuster Special Sales at 1-800-456-6798 or business@simonandschuster.com

Authors' Note

Throughout this book, we illustrate our research findings through the use of actual cases from our ten-year, two-hundred-couple study. We requested, but did not require, that couples participating in our study consent to our using relevant events from their lives in this book and other publications. Permission was required from both partners. Most couples gave us permission. Only those who did are described in this book.

We made every effort to protect the anonymity and confidentiality of those who participated in our research. When cases are described, names, locations, and other details are altered or disguised in such a way as to preclude the recognition of these people by outsiders. However, we did not change any significant details about their relationships: the content of the arguments, the words that are used, and the narratives about violence and emotional abuse are unaltered.

We used statistical procedures to verify the accuracy of couples' narratives regarding their violent histories and episodes, even though we did not witness any acts of physical abuse. We were the first investigators to actually observe the nonviolent arguments of severe batterers and their battered wives. Thus, we could see for ourselves what their nonviolent arguments looked like. We also collected detailed narratives regarding both violent and nonviolent arguments that occurred at home.

We found that partners' descriptions of nonviolent arguments at home corresponded quite closely to what we observed in the laboratory. Therefore, we were able to infer that their descriptions of the nonviolent arguments at home were accurate. There was good agreement between husbands and wives regarding details of both violent and nonviolent arguments. Since husbands and wives agreed on the violent arguments, and their reports of nonviolent arguments corresponded quite closely to what we observed in the laboratory, we are confident that the narratives described in this book are accurate.

Acknowledgments

We would like to express our gratitude to Judy Woodburn, our "freelance" editor, who read and thoroughly critiqued each chapter in this book before Simon & Schuster ever had a chance to see it. Judy's editorial feedback was invaluable, and we don't think we could have written this book without it. Judy's tremendous gift for seeing the prose from the perspective of the reader sent us tumbling off the ivory tower. She helped us sharpen our thinking, improve our organization and structure, and bring some of the experiences of the batterers and battered women to life. We had no professional writer: it was just us, and Judy.

We would also like to express special thanks to Sara Berns, the research assistant who assembled our biographical material. Without the hours and hours she spent watching tapes of our exit interviews, observing videotaped interactions, and assembling material from the interviews, we would have had great difficulty putting together all of the pieces to present integrated cases.

We had help from many in the conducting of this research project. In addition to Sara Berns, special thanks to Eric Gortner, who was up until 2:00 A.M. on many an evening finding mistakes in the data, fixing them, and helping us interpret what we found. Our original project coordinators, Jennifer Waltz and Regina Rushe, helped us get the project off the ground, and also worked overtime to ensure that everything ran smoothly. Peter Fehrenbach, a psychologist at the Seattle VA Hospital, was an excellent clinical consultant, and we appreciate the help we received from Dr. Ann Ganley in designing our study in a way which minimized the risks for battered women. Finally, Dr. Amy Holtzworth-Munroe, now at Indiana University, was instrumental in helping us procure the federal funds necessary to conduct the study.

Our editor at Simon & Schuster, Bob Bender, has handled us as well as our manuscript with skill, patience, and encouragement from the beginning. All through the process, our agents—Katinka Matson and John Brockman—were optimistic, encouraging, and supportive. And, of course, the bottom line: they got us the book contract. Here in Seattle, Judith Kelson whipped the manuscript into publication readiness. We are also lucky enough both to be married to social scientists—Virginia Rutter and Julie Gottman—and thus received not only emotional support, but substantive feedback from beginning to end. Last but not least, we thank Hara Marano for helping us draft the original book proposal, so that Katinka and John could impress Bob, so that we could write this book for Simon & Schuster.

To Virginia Rutter and Julie Gottman

Contents

Contents

1

A Unique Research Project on Domestic Violence

When Vicky returned to Seattle, she had no job, no place to live, no support from her family, and no career. She was twenty-seven, and as she walked down the street, men turned to look at her. She was blond, with high cheekbones, and dazzling blue eyes.

She had no interest in meeting a man, but George had other ideas. He was sitting in a bar with his drinking buddies when Vicky walked in. They all stared at her, smirking, and each one started joking about making this conquest, but it was George who made the bizarre bet. He bet them $100 that he could get her to marry him within six months. Sealing the bet with a handshake, George walked up to her and offered to buy her a drink.

"He was one hundred percent charming," Vicky later recalled. "I fell in love with him almost instantly, and I thought he was falling in love with me. He was perfect. He was wonderful, smart, an undiscovered genius. He told me all about how great his family was, what a wonderful sailor he was, and all of his plans to become an admiral. He fed me all this bullshit about his family values which I bought hook, line, and sinker."

Somehow, says Vicky, even in this first conversation, George was able to ferret out what was most important to her. "He somehow knew that the 'family' thing would hook me. I had spent twelve years rebelling against my family. But deep down inside, a family is what I wanted. That was my dream. And somehow, George knew it.

"Still," said Vicky, "I had no intention of getting married again. I was trying to figure out my life. Where was I going to go to school? Was I going to be an artist? But he really made me feel like he loved me." Vicky wasn't thinking about having children either, but suddenly she was pregnant. George saw to that. After all, he wanted to win his bet. "As soon as I got pregnant," she says, "he proposed. He knew deep down I wanted a family.

"At the time," said Vicky, "the whole thing seemed very romantic: me pregnant and him begging me to marry him. And, almost six months from the day we met, we got married. He was so charming, and so romantic that I thought it was just meant to be."

One of George's friends had told Vicky that George was dangerous, and advised her not to marry him. He told her that she was going to "burn with this guy." They were frightened of him, but Vicky was not. The first sign of real trouble came soon after their daughter Christi was born. Vicky was comforting the baby, but the baby wouldn't stop crying. Suddenly, George yelled at Vicky for not being able to "shut the baby up" and threw a toy at her. Vicky felt a chill run through her. She became very quiet.

A few days after this incident, George began what was to become a familiar refrain. He started quietly talking about his plans to kill three former buddies from his teenage days. He said they were slime and therefore deserved to die. Boasting that there were other people he had already killed, he insisted that his vengeance against the former buddies was not a big deal. George was setting the scene for Vicky to view him as dangerous. What was to become his typical use of violence as a way of intimidating and controlling her had begun.

Martha and Don

This had been a hard day for Don. There were rumors of layoffs, and he could see the handwriting on the wall. His immediate supervisor had been on his case for sleeping late, and Don sensed that he would soon become a liability to this man's inevitable rise to the top. His supervisor had called him in and then told him not to worry, but he had that stupid grin on his face when he said it. Don was getting sick and tired of doing his work well and never getting the recognition he deserved. He was sure he was about to get caught in some kind of vise he had no control over. It had definitely been a miserable day.

Now Don was test-driving the car he had asked his wife, Martha, to pick up from the garage. As he listened to the motor, he knew instantly that he had again been hoodwinked by the garage. They had charged for the tune-up and the work they had done but that damn rattle was still there going up hills, even though he had told them to look at it. As he drove back home his smoldering fury increased. He was so mad when he pulled into the driveway of his home that he almost smashed into his wife's car. She was calmly cooking dinner when he came into the house in a frenzy. "What is it with you?" he said. "Are you really that stupid?" Don railed. "Couldn't you just tell that the damn car wasn't running right, that you'd been had by those damn mechanics?"

"Is something wrong with the car?" said Martha calmly. "It sounded fine to me."

Don continued railing against the garage mechanics and against Martha for not standing up to them. Martha started defending herself, telling Don that even though she knew nothing about cars, she resented being called stupid. He was starting to see red. Don warned her to shut up. Then Martha said that if Don was such a big man why didn't he stand up to the mechanics the last time he thought they gypped him? Don punched her hard in the face for siding with the enemy that way. It was not the first punch of their marriage by a long shot. He kept calling her stupid and hitting her and telling her that all he was asking for was a little empathy about his problems. When Don saw the blood on Martha's face, he knew he had lost it, but he told himself that she deserved it. Only a small part of him, dimly—like a faint whisper in the corner of his brain—wanted to cry like a baby and beg forgiveness. He drove her to the emergency room. Later they had dinner in silence.

By the next day, he regained his old charm and had managed to squelch that dim light of remorse.

Studying Violent Marriages

Both of these couples were participants in a unique study of violent marriages that we have been conducting in Seattle for the past eight years. The purpose of our study was to apply the methods of science to a problem which had rarely been studied by scientists: domestic violence. For over two decades, each of the authors of this book had made his reputation as a scientist studying marriage, and as creators of therapy techniques for helping couples improve their relationships. Thus, we were well aware of domestic violence, as anyone who studies couples must be. But we had never, until eight years ago, taken the detour which has captivated us ever since.

Anyone who decides to inform themselves about domestic violence will have no trouble finding articles and books that address the topic. There are self-help books lining the bookshelves, providing advice for battered women. There are books for academics and professionals written by historians, sociologists, psychologists, and lawyers. But there are few facts, and very little science. The science that has been published is informative. It provides facts about the frequency, severity, and scope of domestic violence.[1] It suggests a great many ways in which Western culture has condoned and even encouraged the battering of women by their husbands, and the more subtle ways in which it still does.[2]

Up until twenty years ago, little was written about domestic violence. It was not identified as a major societal problem, and most battered women didn't know that there was anything out of the ordinary in their marriages. However, with the onset of the women's movement, and the growth of feminism in the 1970s, writers began to draw attention to violence against women, including and especially violence perpetrated by husbands against wives. Psychologist Lenore Walker wrote two extremely influential books that defined the problem, and analyzed it with a combination of scientific procedures and clinical speculation.[3] Sociologists Murray Straus and Richard Gelles conducted two national surveys, which were shocking in their implication—there was so much family violence that many began to wonder whether or not it was the norm rather than the exception.[4]

Since then, domestic violence has captured the attention of some social and behavioral scientists, and slowly a growing body of knowledge has accumulated. At the same time, public consciousness about domestic violence has been raised by the publicity surrounding the O. J. Simpson double-murder trials. In fact, the one clear benefit resulting from the media coverage surrounding these cases has been the discussion of domestic violence that has taken place in the media: through television talk shows, coverage in newspapers and magazines, radio, and commentaries from experts in the field.

In our study we were determined to do something that no one had ever done before: directly observe the arguments of severely violent couples, instead of relying on reports of the arguments.[5] We were also determined to assess, as directly as possible, the emotional experiences of batterers and battered women during arguments. Finally, we wanted to find out what factors determined the demise of abusive relationships, and how the course of domestic violence changed over time.

Why were these scientific methods necessary? First, questionnaires and related reports provided by batterers are always suspect, unless they are verified by observers who can be considered objective. There is a venerable body of research within psychology showing how susceptible participants' reports are to bias and distortion.[6] This is especially true with regard to events from the past. Unless this information is independently confirmed by another more objective measurement of the same phenomena being reported, the answers given by batterers are particularly suspect. People are simply not reliable observers of their own or their intimate partners' behavior. By directly observing arguments rather than simply asking people to report on them, we can verify the accuracy of their perceptions, and judge how trustworthy their accounts of violent altercations are. Although we knew we would not directly observe violent altercations, we could observe nonviolent arguments between batterers and battered women. By determining the accuracy of their accounts of *nonviolent* arguments, we felt we could draw inferences about how trustworthy their accounts of *violent* arguments are.

Second, the role of emotions, especially hostility and fear, in domestic violence has been emphasized in the literature, but, again, we have been forced to rely on reports by batterers and their victims of their emotional experience, typically some time after the episode in question. All of the problems we just discussed are present when we rely on participants to accurately report their emotional experience. Such reports are subjective, often biased, and easily distorted. In contrast, polygraphs and other psychophysiological recording instruments are objective: they don't lie, distort, or report in a biased manner. Because of the technology available for recording heart rate, movement, and other physiological activity, we are able to infer emotional arousal without having to rely on the subjective reports of batterers and battered women. We conducted the first objective measurements of emotional arousal during arguments among batterers and battered women by using sophisticated polygraphs and other psychophysiological recording devices to measure the emotional level of both batterers and battered women during arguments.

Third, even though writers and experts have speculated on how violent marriages change over time, few have directly observed those changes as they occur. People are generally not good at reporting if, why, or how they have changed—either while change is occurring or in retrospect. In order to truly determine what happens to the relationships of batterers and battered women as time goes on, the social scientist has to be there watching them, listening to them, and collecting information as it is occurring. In our study, unbiased observers followed batterers and their partners over time, and using objective as well as subjective measures, measured changes as they were occurring. This way, we can now report on the factors that lead to women getting out of abusive relationships, or those that account for changes in violence over time—either changes for the better or changes for the worse.

What Is Unique About Our Study?

Our study is unique in its use of severely violent couples instead of the low-level violence that characterizes previous studies using multiple measures. It is also unique in its success at allowing for unambiguous interpretation of findings: because of our experimental controls, when batterers and their partners differ from other couples, we can attribute those differences to violence rather than to marital distress. We can do this because we recruited a comparison group where the couples were equally dissatisfied with their marriages but had no history of violence. In previous studies, because violent couples are invariably more dissatisfied with their marriages than nonviolent couples, any differences between them could be attributed to marital dissatisfaction rather than to violence per se.

Our study is also unique in its attempt to do justice to the complexity of emotional experience and the role the various emotions play in battering. Most previous studies have looked at negative emotions as a unit, without distinguishing among them. This is a significant oversight.

For example, ordinary anger serves a positive function in marital relationships, and when it is expressed directly couples face (and eventually solve) problems rather than avoid them.[7] However, provocative forms of anger, such as belligerence and contempt, are much more damaging to a relationship, and are even forms of emotional abuse. These emotional expressions have a very different impact from garden-variety anger, and have to be distinguished from it. Our system of coding marital interaction, the Specific Affect Coding System (SPAFF)[8] allowed us to separate these different emotional experiences and expression.

Why do we place such importance on distinguishing between different emotions? Are these simply arcane academic distinctions, or do they have practical implications for the lives of battered women? The answer to this question lies in the importance of understanding the role of "emotional abuse," a term we introduced in the previous paragraph. Many of our predecessors who have written about domestic violence referred to the ability of batterers to abuse their partners even when they are not being physically violent.[9] These nonviolent forms of abuse are sometimes referred to as "verbal abuse," but more commonly called "emotional abuse." Although not all men who abuse their wives emotionally are batterers, virtually all batterers also abuse their wives emotionally. They do so by verbal threats, intimidating actions such as the destruction of pets or property, humiliating and degrading remarks directed toward their partners, and attempts to rob their partners of their autonomy as human beings. These emotionally abusive behaviors can be extremely intimidating and destructive in their own right. But they become especially significant when they occur in a relationship which includes physical abuse.

Once a woman has been battered, and violence has been established as a method of control, emotional abuse can be especially frightening and controlling. In fact, one of our observations during the collection of preliminary data prior to the study was that emotional abuse can act as a proxy for physical abuse by reminding battered women that they can be beaten at any time. In this way, we suspected that emotional abuse can come to serve the same controlling function that physical abuse does. In order to determine the precise role that emotional abuse plays in a battering relationship, we needed a way of measuring it during arguments that occurred between partners in our laboratory experiments. Thus, we had to develop "codes" that captured this type of intimidating verbal behavior. Many of our SPAFF codes—especially "contempt," "belligerence," and "domineering"—were designed to distinguish between common anger and emotional abuse. Without a sensitive system of observational coding, one that captured emotional abuse, we would not have been able to determine the role such abuse plays in maintaining control, its ability to predict increasing or decreasing levels of violence, and the extent to which it serves controlling functions that resemble the kinds of control exerted by violence per se.

Does emotional abuse signal increased physical abuse? Does its intensity make it unlikely that physical violence will stop? Are men who are very abusive at the emotional level more dangerous and harder to divorce than those who are less emotionally abusive? These and other questions could only be answered by a sensitive system for coding emotions. The use of our SPAFF system and the videotaped recordings of nonviolent arguments to which this system was applied, played a very important role in our study.

Details of Our Study

How We Found Our Subjects. We recruited the participants in our study mostly through public-service announcements in the local media. The sample we obtained was not a random sample of the population, but rather a sample of convenience. This means that we don't know if we can generalize our findings to all batterers, and we must be careful to qualify our results as applying to our sample, not necessarily to battering relationships in general. But we were successful in recruiting a population of severe batterers.

A total of 201 couples was studied. We spent a full year testing our methods before we began studying the couples on whom we report in this book. There were 140 couples whose data we analyzed. They were classified into several groups using our carefully selected measures. There were ultimately 63 couples in our battering group: 27 couples who exhibited some violence, but not enough to be classified as battering couples; 33 couples who were dissatisfied with their marriages but exhibited no violence; and 20 happily married couples. Couples were only classified as "battering" if the wife reported within the past year 6 or more episodes of what we called "low-level violence" (e.g., pushing or slapping), 2 or more episodes of what we called "high-level violence" (e.g., kicking or hitting with a fist), or at least 1 episode of what we called "potentially lethal violence" (the wife was beat up, or the husband threatened to use or did use a gun or a knife).

The sample of battering couples we studied was indeed a severe one, by any standard. Eighty percent of the battered women had been injured by their partners within the past year and injured severely enough to need medical attention. Twenty percent of the batterers had been arrested for domestic violence within the past year. The vast majority of our sample had come into contact with the criminal justice system at some point in the past as the result of battering episodes.

As we mentioned, by comparing the violent couples to nonviolent but equally unhappy married couples we could rule out marital distress as an explanation for any differences found between the two unhappy groups. By comparing the distressed but nonviolent couples to happy couples, we could study the effects of marital stress, controlling for the amount of violence, since neither of these two groups was violent, and only one was experiencing marital distress. Both comparisons were necessary in our study.

We also included what we called a "low-level violent" group of couples to see if some of these couples would, over time, become more violent. If this occurred we could perhaps witness the origins of significant battering. Surprisingly, the husbands among our "low-level violent" couples almost never became batterers, as we defined the term. Instead, we discovered that there is a stable group of couples who periodically have arguments that escalate into pushing and shoving, but never reach the point where we would call the men batterers. These couples exist in large numbers, and often show up in the offices of couples therapists, as we will document in chapter 8. Their low-level violence often goes undetected by therapists, in part because the partners themselves do not consider it significant. It is important to know that such couples exist. It is also a weakness of currently existing couples therapies that such violence often goes undetected. But these couples are not the subjects of this book. Our book is about batterers and battered women, where violence is not "low level," but severe. Battering is physical aggression with a purpose: that purpose is to control, intimidate, and subjugate another human being. Battering is always accompanied by emotional abuse, is often accompanied by injury, and is virtually always associated with fear and even terror on the part of the battered woman.

All couples were paid at least $160 for their participation. Amazingly, we recruited a sample of severely violent couples with a simple public-service announcement (on radio broadcasts and in newspapers) stating only "Married couples, earn up to two hundred dollars in a research study. Seeking couples experiencing conflict in their marriage." The announcement said nothing about physical violence. The fact that this announcement got so many battering husbands to respond is a testament to the alarmingly high proportion of women who have experienced battering in their relationships. One previous study estimated that 36 percent of their sample of 625 newly-wed couples reported at least some violence.[10] Other studies of newlyweds have put the figure closer to 50 percent.[11] Each year at least 1.6 million wives in the United States are severely assaulted by their husbands and at least one-third of all murdered women are killed by husbands, ex-husbands, boyfriends, or ex-boyfriends.[12] The domestic assault of women in the United States is a problem of epidemic proportions.

Our Methods for Observing Nonviolent Arguments. To be confident that we were not putting battered women in jeopardy, we developed a set of procedures to help assess the risk of violence to ensure that no couples left the laboratory until the risk was minimal. We designed our debriefing procedures with the help of Dr. Ann Ganley, a nationally respected clinician specializing in domestic violence. All battered women were given referrals for shelters, and individual psychological and legal counseling after each session. They were asked privately whether they felt safe, and if they felt that the argument in the laboratory would put them at risk of physical aggression. If a woman felt unsafe, we constructed a safety plan. All interviewers were trained on our safety protocol, which included assessing the level of danger present following the laboratory procedures.

All subjects were given a written statement reiterating our position that both verbal and physical aggression are destructive to intimate relationships and that we deplore both domestic violence and verbal abuse. We called the wives in our study following their participation and used a structured interview to probe the extent to which any violence may have been precipitated by involvement in our study. In no cases did the police need to intervene. Many women showed interest in the referrals offered. Most important, in none of the cases were we able to trace violent altercations to our subjects' participation in our study.

Structured Interviews of Both Batterers and Battered Women. We interviewed husbands and wives separately about arguments they had in the past, both violent and nonviolent ones. We asked them about the history of violence in their families growing up, and we conducted a psychiatric assessment of each person. In one portion of our interview we asked about violence that has occurred outside of the current marital relationship. We collected their detailed perceptions about the "play-by-play" of their marital arguments, and tried to understand how they thought about these events, and what led up to the violence. Later, they were called by telephone twice over the following two weeks to obtain reports of the worst argument that had occurred during the previous week.

Assessing Emotional Arousal at the Physiological Level. As we videotaped the couples discussing an area of continuing disagreement in their marriage, we monitored their bodies with electronic sensors that indicated how aroused they were at various points during the argument, how rapidly their hearts were beating, the amount of blood reaching their periphery, how fast their blood was flowing, how much they were moving, and how much they were sweating. After the electrodes were attached and the quality of the signal was verified, subjects were asked to relax with their eyes closed for two minutes so that a baseline set of physiological measures could be obtained. Then, after the interaction, we showed the couples their videotape separately and asked them detailed questions about how they were feeling and thinking about important moments during their conflict discussion.

Methods of Analysis. We later transcribed the videotape verbatim, and we analyzed each person's behavior with very detailed systems that classified visual gaze, vocalizations, attempts to influence one another, and their emotional expressions. We synchronized these behaviors with the physiological responses we had observed.

Two Years Later: A Second Visit to the Laboratory. Because we were interested in the stability of these marriages and the changes in patterns of abuse over time, we brought couples back into the laboratory two years later and repeated most of our experimental procedures. We found out which couples were still together, and of those couples who remained together, in which cases violence decreased. We also examined changes in the quality of their arguments and the husband's level of emotional abuse.

Cobras and Pit Bulls

One Saturday night, after our data had been collected, we were sitting at the computer very late, and made a startling discovery. Typically, when people start arguing, they become aroused internally: their heart rates go up, they sweat, and they exhibit other signs of emotional arousal that correspond to the observed verbal aggression. However, we noticed that there was an enormous range in the heart rates of the men we were studying as they became aggressive during the arguments. We were astonished to find that in 20 percent of the batterers, there was a *decrease* in heart rate as they became more verbally aggressive. This discovery was counterintuitive. These men looked aggressive, they sounded aggressive, and they acted aggressively: yet internally they were calming down. We then discovered something that was even more astonishing: when we separated the batterers who were internally calm from those who became internally aroused, there were profound differences between the two groups. We had stumbled onto something quite new.

We found that the men who lowered their heart rates during marital interaction were far more emotionally aggressive toward their wives at the very start of the interaction than other men. They began the conversation being immediately belligerent, defensive, or contemptuous. If you were to watch these men on the videotape, you would think that they were so stirred up that you would probably pick them out as good candidates for a stroke or a heart attack. And yet the physiological data we were collecting in the control room were telling us that they were calm, calmer than they had been when we had asked them to close their eyes and relax. Like the cobra who becomes quite still and focused just before striking its victim at more than 100 miles an hour, these men were calming themselves internally and focusing their attention, while striking swiftly at their wives with vicious verbal aggression.

When we examined the type of battering the two types of men displayed at home, the men we came to see as Cobras were more likely to have used or threatened to use a knife or a gun on their wives than the other batterers. In general, the Cobras were more severely violent than the other batterers. Furthermore, when we analyzed our interactions, we found that the net effect the Cobras' peculiar way of marital attack had on their wives was to suppress their expression of anger, increase their level of fear, and produce significant amounts of sadness.

The men who increased their heart rates as they became verbally aggressive were quite different. They exhibited anger as a kind of slow burn, gradually increasing it in a domineering and threatening fashion over the fifteen-minute conflict discussion, but never letting up. In this respect, these men reminded us of Pit Bulls, creatures that grew increasingly aggressive until they finally attacked. Their wives did not appear as intimidated by them as did the wives of the Cobras. In fact, the wives of Pit Bulls often argued as vociferously as their husbands did.

The Cobras showed evidence of severe antisocial, criminal-like traits, and were also highly sadistic in their aggression. They were also more violent toward others in their lives: friends, relatives, strangers, coworkers, and bosses. They were much less emotionally dependent on others than the Pit Bulls. This means that the Cobras were not particularly clingy, jealous types. They encouraged their wives to be independent. They kept teasing the wives and taunting them to leave or have an affair. The Pit Bulls, on the other hand, were much more insecure. They saw potential betrayal in their wives' every move. They feared being abandoned.

We continued to examine these two subtypes of batterers, and the closer we looked, the more differences we found. Two years later, not a single Cobra was separated or divorced from his battered wife. In contrast, the marriages of the Pit Bulls were highly unstable, and almost half of them had dissolved within the two years between their first and second visits to the laboratory.

George is a Cobra. His intimidation of Vicky was cold and systematic, a way of controlling her and getting her to do his bidding. It was a tactic he had been using with everyone in his life and he knew that it worked. It only failed when the other guy got there first and was meaner and tougher. With women it was second nature for George, that combination of sweet talk and threat, and an uncanny sense of how to get to some of them and turn them into true believers. In the early stages of their marriage Vicky saw this cynical side but interpreted it as a sign of vulnerability. That was how she developed her dream. She made it her mission to reform his views of people and to bring out the tender, charming, loving side of George that had initially won her admiration and love.

Don is a Pit Bull. With him the violence was due at least in part to his emotional dependency on Martha. He was prone to fits of jealous rage. He seemed to be terrified that she would leave him, and then became terrified of his own dependency. He took it all out on Martha. He blamed her not only for the violence, but for the dependency. Don wasn't one of those men who gets so wrapped up with other aspects of his life that he takes his wife for granted. Don was very involved with Martha. In fact, he knew all of her movements during the day, and he would call her often, to check up on her and make sure she was where she said she would be. Don could be very impulsive but very romantic as well. He was a generous man, and he liked to buy Martha things and take her to fancy places. He liked to see her dressed up to go out. But he hated other men staring at her, and he thought he saw them doing that all the time. He liked to keep her everyday movements strictly under his control.

Does the Violence Ever Stop on Its Own?

As we have already mentioned, one of the primary purposes of our study was to see what happens to these couples as time goes on. When do they stay together? When do they split up? When does the violence continue? When does it stop? When the violence decreases, does the emotional abuse decrease as well?

We were interested in these long-term processes in part because they might have implications for the rehabilitation of batterers and methods for counseling battered women. Perhaps, in the midst of all this data collection, we could ascertain how battered women might be best advised, and how batterers might be punished or educated. We knew that in embarking on such questions, we would inevitably be entering delicate and potentially dangerous territory. We knew that we had to be careful, because not all factors that predict these changes are easily translatable into advice for battered women. We recognized that the steps taken to get out of an abusive relationship could also place battered women at increased risk. The risk of severe assault, and even homicide, increases dramatically when battered women leave their abusive partners.[13] Nevertheless, we hoped that we might find out some things that would provide hope to battered women, and even some clues as to how to reduce battering.

Although we will be discussing our discoveries regarding these important questions in chapters 6 and 7, we can say here that our preliminary results were somewhat confusing and ambiguous. Our profile of batterers whose relationships broke up suggest that these men are quite emotionally abusive and extremely preoccupied with their partners. Most of them are Pit Bulls. The battered women who leave tend to be deeply dissatisfied with the overall quality of their marriages, not just with the violence but with just about everything about their partners. They also tend to fight back and defend themselves verbally, despite their husbands' capacity for brutality. The wives of Cobras were much less likely to get out, in part because—at least in the short run—they recognized the danger of trying to leave a Cobra; but also, the wives of Cobras were much more attached to their husbands, despite the severity of the abuse, than were the wives of Pit Bulls. In chapter 7, we tackle the equally important question of when does the violence increase, decrease, and cease altogether. We found that in our sample, violence rarely stopped on its own in the absence of either therapy or criminal sanctions. Even when batterers are held accountable, through either a criminal conviction or court-mandated treatment, it is not clear that such interventions are reliably effective.

However, there were gaps in our findings, and they raised as many questions as they answered. We realized that no matter how rigorous our design, and no matter how comprehensive our measures, they did not tell us the entire story. In anticipation of writing this book, we decided that we needed more information to help fill in the blanks, and we recontacted many of the battered women three years after our two-year follow-up. Some of these women had left their abusive partners. Others were still being abused. We also called back some of the husbands. We spent hours with each "exit interview," testing some of our ideas and generating others, combining structure with open-ended questions as much to get new ideas as to confirm previous ones. These exit interviews will figure prominently throughout the book. They add a richness in detail that cannot be captured by purely quantitative methods. These interviews answered many questions for us and raised still others.

When we first decided to write this book, we were going to emphasize the characteristics of batterers. And we devote much of this book to a discussion of what batterers are like. But once we began our exit interviews, we became more and more interested in the women: we found them to be resourceful, courageous, and in many ways heroic. We hope that their heroism emerges clearly in these pages. Above all, we hope our findings help contribute to the growing efforts of many in our society to stop violence against women.

2
Basic Facts About Battering: Myths Vs. Realities

During and following the O. J. Simpson trials the media were full of information about domestic violence. One of the few positive outcomes of the O. J. Simpson murder trial was that the public consciousness about domestic violence greatly increased. Unfortunately, this increased consciousness was a double-edged sword, as misinformation competed with facts, and misinformed opinions often substituted for reality.

Domestic violence is a problem of immense proportions. Unfortunately, there is much that is still not understood about the nature of battering, despite the plethora of opinions and speculative theories. In our presentation of basic information about battering, we hope to begin the process of separating fact from fiction and myth from reality.

Myth #1: Both Men and Women Batter

There has been a backlash against the advocacy movement on behalf of battered women, a backlash that says, "Wait a

34

minute! It is not just women who get battered. It is men too."
O. J. Simpson referred to himself repeatedly as a battered husband. There are even those who claim that a huge underground movement of battered husbands refuse to tell their
stories because they are reluctant to be identified as "wimps."

In support of these claims, some people cite statistics from
two national surveys conducted by sociologists Murray Straus,
Richard Gelles, and their colleagues.[1] These statistics show
that the *frequency* of violent acts is about the same in men and
women. However, these statistics do not take into account two
aspects of violence that are crucial to understanding battering:
the impact of the violence and its function. According to statistics from the national surveys of domestic violence conducted
by the New Hampshire Family Violence Research Center[2] as
well as research reported by Dr. Dina Vivian and her colleagues
at the State University of New York at Stony Brook,[3] male violence does much more damage than female violence: women
are much more likely to be injured, much more likely to enter
the hospital after being assaulted by their partner, and much
more likely to be in need of medical care. Wives are much more
likely to be killed by their husbands than the reverse; in fact,
women in general are more likely to be killed by their male partners than by all other types of perpetrators combined.[4]

Because men are generally physically stronger than women,
and because they are often socialized to use violence as a
method of control, it is hard to find women who are even *capable* of battering their husbands. However, battering is not just
physical aggression: it is physical aggression with a purpose.
The purpose of battering is to control, intimidate, and subjugate one's intimate partner through the use or the threat of
physical aggression. Battering often involves injury, and in our
sample, it was usually accompanied by fear on the part of the
victim. As we shall show more conclusively in chapter 3, fear is
the force that provides battering with its power. Injuries help
sustain the fear. The vast majority of physical assaults reported

in the national surveys were pushes, shoves, and other relatively minor acts of violence. They were not the kinds of battering episodes that typically end up in the criminal justice system.

All indications are that in heterosexual relationships, battering is primarily something that men do to women, rather than the reverse. However, as we will show, there are many battered women who are violent, mostly, but not always, in self-defense. Battered women are living in a culture of violence, and they are part of that culture. Some battered women defend themselves: they hit back, and might even hit or push as often as their husbands do. But they are the ones who are beaten up. On a survey that simply totals the frequency of violent acts, they might look equally violent. But there is no question that in most relationships the man is the batterer, and the woman is the one who is being battered.

Myth #2: All Batterers Are Alike

Although there is still a tendency for professionals to talk about batterers as if they were all alike, there is growing recognition that there are different types of batterers. There are at least two distinguishable types that have practical consequences for battered women, and perhaps more. Each type seems to have its unique characteristics, its own family history, and perhaps different outcomes when punished by the courts or educated by groups for batterers. Based on our findings of a distinction between the Cobras and the Pit Bulls, and the work of Dr. Amy Holtzworth-Munroe and Gregory Stuart,[5] we think a compelling case can be made for at least two subtypes, roughly corresponding to our distinction between the Cobras and the Pit Bulls.

Cobras

Cobras appear to be criminal types who have engaged in antisocial behavior since adolescence. They are hedonistic and impulsive. They beat their wives and abuse them emotionally, to stop them from interfering with the Cobras' need to get what they want when they want it. Although they may say that they are sorry after a beating, and beg their wives' forgiveness, they are usually not sorry. They feel entitled to whatever they want whenever they want it, and try to get it by whatever means necessary. Some of them are "psychopaths," which means they lack a conscience and are incapable of feeling remorse. In fact, true psychopaths have diminished capacity for experiencing a wide range of emotions and an inability to understand the emotions of others: they lack the ability to sympathize with the plight of others, they do not experience empathy, and even apparent acts of altruism are actually thinly veiled attempts at selfishness. They do not experience soft emotions such as sadness, and rarely experience fear unless it has to do with the perception that something bad is about to happen to *them*.

But not all Cobras are psychopaths. Whether psychopathic or merely antisocial, they are incapable of forming truly intimate relationships with others, and to the extent that they marry, they do so on their terms. Their wives are convenient stepping-stones to gratification: sex, social status, economic benefits, for example. But their commitments are superficial, and their stance in the relationship is a "withdrawing" one. They attempt to keep intimacy to a minimum, and are most likely to be dangerous when their wives attempt to get *more* from them. They do not fear abandonment, but they will not be controlled. Their own family histories are often chaotic, with neither parent providing love or security, and they were often abused themselves as children.

As adults, they can be recognized by their history of antisocial behavior, their high likelihood of drug *and* alcohol abuse, and the severity of their physical and emotional abuse. Their wives fear them, and are often quite depressed. But fear and depression do not completely explain why the women are unlikely to leave the relationship. Nor is it simply that they lack economic and other resources: indeed, Cobras are often economically dependent on their wives. Despite the fact that they are being severely abused, it is often the women rather than the men who continue to fight for the continuance of the relationship. It is these couples where the men exude macabre charisma.

Pit Bulls

The Pit Bulls are more likely to confine their violence to family members, especially their wives. Their fathers were likely to have battered their mothers, and they have learned that battering is an acceptable way to treat women. But they are not as likely as the Cobras to have criminal records, or to have been delinquent adolescents. Moreover, even though they batter their wives and abuse them emotionally, unlike the Cobras the Pit Bulls are emotionally dependent on their wives. What they fear most is abandonment. Their fear of abandonment and the desperate need they have *not* to be abandoned produce jealous rages and attempts to deprive their partners of an independent life. They can be jealous to the point of paranoia, imagining that their wives are having affairs based on clues that most of us would find ridiculous.

The Pit Bulls dominate their wives in any way they can, and need control as much as the Cobras do, but for different reasons. The Pit Bulls are motivated by fear of being left, while the Cobras are motivated by a desire to get as much immediate gratification as possible. The Pit Bulls, although somewhat less violent in general than the Cobras, are also capable of severe assault and murder, just as the Cobras are. Although one is safer trying to leave a Pit Bull in the short run, Pit Bulls may actually be more dangerous to leave in the long run. Cobras strike swiftly and with great lethality when they feel threatened, but they are also easily distracted after those initial strikes and move on to other targets. In contrast, Pit Bulls sink their teeth into their targets; once they sink their teeth into you, it is hard to get them to let go!

It is not clear how Cobras and Pit Bulls are apportioned within the battering population. In our sample, 20 percent of the batterers were Cobras. Interestingly, Dr. Robert Hare, an internationally renowned expert on psychopaths, estimates that 20 percent of batterers are psychopaths.[6] This correspondence is provocative. However, our guess is that Cobras constitute a larger percentage of the clinical or criminal population of batterers than the 20 percent found in our study. The Cobras fit the profile of the type of batterer who comes into contact with the criminal justice system much more than the Pit Bulls do. The profile of the Cobra also describes those referred by judges to treatment groups much better than the profile of the Pit Bull.

Myth #3: Battering Is Never Caused by Drugs and Alcohol

Dr. Kenneth E. Leonard reviewed a body of literature in 1993 suggesting a strong relationship between alcohol use and battering.[7] However, there was at that time a great deal of ambiguity about the extent to which drug and alcohol abuse causes men who would otherwise not be batterers to beat their wives. In 1996, Dr. Leonard conducted the most definitive study to date on the role of alcohol in physical aggression by husbands toward wives.[8] In this study of newlyweds, Dr. Leonard reported that alcohol use was one of the strongest indicators that men would be physically aggressive during their first year of marriage. Although the research on drug abuse has been less extensive, it is clear that batterers are a great deal more likely to be drug abusers than are men who do not batter.

None of this research proves that alcohol or drugs "cause" battering. It simply suggests that batterers tend to have drug and alcohol problems. Because of this connection, battered women who haven't given up the dream often see treatment for drugs and alcohol abuse as the ray of hope: "If only he would stop drinking [or shooting up, or snorting coke], everything would be fine." It is easy to understand how it is that battered women develop this belief. Indeed, it may be true that for some batterers, stopping the substance abuse *will* lead to an end to battering.

However, the relationship between substance abuse and battering is an extremely complicated one. First, a substantial portion of batterers are not alcohol or drug abusers. Although battered women married to batterers without drug and alcohol problems would not be inclined to see treatment for substance abuse as relevant, the point is worth making because many people assume that the substance abuse is more connected to battering than it really is. Some batterers use alcohol; some don't. Some batterers abuse illegal substances; others don't.

Second, just because batterers abuse drugs or alcohol doesn't mean that they batter only when they are intoxicated. A battered woman may be just as likely to be beaten when a substance abuser is sober as she is when the batterer is under the influence of these substances.

Third, even when battering episodes typically occur while the batterer is high on drugs, it is not always the intoxication itself that increases the likelihood of battering. The majority of men with drug and alcohol problems do not batter their wives. Alcohol and drug intoxication may lower inhibitions, but they also make for handy rationalizations. Some batterers in our sample got high in order to provide a way of justifying the beating that they had planned before getting high. Many men we talked to attributed their violence to drugs and alcohol: when they did so, it was an attempt to minimize the significance of the battering per se to deny that violence was a problem beyond the other problem of drug abuse, and to distort the cause of the violence, which was the need for control.

Too much focus on drug and alcohol abuse leads us away

from the central issue: battering is fundamentally perpetuated by its success in controlling, intimidating, and subjugating the battered woman. The types of men who abuse their partners are also the types of men who abuse drugs and alcohol. Alcohol and drug abuse are part of the lifestyle of the batterer. But it would be a mistake to assume that the drug use causes the violence.

However, it is also true that substance abuse can be one of the causes of violence, and to see it as nothing but an excuse is to oversimplify a complex relationship. We believe that in rejecting alcohol and drug abuse as causal explanations for battering, many theorists in the field of domestic violence have thrown the baby out with the bathwater: in fact, some batterers *do* only batter while intoxicated *because* the state of intoxication transforms them. But these men should not be allowed to use the substance abuse as a justification for the violence. The fact that the batterer was intoxicated should not be grounds for legal exoneration, or a "diminished capacity" defense if the batterer is charged with a battering-related crime. The batterer's accountability should not be affected by whether or not he is sober while battering: a batterer should *always* be held accountable for battering. Nevertheless, any insistence on separating substance abuse from domestic violence results in lost opportunities for combining what we know about stopping substance abuse with what we know about stopping violence.

As things currently stand, the substance abuse and domestic violence experts typically study one or the other but not both. Rarely do experts from the different fields communicate with one another. If leading figures in the field of substance abuse worked together with leaders in the prevention of domestic violence, it might be possible to develop more effective ways of reducing both problems. And it is entirely possible that if men can be successfully treated for substance abuse, some of them *will* stop battering. It is perfectly consistent to hold the position that drug and alcohol abuse can be one of many causes of battering on the one hand, and continue to hold the batterer responsible for the violence on the other hand.

Myth #4: Batterers Can't Control Their Anger

This is a complicated issue, because there is a sense in which all behavior, even behavior that we think of as voluntary, is actually caused by past and current events in our environment. We are all products of our own unique history, and that history helps to explain how we respond in particular situations.

But voluntary behavior involves a choice, and depending on the outcome one seeks, different choices will be made. Battering is usually voluntary. There are some people with temporal lobe epilepsy whose brains literally trigger violent outbursts that bear no relationship to anything that is going on in the environment. There are some batterers (a small minority) whose battering rampages are truly impulsive and uncontrollable, at least in the early stages of each incident. But in the vast majority of cases, battering is a choice in the same sense that all other voluntary actions are. With Cobras, their physiological responses to conflict are consistent with increased concentration and focused attention. Their lowered heart rates during arguments probably function to focus their attention, to maximize the impact of their aggression. We suspect that Cobras are not only in control, but that they use their control over their own physiology to strike more effectively. But even Pit Bulls, who are highly aroused when they strike, still choose to strike.

Psychologist Donald Dutton and others have written of the "dissociation" often associated with violent episodes.[9] Dutton is talking about the type of batterer whom we would classify as a Pit Bull, and provides some anecdotal evidence that some of them experience an altered state of consciousness during battering episodes. In extreme cases they do not even remember the episodes afterward. Although dissociative states are consistent with the interpretation that they are "out of control" when they batter, few of the batterers in our sample described their episodes of violence in a manner that suggested dissociation. They remembered the episodes but either minimized their significance or denied responsibility for them. Occasionally, they would deny that the violence had occurred. Our interpretation of this denial is that these batterers are lying, using another method of extending their control over their battered wives. The relationship between voluntarily lying and dissociation (truly not remembering) remains an unresolved issue, to be determined by future research. But in the vast majority of violent episodes that occurred among our sample, although the batterers may have been behaving impulsively, they were not out of control.

Myth #5: Battering Often Stops on Its Own

Chapter 7 is entirely devoted to this topic. We will show that battering seldom stops on its own. We found in our research that while many men decrease their level of violence over time, few of them stop completely. And when they do stop, the emotional abuse usually continues.

This is quite important, because most research considers only physical abuse. But emotional abuse can be at least as effective a method of maintaining control, if the physical violence was once there. Once a batterer has achieved dominance through violence and the threat of more violence, emotional abuse often keeps the battered woman in a state of subjugation without the batterer having to use physical force. Since the violence is used in order to obtain control, it is more convenient for the batterer to restrict himself to emotional abuse. That abuse reminds her that the threat of violence is always present, and this threat is often sufficient to retain control. Any intervention which defines success without taking emotional abuse into account will inflate its effectiveness. In our sample, although many batterers *decreased* the frequency and severity of their violence over time, almost none of them stopped completely *and* also ended the emotional abuse.

Frank stopped being violent for eighteen months, and Jane, his wife, was quite happy about it. If we hadn't also studied emotional abuse, they might have looked like a couple whose problems had been solved. But, if anything, we found that Frank was even more emotionally abusive two years later than he had been initially, despite ceasing the physical violence. He was more insulting, more verbally threatening, drove more recklessly when angry, and humiliated Jane at every opportunity. All of these emotionally abusive acts were extremely hurtful and degrading to her. But they served an additional function: they reminded her of the violence, and the tightrope she had to walk to avoid recurrences of that violence. These reminders were all she needed. Frank maintained his control without having to risk breaking the law. Emotional abuse, as destructive as it is, is not against the law.

Myth #6: Psychotherapy Is a More Effective "Treatment" Than Prison

Our prisons are overcrowded and judges are constantly looking for alternatives to prison when given discretion in sentencing. Because psychotherapy is available for batterers, judges often find some referrals for court-mandated treatment irresistible as alternatives to imprisonment, especially since domestic assault charges are often misdemeanors rather than felonies.

Unfortunately, what appears at first glance to be an enlightened alternative to imprisonment is often a mistake. There is very little evidence that currently existing treatment programs for batterers are effective, and much reason to be concerned that in their present form, they are unlikely to stop the violence and even less likely to end the emotional abuse.[10] Yet people in our culture believe in psychotherapy, and battered women are no exception. Therefore, when their husbands are "sentenced" to psychotherapy they may be lulled into a false sense of security, thus leading them to return home from a shelter falsely convinced that they are now safe.[11]

As a matter of fact, Roy had been to therapy once, and Helen received glowing reports from the anger-management therapist. Roy received sixteen weeks of group therapy, and his therapist wrote the following during an evaluation at the conclusion of these sixteen weeks:

"In my professional opinion, Roy no longer constitutes a danger to his wife, Helen. He has been a model patient. He has accepted responsibility for being a batterer, has shown no inclination to repeat the violence from the past, and even stands a chance of qualifying for work as a therapist himself, working with batterers who have not yet developed the insight that has changed Roy's life."

Naturally, Helen was quite excited to make things work with the new Roy. But Roy's therapist had been conned. And Roy's therapist had inadvertently misled Helen. Less than two months after the group treatment had ended, Roy came at Helen with a knife, nearly killing her.

Violent criminals who assault strangers are seldom offered psychotherapy as an alternative to prison, in contrast to perpetrators of wife battering. What does this tell us about the criminal justice system and how it views "family violence"? Family violence is still regarded as less serious than violence against strangers, even though most women who are murdered are not killed by strangers but by boyfriends, husbands, ex-husbands, and ex-boyfriends.[12] But accountability is a prerequisite to decreased violence. We believe that referrals to psychotherapy, in the absence of legal sanctions, send the wrong message to batterers: they have gotten away with a violent crime with nothing but a slap on the wrist. O. J. Simpson is an excellent example. In 1989, he pleaded "no contest" to the charge of misdemeanor assault, after beating his wife

Nicole Brown Simpson on New Year's Eve. He received a small fine and was ordered to seek treatment. The treatment ended up being nothing more than a few sessions, some of which were conducted by telephone. We now know just how ineffective this "punishment" and the treatment that was required of him were.

We have no illusions about the rehabilitative power of prison, but at least prison stops the violence temporarily and gives the battered woman time to make plans. It also sends a powerful message to the batterer.

Consider also the ability of the most violent batterers—like Roy and George, both Cobras—to con judges, police, probation officers, and therapists. The Cobra will figure out what the therapist wants him to say, sound contrite, be counted as a success, and yet all that has been accomplished is that the system has been exploited by the Cobra. We believe that some form of treatment, either education or group therapy, should be offered to all convicted batterers on a voluntary basis, but it should never be mandated and it should never be offered as an alternative to the appropriate legal sanctions. We also believe that after the first offense, domestic assault should automatically be a felony. There is no reason to give up on education and treatment. But there is even less reason to allow batterers to use them as additional methods of control: control of the criminal justice system as well as the partner. The message has to be clear and unambiguous: violent crime will not be tolerated, whether the victim is a stranger or a family member.

Myth #7: Women Often Provoke Men into Battering Them

This myth is held by most batterers, many members of the general public, and even by some professionals. But as we shall show in chapter 3, men initiate violence independently of what their wives do or say. One husband came home from work after being criticized by his boss, and as his wife came to greet him at the door, he punched her in the face, knocking her unconscious. Drs. Lenore Walker and Donald Dutton have both described the internal build-up of tension that seems to occur in many batterers, regardless of what the battered woman is doing or saying.[13] Ultimately, this tension leads to an explosion of violent rage.

One of the couples in our sample had been in treatment with a family therapist. The husband and wife both quoted the therapist as saying to the wife: "If you would stop using that language, perhaps he wouldn't get so out of control." The husband wore this therapist's comment as a badge of honor and even referred to her use of profanity as "violence." In his view, she started the violence whenever she swore at him. The therapist appeared to be supporting this view. The wife never felt understood by the therapist, but the outcome of treatment was that she blamed herself for the battering and thought that the solution was "to be a better wife."

Holding the husband accountable for using violence, regardless of what the wife does or says, is a necessary step for the violence to stop, but it is not sufficient. The batterer has to "feel" accountable in order for the violence to stop. Feeling the accountability means that in addition to the batterer being punished, he must feel that his punishment is justified. It is the rare batterer who feels this way, which helps to explain why battering infrequently stops on its own. Instead of holding themselves accountable, batterers minimize the severity of their violent actions, deny that they are responsible for them, and distort them to the point where they become trivial, as George did when he said after beating up Vicky, "I didn't think nothing of it because it wasn't important."

In those rare instances where the husband feels accountable, the violence as well as the emotional abuse might stop. One of the few batterers in our sample to stop the abuse entirely told us from the beginning that, "I never felt right about it. Even while I was doing it. When I was arrested I deserved it. No man has the right to hit a woman unless she's trying to kill him."

Thus, even if the husband's violence is a response to remarks made by the wife, it is a mistake to think of these remarks as "provocations." Provocation implies that "she got what she deserved." George believed he was justified in beating Vicky because she had an "attitude" about his being late for dinner. Batterers make choices when they beat their wives. There is no remark or behavior that justifies a violent response unless it is in self-defense.

In our sample, men were rarely if ever defending themselves when they started battering. Nothing a woman says to a man gives him the right to hit her. Therefore, women couldn't possibly precipitate male battering unless they initiated the violence, which they rarely did in our sample. And even if they do initiate physical aggression by pushing their husbands, punching them in the arm out of frustration, or throwing something at them, they haven't provoked a beating. Husbands have a right to defend themselves: when they are punched, they can deflect the blow; when they are pushed, they can hold their wives so that they stop; and when something is thrown at them, they can duck and yell at their wives to stop. None of these physically aggressive behaviors constitute battering. However, they are commonly used by batterers as excuses for battering that would have occurred anyway.

Sam gave Marie a black eye when she shook him in the middle of the night, waking him up. She couldn't sleep because he had been flirting with another woman at a party, and in fact had been dancing with her in a way that was blatantly sexual. He got angry when she woke him up, refused to discuss it with her, and when she hit him with a pillow out of frustration, he punched her in the face.

There is a philosophy of marriage inherent in the view that women provoke men to be violent. It says that the man is the head of the household, the boss. In the old days, being the boss meant having the right to beat and even kill your wife, the way masters had the right to kill their slaves. Now, it means viewing the wife as someone who deserves to be beaten under certain conditions. Wives never deserve to be beaten by their husbands. Battering is a criminal act, and verbal challenges from the wife do not constitute mitigating circumstances.

Harry, one of the husbands in our sample, almost choked his wife Beth to death after she taunted him: "You're probably a fag, just like your father." What she said was wrong, but she didn't deserve to be choked for it. Harry should have been charged with attempted murder.

Myth #8: Women Who Stay in Abusive Relationships Must Be Crazy

This myth actually assumes a fact, namely, that most battered women *do* stay in abusive relationships. In our sample, within two years of their first contact with us, 38 percent of the women had left their husbands. When you consider that about 50 percent of couples divorce over the course of their lives,[14] 38 percent in two years is very high indeed! Many battered women *are* getting out of abusive relationships. Abused women ought not to be blamed for not leaving. In fact, they do leave at high rates. And their leaving is often an act of courage because it means having to cope with enormous fear as well as financial insecurity.

But what about those who haven't left yet? Does this mean that there is something wrong or odd about them? The answer is no. It is much easier to get into an abusive relationship than it is to get out of one.[15] Women are often afraid to leave, and with good reason. Their chances of getting seriously hurt or killed increase dramatically for the first two years after they separate from their husbands.[16] Leaving is risky, and often staying is the lesser of two evils. Tracy Thurman went all the way across the country to escape from her abusive husband. But he tracked her down in rural Connecticut, and came after her with a knife, disabling her for life and almost killing her. Police and neighbors watched the slaughter. Her case was a watershed in the quest of advocates for mandatory arrest laws, laws which require that arrests are made when the police find probable cause for a domestic dispute.

Second, women often can't afford to leave, especially if they have children. They are economically dependent on their husbands, and that economic leverage is part of the control exerted by the batterer. Vicky had to wait a long time after she had decided to leave George until she was financially able. So did Clara, who was a homemaker married to a university professor. He controlled all the finances, and whenever he thought she might be contemplating leaving, he would remind her of his resources to hire the best divorce lawyer in town. He assured her that he would settle for nothing less than full custody of the children, and that she would get nothing. Clara was trapped by economic dependency.

Third, after being subjected to physical and emotional abuse for a period of time, women are systematically stripped of their self-esteem, to the point where they falsely believe that they need their husbands in order to survive, despite the violence. This lowering of self-esteem is often part of a constellation of symptoms that are common to survivors of trauma.

Battered women experience trauma similar to that of soldiers in combat, abused children, and rape victims (many battered women *are* also raped by their husbands). These symptoms include depression, anxiety, a sense of being detached from their bodies and numb to the physical world, nightmares, and flashbacks of violent episodes. The syndrome characterized by these symptoms is "post-traumatic stress disorder" (PTSD).[17]

Many battered women suffer from mild to severe versions of PTSD, and as a result are not functioning well. Their parenting is affected, their problem-solving abilities are impaired, and their ability to plan for the future is disrupted. Given this common experience of trauma, it is amazing that battered women manage to be as resourceful and resilient as they are, especially since their lives and the lives of their children are often at stake. The corrosive and cumulative effects of battering go a long way toward explaining how hard it is to get out of an abusive relationship.

Erin had long ago stopped loving her husband, Jack. But Jack had convinced her that she lacked the ability to survive without him. He was constantly telling her that she was stupid, disorganized, ugly, and needed him around in order to get through the day. After years of public insults, severe beatings, and successful attempts at isolating her from the rest of the world, Erin began to believe him. She stayed.

Another thing that keeps some women in violent relationships is that they are holding on to a dream that they have about what life could be like with these men. They love their husbands and they have developed a sympathy for them and their plight in life. They hope that they can help their men become normal husbands and fathers. These dreams can be powerful and are very hard to give up.

Some Cobras exude an inexplicable type of charisma for their partners. Battered women stay in these relationships because they are quite attached to and love their husbands, not because of the violence, but in spite of it. They are afraid of their husbands and want the violence to stop. But to them, violence is not a sufficient reason to leave the relationship. In fact, the wives of Cobras are often *more* committed to maintaining the relationship than their husbands are, despite the severe beatings.

Although as outsiders, it is hard for us to understand this attachment, it helps to remember that violence is normal in many subcultures within North America. When violence is all around you, it tends to be accepted as a fact of life. As hard as it might be to imagine, many battered women assume that violence is part of marriage. They don't like it. They continue to try to change it. But they don't view it as a reason for getting out. They have accepted the culture of violence.

Cobras seem to choose women who are especially vulnerable to their macabre charisma. They also figure out quite quickly where the woman's particular vulnerabilities lie. George, for example, figured out quite quickly that Vicky had a dream, and he altered his presentation of himself so that it would be in accord with that dream. He also happened to meet Vicky at a unique time in her life: she was vulnerable not just because of her dream, but because her self-esteem was at an all-time low, and her life was in shambles. Vicky is no longer vulnerable to the Georges of the world. She has become streetwise. In fact, she would have probably resisted his "charms" at an earlier time. But George met her when she was uniquely available to join with him in the relationship that was to become her worst nightmare.

Another couple with a similar dynamic was Roy and Helen. They had met in prison, where he was serving time for armed robbery, and she was visiting her boyfriend, who had been locked up for sexually abusing Helen's daughter. Helen was one of the most severely battered women in our sample. When they first came into contact with us, Roy and Helen were homeless, although she held a job as a hotel receptionist. He had broken her neck and her back on separate occasions, caused eight miscarriages by beating her whenever he got her pregnant (he refused to use birth control), and he had even stabbed her once or twice, "not to kill her, just to scare her." He was an alcoholic and a heroin addict, and refused to enter treatment for either. He also engaged in frequent extramarital affairs. Yet even though she had made it to a shelter on one occasion, she didn't stay because they "tried to talk me into leaving him." As she put it, "I don't want to leave him; I just want him to stop beating me." She loved him and was committed to him not *because of* the violence, but *in spite of* it. What Vicky once told us about George's mother was probably applicable to Helen: "She never knew that there was anything different; where she was brought up, men beat women. They don't know that they deserve better. They don't even know that there is anything better."

A small percentage of the battered women in our study married to Cobras were themselves antisocial before getting involved in their current abusive relationships, just like their husbands. These women were themselves impulsive and often had criminal records going back to childhood. Helen was one of these women. She and Roy hit it off, immediately decided to live together, and soon after that they were married. Their marriage was both volatile and violent.

Some women in our sample expressed a preference for romance "on the edge," unpredictable and potentially both dangerous and adventurous. They would have it no other way. Even though they did not want to be battered, they found their husbands charismatic and attractive, and had no interest in leaving them. Often they stay against their family's advice and the advice of their friends. By their own account, they had no interest in relationships with boring nice guys.

Myth #9: Battered Women Could Stop the Battering by Changing Their Own Behavior

By now, it should be clear that battering cannot be changed through actions on the part of the victim. Battering has little to do with what the women do or don't do, what they say or don't say. It is the batterer's responsibility—and his alone—to stop being abusive. We collected and analyzed data on violent incidents as they unfolded at home, and examined sequences of actions that led up to the violence. We discovered that there were no triggers of the violence on the part of the men, nor were there any switches available for turning it off once it got started.

Countless women from our sample still believed that it was their job to stop the husbands' violence. Helen was a perfect example. She would defend Roy when given the opportunity, usually by blaming herself. "He is a good man who is easily stressed out. I work hard to make it easier for him, but not hard enough. Like when he wants to have sex. I should be there for him more because I know a lot of this has to do with sexual tension. And I like to drink. If there wasn't alcohol around, he probably wouldn't hit me as much."

Because battering has a life of its own, and seems to be unrelated to actions on the part of the woman, couples therapy makes little sense as a first-line treatment. One would not expect couples therapy to stop the violence, since the violence is not about things that the women are doing or saying. Couples therapy has other disadvantages. First, it can increase the risk of violence by forcing couples to deal with conflict on a weekly basis, leaving the batterer in a constant state of readiness to batter. Second, when the couple is seen together, the therapist implies that they are mutually responsible for the violence. This implication is handy for the batterer, since it supports his point of view: "If she would just change her behavior, the violence would stop." The victim ends up being blamed for her own victimization.

Couples therapy can work for couples where there is low-level physical aggression without battering. It might also work in relationships where the husband has demonstrated the ability to stop being abusive for one or two years. But we would never recommend couples therapy as the initial treatment strategy for batterers, even in those instances where psychotherapy of some sort might be appropriate.

Myth #10: There Is One Answer to the Question "Why Do Men Batter Women?"

There are many competing theories among social scientists, legal experts, and advocates about what causes battering. The theories are often pitted against one another as if one is correct and another incorrect. In fact, no one knows what causes battering, and there is in all likelihood no one cause. We are not attempting to answer that question in this book. Instead, we are describing what we have learned about the dynamics of battering by looking intensively at the relationships between batterers and battered women, and we recognize that any complete understanding of battering has to include analyses that are beyond the scope of this book.

Most important, any complete understanding of battering has to take into account the historical, political, and broad socioeconomic conditions that make battering so common. The subordination of women to men throughout the history of our civilization, and the resulting oppression, is pivotal in this analysis. Our culture has been patriarchal as far back as we can trace it. As we describe in more detail in chapter 10, patriarchy has sanctioned battering historically and continues to operate to perpetuate battering today: the continued oppression of women provides a context that makes efforts to end violence against women difficult if not impossible.

Battering also is intimately related to social class. It is much more common in lower socioeconomic classes than it is in middle and upper classes. Where violence in general is common, so is violence against women. All of the economic forces which operate to perpetuate class differences, racism, and poverty contribute to high rates of battering. The fact that our book is not about these class differences does not mean that they are not important. They are.

Finally, it should be noted that our sample was 90 percent Caucasian. Although the couples in our sample were predominantly working class and lower class, there were few African American, Latino, and Native American couples in our sample. Therefore, we are unable to discuss potentially important cross-cultural differences in battering, and are forced to discuss battering without taking into account possibly unique dynamics among ethnic and sexual (gay and lesbian) minorities. This is a crucial area for future research.

In short, battering occurs within a patriarchal culture, and is made possible because such a culture dominates American society. It is further fueled by poverty, racism, and heterosexism. Our focus is on individual differences within the broader society. Not all men are batterers, despite the culture. Therefore, we think our intensive focus on the dynamics of relationships is one crucial area where understanding is needed. But it is only one of many foci that are necessary for a complete understanding of battering.

Although not all or even most men are batterers, most batterers in heterosexual relationships are men. Batterers come in different shapes and sizes. Drug and alcohol abuse are often important components of violent episodes. However, most batterers do not commit their beatings in a state of uncontrollable rage.

As we shall document in chapter 7, battering can and often does decrease over time, but it seldom completely stops on its own. Until batterers are consistently punished by the criminal justice system in a way that is commensurate with the crime committed, the rates of domestic violence are likely to remain staggeringly high. Women do not, cannot, and should not be implicated, either directly or indirectly, as contributors to the problem of battering, even when they challenge their husbands verbally or stay in abusive relationships. In fact, there is little women *can* do to change the course of a violent episode, or affect its onset.

However, we have personally witnessed many heroic and resourceful steps taken by battered women that have ultimately freed them from their violent relationships, or in other cases turned the relationships in a positive direction. Even though stopping the abuse is the husband's responsibility, these heroic initiatives taken by women despite dangerous and traumatic circumstances inspired us to write this book. We will describe these actions in chapter 6.

For now, having laid to rest some common misconceptions about domestic violence, we want to put the dynamics of battering episodes under a microscope.

3

The Dynamics of Battering: The Anatomy of Violent Arguments

In this chapter we want to put violent arguments in abusive relationships under a microscope. We will see what arguments among Pit Bull and Cobra couples have in common, how they differ, and the ways they conform and diverge from the arguments that nonviolent couples have.

All of these arguments were told to our interviewers when couples first came to the laboratories. We have reconstructed these arguments from interviewees' descriptions, which were, for the most part, congruent with one another. As we go along, we will provide commentary, followed by a listing of the "stages" of the arguments that culminated in violence.

George turned on the TV, looking forward to some "tits and ass." He liked watching shows that Vicky referred to as "bikini reviews." They relaxed him, sometimes aroused him, and since it was his house, he would watch what he pleased. He had two or three beers before settling in, and just wanted to be left alone.

George and Vicky lived in a small apartment for ensigns and their spouses. The kitchen was rectangular, with only a partial wall separating it from the living room. Vicky could hear the TV, and the show annoyed her. Even though Vicky was a battered woman, and George was never easy to reason with, she always stood up to him when she felt he was not behaving properly. She was annoyed that he got off on what she considered to be female exploitation. Here she was, making his dinner in the kitchen, acting like the housewife that she had never pictured herself as, and George was sitting there "watching these women walk around like a dog show in bathing suits." Vicky found the whole situation insulting. She had told George from day one that she was flat out intolerant of the way media objectified women's bodies, and she wouldn't have it in her house.

Vicky spoke up, as she usually did: "How can you watch that stuff while I'm in here cooking. I find it so degrading!"

George's response was typical: "You're so stupid. I don't understand why you have a problem with this. I'm only looking at them."

Vicky, despite the contempt in George's voice, remained calm, almost as if she had taken a course in constructive communication: "The point is that I'm very sensitive about this. And I told you when we first met that I was and I didn't want it in my house and you agreed to it."

George calmed down internally, but you never would have known it: "You just can't fit into one of them bathing suits anymore, that's why you can't stand me watching them. Even if you could, you're too ugly to walk around in one. And I don't agree to that fucking rule anymore. I can have any fucking thing I want in this house or bring Playboy bunnies here if I want to."

Vicky was angry now, so angry that she temporarily forgot what a dangerous man George could be. She charged into the living room and turned off the TV. George's response was quick, and it was ferocious. He broke the glass coffee table by

smashing it with his fist. This was a reality check for Vicky. The
ferocity woke her up. Her whole body was transformed, and
she was now afraid. She tried to walk out of the living room
back into the kitchen, but George followed her. He threw a
beer can at her. He was yelling at her, calling her a "stupid
bitch." Their daughter, a toddler, was in the kitchen, watching
all of this. She witnessed George grab Vicky by the neck, slam
her against the window, and start throwing kitchen utensils at
her. As Vicky began to feel that familiar combination of pain
and numbness (almost as if this was happening to someone
else), scared that he was going to kill her, he left the room, but
continued screaming and yelling as he marched through the
apartment. Vicky was shaking with fear, crying with sadness,
and at the same time trying to soothe her little girl. George
then came back into the kitchen, grabbed Vicky by the hair,
and started throwing her around the kitchen. As he was throwing her around, he uttered the refrain "stupid bitch" again and
again. She went down into a fetal position, and George kicked
her. Then he left the apartment. He didn't flee, but he left
screaming, "I'm not going to stay here and take this shit," as if
he were the injured party. Meanwhile, battered one more time,
Vicky cleaned up the mess, gave her daughter a bath, com-
forted her, and put her to bed.

This was not the most severe violent episode that George
and Vicky ever had. But the episode had special significance
for her. She vividly recalled the swiftness of her shift from
anger to fear. She remembers begging him to stop, and how little effect the begging had. She felt, as she had so many times
before, that her life was in his hands. And it literally was. But
the significance was also in the substance of the issue. In her
dream George would have responded like Ward Cleaver. He
would say, "I'm sorry, I understand that this TV show really
upsets you, and I won't watch it." Even at his best, George did
a very poor Ward Cleaver imitation. Somehow, this fight stood
out because it provided a stark contrast between his need for

immediate gratification and his lack of sensitivity toward her. Not only was George indifferent to Vicky's discomfort, but he sadistically added insult to injury by calling her fat, ugly, and stupid. Not only did the vicarious sexual rush of the TV take precedence over Vicky's vulnerability, he accentuated the contrast by the content of his verbal abuse.

George, like most batterers, escalated the situation (Vicky's attempt to influence him) extremely rapidly, using both physical and verbal abuse in the service of control, intimidation, and subjugation. He was in her face twice as fast as she ever expected. Battering is not *just* physical aggression, but physical aggression that serves a function. That function is control. But there are different kinds of control, and different experiences that generate perceived challenges to that control. For both happily married and unhappy but nonviolent couples, a direct request, expressed in a neutral tone, will lead either to run-of-the-mill disagreement, criticism, defensiveness, or compliance. George's first response was verbal abuse. This is typical of the Cobras, who are quick to strike with belligerence and emotional abuse because it often quiets the partner quickly and with minimal effort. If Vicky had been less heroic, less willing to stand up for herself, the argument would have ended. George would have been left alone, which is all he wanted.

But Vicky still had her dream, and George was a major player in that dream. And it was still early in their relationship. She had been insulted, and her method of striking back was to turn off the TV. After all, she and George had agreed that he would not watch sexist television shows in their home, and she expected him to honor this agreement. But Vicky was in a bind: she could have given in, thus further consolidating emotional abuse as a method of control, or she could have shown him that she would not be treated like that.

She chose the latter course but she would have lost either way. Her choice triggered in George a primal, visceral sense of outrage: "his woman" was telling him what to do in "his house." In George's mind this could not be tolerated. He didn't care about any agreements he made in the past, during the days when he was conning her into marrying him. He didn't care if she felt degraded or insulted: in fact, the lower her self-esteem, the easier she would be to control. All he cared about was being able to do what he wanted when he wanted to do it. She was an obstacle, and she had to be stopped. His outburst was an attempt to teach her a lesson. No woman was going to influence him! No woman was going to control him! There would be no more turning off the TV unless he was the one to turn it off. He struck ferociously, quickly, and without regard for their daughter.

To him, this incident "was not worth remembering." To him, it was unimportant. He didn't even remember what the fight was about.

The Stages of the Argument

Unpredictability. For the vast majority of couples in our sample it was extremely difficult to predict when the batterer would strike. Batterers are not violent twenty-four hours a day, seven days a week. Seldom does the battered woman know just when the batterer will strike. For example, George preceded his physical abuse with emotional abuse. But emotional abuse is not a reliable sign of impending physical abuse. Emotional abuse is so common in batterers that, in the majority of instances, emotional abuse is *not* followed by physical abuse. Because it is such a common feature of these relationships it is an unreliable sign. When Vicky turned off the TV while George was watching it, on another day he might have just stomped out of the house, or withdrawn into the bedroom. Not only is the violence unpredictable, but it is also uncontrollable by the battered woman. We discovered from our detailed study of the anatomy of violent episodes that once a violent episode starts, there is nothing she can do to affect its course.

The unpredictability and uncontrollability of battering is part of what makes it so frightening. The fear for one's physical safety is, of course, terrifying in and of itself; this fear is magnified dramatically when there are children involved.

Holding onto the Dream. The women in our study did whatever they needed to do to survive, but they did not as a rule become passive, docile, or submissive. In fact, we discovered that as a group they were resourceful, heroic, and consistently held their ground. What we saw, again and again, were women trying to inject as much normalcy into their lives as possible. When Vicky was offended by a TV program that George was watching, she told him so in a way that would not threaten most men. She did not hold back because of an anticipation of danger. The underlying attitude is best summed up as follows: "I am going to fight for the kind of family life that I want. I am not going to avoid asking for change when I want it. I am not giving up." This is what we mean by "holding on to the dream." This is a very bold stance.

The Batterer's Unwillingness to Accept Influence. We discovered that batterers were unable to accept any influence from women, no matter how reasonable and gentle the influence attempt was. We kept hearing about men asserting their authority, teaching their wives a lesson, being outraged that their wives were suggesting rules of conduct. And we observed even in the laboratory that they became more aggressive when their wives asserted themselves, usually beginning with emotional abuse. In all the videotapes we made in our laboratory, never did we hear a batterer say to his wife anything like, "That's a good point," or "I never thought of that," or "You are starting to convince me." Accepting influence is something most men (and most women) do all the time in marriages.[1] For example, a woman might ask her husband not to work on Thursday night because her mother is coming over this weekend. He will say something like, "Sure, I'll see if I can do the work Sunday night after she leaves." But for the batterers in our study this process seemed to represent a loss of face, an assault to their sense of honor.

The Wife's Response: Anger versus Fear. Even when the batterers reacted to normal, everyday requests with emotional abuse, the women typically responded calmly. They didn't ignore the abuse. In fact, it made them angry. And they didn't let it go. But their initial responses could hardly be considered provocations, especially considering the fact that they were themselves *reacting* to abuse. Vicky turned off the television. It is important to remember that during abusive episodes, women are insulted and degraded before as well as during the beating. Most people get angry when they are insulted and degraded. So do battered women. Even though they are frightened and in pain from physical assault, they remain angry and outraged. Furthermore, they have to keep coping. Vicky tried to take care of her daughter, even while her husband was in the middle of a rampage.

Battered women experience a variety of emotions all at once. Often, the emotions seem contradictory. When most people are angry, they are too angry to be scared. When most people are sad, they are too sad to be scared. Yet battered women live in a constant state of competing emotions, and the competition is simply magnified during an abusive episode.

The Absence of a Withdrawal Ritual in Battering Couples. When happily married or unhappy but nonviolent couples have an argument, there is an invisible line that they do not cross. The arguments of these couples do not become violent. At some point, the escalation process stops or reverses itself. We call this process a "withdrawal ritual." Some couples take breaks, other couples compromise, still others—in fact most others—do a combination of both. Some couples simply stop, and come back to the issue another time. Others sweep the problem under the rug when it gets to a certain point of heightened intensity.

Battered women are typically quite willing to stop at the point where they start to sense danger. But once the husbands are activated, they cross a line. Since violence is unpredictable, we don't know when that line is crossed. But we do know that once it is crossed, violence follows. And once violence begins, there is nothing the woman can do to affect its course. The men lack the ability or the motivation to stop the escalation process. And, no matter how the women try to induce a withdrawal ritual, it has no effect once the violence starts.

In our laboratory, there were numerous safeguards against the violence occurring during the videotaped arguments. All of the scientific trappings, the psychophysiological equipment to which they were attached, the videotaping of the arguments, and the presence of technicians served to contain the arguments and limit them to emotional abuse. Furthermore, we had a procedure after the arguments that helped to calm couples down, so that they would not have a violent episode that resulted from participation in our study.

However, we believe that we saw behaviors on the part of batterers that signaled the crossing of that line, and that if it hadn't been for our procedures, violent episodes might have resulted. To understand these behaviors, we need to remind you that all of our laboratory interactions were analyzed using our Specific Affect Coding System (SPAFF). Technicians who were not told anything about the study were trained to code emotional expressions and units of speech based on what the spouses say, their body language, voice tone, and facial expressions. "Belligerence" and "contempt" are two of these codes. "Belligerence" refers to taunting, challenging remarks designed to provoke another person. George's statement that he could bring Playboy bunnies home if he wanted to was a classic example of belligerence. Contempt refers to insulting, demeaning behavior directed toward the partner. We found that batterers were much more likely to be belligerent and contemptuous in the laboratory than nonviolent husbands were. Similarly, belligerence and contempt commonly occurred prior to violent episodes. When belligerence and contempt are combined with another SPAFF behavior, "domineering," we believe that the batterer is signaling that he is close to crossing the line. "Domineering" distinguished between batterers and other men and women much more reliably than any other. To dominate during an argument is to squelch, to control, to suppress the behavior of another. Even in the restrictive conditions of our laboratory, the controlling behavior on the part of the batterer was obvious.

Cobras are especially likely to cross the line when they experience the partner as trying to control them. Their domineering behavior was the closest we found to battering in the laboratory. It was so common in batterers, and so uncommon in nonviolent men, that we see it as the closest batterers can come to being violent without actually getting physical, the signal that a batterer is close to initiating violence. Batterers hold battered women on a tight leash. In the laboratory, where violence is impossible, the easiest way to assert control is to squelch the other's attempts to be a partner in conversation.

The Violence Commences. In the laboratory, we found that the battered women were just as angry, if not angrier, than their husbands were. These results were consistent with couples' descriptions of violent altercations. Women subjected to a history of violence are understandably angry; they certainly have more reason to be angry than their husbands do, so it isn't surprising that anger leaks out during the laboratory interactions. However, we were surprised to find that both in the laboratory and at home, battered women expressed as much belligerence and contempt as their husbands did. In violent altercations, women get angry when their husbands begin to abuse them—and often fight back, at least verbally. Even though it doesn't have any impact on the course of the husband's violent episode, at times it appears that the anger is simply overwhelming.

In fact, battered women appear to respond during arguments—both violent and nonviolent—much as one would expect. When you're being abused, you are bound to be scared, but you are also bound to be angry. We saw much effort on the part of battered women to contain their anger, but it tended to leak out anyway. At the same time, even as they were feeling the fury and the frustration of trying to reach this unreachable man, they were fearing for their safety. The Cobra is trying to teach the wife a lesson: he has control, and she must not forget that. The battered wife is frightened, angry, and has no effective way of stopping the violence until it runs its course.

The Reestablishment of Control. George stopped his violence toward Vicky once he felt that she had been taught a lesson: "Don't try to tell me what to do." Then he left the house. The departure was the icing on the cake. The violence ended when control was reestablished. Vicky never made an issue out of the "tits and ass" shows again, at least not for a number of years. Of course, nothing was resolved. The issue was just never discussed again. There was never an apology by George; he minimized the whole incident. Vicky strove to return to normalcy as quickly as she could. Among Cobras, this is the way violent altercations usually go. They end when the Cobra decides to end the violence. The battered woman, as long as she still holds on to the dream of a normal relationship, tries as quickly as possible to erase the incident and return to the status quo prior to the incident. In Vicky's case, this meant cleaning up, caring for her child, and going to sleep.

Carl: An "Out-of-Control" Cobra

For some Cobras, their battering seems truly impulsive, as if the batterer really *is* out of control. Unlike George, who struck quickly and ferociously but never seemed to lose control, not all battering among Cobras looks so clearly calculated to maintain or reestablish control. There has been a tendency in the professional literature to deny the importance of losing control among batterers, because that interpretation appears to let the batterer off the hook, like the diminished-capacity defense in a criminal trial. How can someone be held responsible for an involuntary reaction? Despite the fact that battering is often impulsive, batterers choose to be violent at particular times, and for particular reasons. In the case of the Cobra, the brutality is typically cool and calculated. But not always.

Carl's battering was explosive. When he battered, he looked out of control. His anger came on suddenly, without warning, and often seemed to occur out of the blue. In our view, he "lost it" when he was upset with himself. The anger served a cleansing function for him. It was cathartic. He felt better afterward. And, more than either Pit Bulls or most Cobras, something really snapped when he became violent. Carl is no less responsible for the battering because of this snapping process. Like all batterers, Carl should be held accountable for it. But there are two distinct battering dynamics in Cobras: the calm ferocity manifested by George; and the explosiveness which characterized Carl. There were more Cobras like George than there were like Carl, but the Carls do exist.

Carl drove recklessly, especially when he was angry. In the fall of 1989, he and his wife Liz were on vacation in Egypt, and Carl was at the wheel. He wasn't driving well, and Liz was getting nervous.

They were trying to find the U.S. Embassy to get a form notarized. She was asking him a technical question about the form, and he wasn't answering. After ten minutes of silence, he answered her question. She asked him why he didn't answer her right away, and he started punching her on the arm—while he was driving! The same spot on the arm, six painful blows, driving the car with one hand, recklessly punching her with the other. She was angry, and expressed it so quickly that she didn't have time to suppress it for fear of the violence getting worse. "What the hell are you doing?" she screamed at him. "That *hurts.*" He later explained: "She's asking me idiotic questions when I'm trying to find this shithole in a strange land, and she's digging into me. I was sick and tired of her distracting me with her verbal nonsense. I'm trying to focus and she's coming out of left field. I want it quiet when I'm concentrating on the road. You can't focus on conversation and drive at the same time. You want quiet, she won't be quiet, and it gets on my nerves."

He was wound up, angry at himself for being lost and not knowing the directions, and was taking it out on her. She stopped speaking to him: she was angry, and her arm hurt. He never apologized. They never talked about the incident later. She cried as she remembered the black-and-blue bruise on her arm. But she told us that she lets these things go because it does no good to bring them up later.

He mocked her. Even though she never accused him of being abusive, he would admit to it: "Yeah, I'm a batterer, big fucking deal," he would say in a taunting tone of voice.

In the end, she was intimidated and afraid. Carl was not thinking, just acting. Self-insight and reflection were never his strong suits. He had a serious problem with his own hatred of himself and it made him very mean. His contempt for himself often turned into violence toward Liz. He remembers *her* accusing him of being abusive, and quotes himself as saying, "So what? I haven't killed you, have I? That wouldn't be hard, you know. So don't make a mountain out of a molehill." He mocked her to us for staying with a man who was willing to admit that he was a wife beater.

He told us that she ridiculed him, badgered him, and carped at him. He didn't see his response as an overreaction. He didn't see himself as a walking powder keg, although we did. Cobras cannot always be judged by the trail of blood left behind. Carl was like a grenade, exploding with self-loathing and inflicting the consequences on others, especially Liz. He and Liz were in complete agreement about what happened. But whereas Liz was deeply affected by the incident, Carl shrugged it off. He engaged in the classic minimizing that Cobras do, much in the way that George did. Carl told himself that it was no big deal. She deserved this beating. She was intimidated, controlled, and subjugated by this and the incidents that followed, none of which were a big deal to him.

Carl was not plotting a control coup against Liz. He saw the world through a prism which distorted and greatly limited his awareness. His behavior was an externalization of his self-loathing. His self-loathing meant that he could go off at any time. His violence was not predictable because it didn't depend on what Liz did or didn't do. His violence was a smoldering ember, ready to flare up, and he felt better after letting off some steam, and in the process subjugating Liz.

The more he was able to diminish her in his eyes, the less he had to focus on his contempt for himself, which for him was an awful and constant feeling. He didn't fear abandonment, like a Pit Bull, nor was he as cold and calculating as some of the other Cobras, such as George. He was a batterer who conformed to that old stereotype: he couldn't control his anger. His battering was about anger, and about lack of impulse control. But just like all the other Cobras, control over another made him feel better.

Pit Bull Anger: Control Driven by Fear of Abandonment

As we stated at the outset, there is no one typical pattern in a violent altercation. Battering is always about the establishment of control, and batterers are men who not only have an extraordinary need for control, but who grow up convinced that whatever they need to do to control their partner is justified, including battering. Cobras usually gain control through a ferocious, cold, calculating method of abuse; occasionally, they gain control through their sheer explosiveness. In the next incidents, we describe the two major ways that Pit Bulls establish control over their partners. One method, which allows us to revisit Don and Martha, a couple whom you met in chapter 1, is through constant scrutiny and attempts at isolation, so that the batterer is always "in the face" of the battered woman, and she ends up feeling that she is being battered constantly, even when he is not there. The other method involves total mind control, to the point where the battered woman begins to doubt her own sanity.

Martha had been out with a friend, and it was getting close to midnight. Don was getting agitated. He couldn't sleep. Where was she? Was some guy hitting on her? Did she have something going on the side? His fantasies were playing games with him. He had her tried, convicted, and sentenced by the time she walked in the door. Martha assumed he would be asleep, and was quiet so that she would not awaken him. She went into the bathroom and started to wash her face.

Suddenly, Don slammed open the door, hitting her on the side. "Why did you do that?" asked Martha. Don attempted to be casual: "No reason. You are being kind and considerate, as usual." His voice was dripping with sarcasm.

Martha asked him why he was acting like this, why couldn't he just leave things alone? "Don't you *ever* talk to me like that!" Don threatened. Martha became enraged, as the ramifications of his behavior and the reasons for it suddenly became apparent to her, like an unexpected gust of wind. But even an observer would have guessed what was going on with Don when he screamed, "Where have you been until midnight?" She told him whom she was with, containing her anger to gently explain that they had been out to dinner, that he knew she was working late, that it was, under the circumstances, not surprising that she wasn't home until midnight. Why didn't she call? Because there was no reason to.

He acted like a victim at first, switching courses to sound momentarily like an understandably concerned spouse. But by this time Martha was also dripping with sarcasm: "So you were worried about me?" He told her to shut up, and she could have stopped there, just as Vicky could have tolerated George's television viewing. But she was more angry than she was scared, and she thought that maybe they could work through this issue once and for all. So she pressed him because she wanted him to be rational, to understand, to sympathize with her, to acknowledge that she had done nothing wrong. Battered women like Martha and Vicky are in no-win situations as long as they hold onto their elusive dream. She forced herself to remain calm, and asked him why he couldn't just trust her and believe her.

It was then that he started hitting her on her head with his fist. He was pulling her hair, punching her in the face, and leaving those familiar, telltale signs of his abuse around her eyes and on her chin. Martha was crying during this barrage, but Don kept at it, yelling, hitting, and screaming at her to pack her stuff and get out. Of course, every time she had actually tried to do that, she had been beaten for it. At this moment, to obey or disobey was immaterial, as he was giving her no opportunity but to deflect the brutal assault. She started to fight back, yelling, "Leave me alone! You can't do this."

At some point, he did go into the bedroom and started to pack her things. But he was actually doing little more than creating a mess—throwing random items in boxes, throwing her clothes on the ground, breaking things on her dresser. She just kept screaming, "Why?" And the more she screamed, the harder he threw, and the harder he threw, the more she screamed. She later recalled how incredibly loud the encounter was. She was crying, and screaming, and yelling, and then—to shut her up, he later told the police—he began to choke her.

As he was choking her, he said, "You want to die? You do, don't you? You're going to end up dead someday. I'm going to kill you if you don't shut up." Martha later told us that she had never been quite as frightened as she was at that moment because she was totally dependent on his mercy. She couldn't breathe, and she thought he was, in fact, going to kill her. But he let go after a few seconds.

She told him that she was getting out of the house to spend the night at her brother's house. He said, "Just get out of here." They were both dazed by what had happened, and they wanted to be rid of one another. She took some of her clothes, and as she was packing she noticed that the house looked like it had been struck by a tornado. But she didn't care. She had to get away. She couldn't stand the helplessness, the fear, but in recounting the incident, what she said was most intolerable was the *control* he had over her—including whether she lived or died.

She didn't speak to him for forty-eight hours after that incident. When he called at her brother's, she said that she wasn't coming back. Then he came by to apologize and was as charming as he typically became after beating her, which was quite charming indeed. But nothing changed. He was very affectionate for a few days, but there was no discussion of the incident, no apology.

Martha sustained several injuries during this incident, including bruises all over her face and on her neck from the strangulation. Things were better for a brief period of time, but soon returned to normal, with three or four instances of battering per week.

Don didn't like it when Martha went out without him. He often referred to her friends as a "bunch of whores." Once when he said that she responded sarcastically, "Oh, you think that my friends have sex for money?" He slapped her across the face, calling her a "smart ass." *He* told us about this incident, to exemplify what he was up against: "See what I'm dealing with? Who would put up with that shit?" He told us about another incident, which culminated with his arrest, to show us how unfair the system was, because after all, why should a man be arrested when his own wife is humiliating him? How was she humiliating him? By manipulating him into fits of rage. From his perspective, she was in control.

Don was a Pit Bull. Control was just as important to him as it was to George and Carl, but for different reasons. Don genuinely felt, throughout his body, that he would be abandoned. He hated Martha because the fact of her existence made him feel vulnerable, and he couldn't tolerate the intimacy which led to his fear of abandonment. But the possibility of abandonment scared him even more than the intimacy. He blamed Martha for his own neediness, and punished her for it almost every day they were together. George's "needs," in contrast, were always transitory. So were Carl's. They didn't want anyone to get in their way at certain times, especially not their wives. With Don, the needs were constant; Don needed Martha to fill a void that could never be filled. The void was a consequence of Don's inability to form an emotional connection with another human being, despite a compelling need to feel connected to others. The only way that Don could connect with Martha was through violence. One difference between Don and the Cobras was in how Don saw himself as a victim. George and Carl knew that they were not victims, and they didn't care that Vicky and Liz *were*. Don sincerely felt like a victim.

Power and control come in many varieties. But however the control is experienced, it is the batterer who holds the cards. Cobras know that they hold the cards. Pit Bulls don't know it, and they seem pathetic for that. But in the end, if you consider the incident we just described between Don and Martha, the similarities to the Cobras are greater than the differences. All three men did what they felt they had to do in order to sustain control. Because of their dream of a normal life, all three women responded by treating the men as if they were like other people, people who could be reasoned with. Vicky, Liz, and Martha all paid dearly for that. They felt sheepish, and even somewhat ashamed in retrospect, long after leaving these relationships. How could they have been so blind? None of the batterers experienced shame. Pit Bulls and Cobras are quite different, and we will be illustrating and describing these differences throughout the book. But in this most important way, they are identical: they are all batterers, and they are dangerous.

Similarities and Differences

The incident between Don and Martha shows many of the same characteristics of those involving the Cobra couples: the unpredictability, the seemingly inconsequential act, the combination of anger and fear on Martha's part, the inability to defuse the situation, and the use of violence as a method of reestablishing control. But we also saw some important differences between this argument and the ones described between the Cobras and their partners.

Control Driven by Dependence. For George and Carl, "control" meant being left alone and not accepting influence from a woman. For Don, "control" meant turning Martha into a puppet, stifling her independence, taking away any life she may have had apart from him. He was tortured by the fear that she would abandon him, and no matter how hard he tried to squelch that fear by asserting control, the fear never left him. This helps to explain why Don was battering Martha practically every other day, rather than episodically. He felt constantly vulnerable to losing her, and he released the demons of his vulnerability through violence. Whereas George and Carl fought to be left alone by their wives, Don fought to intensify the attachment between the two of them.

The False Perception of Victimization. Don felt like a victim even though he was the perpetrator. He thought of Martha as the perpetrator because he saw her as the person in control of the situation. Martha was screaming and yelling at Don even as she was being beaten. When Martha tried to drop the subject, Don felt victimized and provoked: to him, he was being dismissed and psychologically abandoned. As O. J. Simpson wrote in his so-called suicide note, "Sometimes I felt like a battered husband."

The Batterer Who Makes "Demands" of His Partner. George and Carl were fiercely independent and struck quickly and ferociously when that independence was challenged. Vicky and Liz sought the intimacy and involvement that people commonly look for in relationships. The desire for a normal family life was part of their dream, and so they attempted to get their battering partners to act like normal husbands and fathers. Both George and Carl were prone to violence as well as emotional abuse as methods of resisting influence. Cobras are less likely to place demands on their wives as long as they are left alone. They become dangerous when they don't get what they want at the time they want it.

Don, however, was doing more than resisting influence: he was demanding *change* from Martha. Because he was emotionally dependent on her and terrified of abandonment, he tended to be chronically dissatisfied with the amount of intimacy and emotional involvement she provided. For example, Don demanded that Martha spend all of her leisure time with him, and he was chronically suspicious that she was having an affair.

The Fight That Never Ends. Because Don was never satisfied that he was loved enough, and because fighting was his only way of making an emotional connection with Martha, their fights never ended. Hence, there was almost constant violence and emotional abuse. Unlike the two Cobra couples, where the fights would end when control was reestablished, Don's beating was interrupted by the police, and there were never more than a few days of grace between episodes.

Total Mind Control: Making Battered Women Feel Crazy

Ruth's sister had been living with Ruth and Gene for six months. The sister got on Gene's nerves. Gene resented not having time alone with Ruth, but Ruth didn't seem to mind. Gene would fume at the reminder that before Ruth, a room-mate had been renting the downstairs apartment. Why was Ruth not upset that they had so little time together? Gene was a Pit Bull, and like Don, didn't want to share his battered partner with anyone. He was another example of the demanding, emotional dependency that generates both the possessiveness and the need to control.

On one particular night, Gene started to complain about Kay living with them: she should pay more rent, she should stop running up the phone bill, she should eat her own food. Ruth had no gripes about Kay, and she told Gene that he should talk to her himself if he was dissatisfied with her behavior. Thus, Ruth, despite living with a batterer, and knowing that he was capable of hurting her, stood up to him. She was calm, but assertive. He disagreed, claiming that since Kay was her sister, Ruth should be the messenger. Ruth held firm: "I find it helpful to have her around. I don't have a quarrel with her. I don't want to be a go-between. You can discuss things as easily as I can. You can communicate with her."

The stalemate was familiar to both of them. Up until now, this disagreement might seem fairly normal for a couple without a great deal of money or space. Ruth was a battered woman; yet she held her ground, and she was sure she was right. But even now, the disagreement had a bizarre quality to it, one that is typical of arguments that Pit Bulls have with their partners. Gene was not just disagreeing; he was being emotionally abusive *as* he was disagreeing. In this incident, as in all of the fights between Gene and Ruth, emotional abuse was immediately part of the argument, as soon as she disagreed with him, no matter how calmly she did so. Ruth became irate at the insults, and feeling a need for space, she tried to leave the house. She was searching for a withdrawal ritual.

Gene wasn't about to let her leave. He grabbed her to prevent her from leaving and continued swearing at her. He twisted her arm in such a way that if she continued to wriggle free, her arm would break. She asked him to let go, and she stopped wriggling. He let go, but stood between her and the door and ordered her not to leave. She ran into the bedroom and hid in the closet. He kicked her in the stomach once he found her: he kicked her even though she was pregnant, and he did it *in* the closet. It was more unreal for her than painful. She couldn't believe that her husband was kicking their child in their closet. She remembers worrying about a miscarriage.

Kay, the subject of their argument, eventually pulled him off Ruth and calmed him down. He left for the evening, and came back late that night, spending the few remaining hours of darkness on the couch.

What happened the next morning distinguishes this argument from the one between Don and Martha. Gene apologized for being angry, but *denied* that he had beaten Ruth up. Even when Kay confronted him with his beating, he screamed, "You're both conspiring against me. You know as well as I do that nothing happened." Ruth and Gene didn't talk much over the next couple of days. Ruth didn't know what to think.

Four years later, Kay died of AIDS. At her funeral, Ruth brought up the incident for the first time since that morning. He denied ever touching Ruth while she was pregnant. Perhaps he didn't remember. But a memory lapse would hardly explain the time he hit her at a bar, in front of his friend, and then denied it the next day. Ruth remembered calling his friend, and the friend also denying it.

A violent argument for some Pit Bulls lacks a discrete beginning and a discrete ending. In this particular incident, Gene's denial the following day was the climax of the argument, a method of mind control that not only affected Ruth's perception of the argument the night before, but gradually, over time, created in her a state of confusion. Ruth remembered each and every episode as if it were yesterday, and Gene continued to deny that these episodes had occurred.

Ruth remembered cramping in her stomach for a couple of days after the closet encounter, but explained that she still felt the baby moving, so she didn't go to the hospital. But his denials were so persistent and so persuasive that she began to doubt her sanity. She eventually had a hard time knowing what was true and what wasn't. In this way, Gene was using a strategy that was designed to and gradually succeeded in gaining control over Ruth's mind.

In some ways, this pattern was like our previous examples. Gene was a Pit Bull, and he was jealous. He even became jealous of his children once they demanded Ruth's attention. But Gene illustrates a new element, denying the woman's experience of reality. Pit Bulls often deny their partners' experience of reality; at times, the denial is so effective that—when used in combination with methods to isolate the woman from other people—battered women sometimes begin to doubt their own sanity. Sometimes the men actually believe their own denial; at other times it is a manipulative ploy. But it is an important element of control: battered women become more dependent on their battering husbands when they begin to doubt their own views of reality. Sometimes they become convinced that they need their husbands to take care of them because their husbands have systematically eroded their autonomy as well as their identity. This denial method, crude though it might sound, is very effective and therefore a key component of the mind control in abusive relationships.

Similarities and Differences Between Arguments Perpetrated by Batterers and Those of Nonviolent Couples

All couples argue. Sometimes the arguments get pretty heated, even when couples are happily married. So what is it that makes the relationship between the batterer and the battered woman such a powder keg? Nonviolent couples tend to withdraw from arguments before the arguments escalate into violence. A woman in a relationship with a batterer cannot predict when an argument will turn violent and therefore she cannot withdraw beforehand.

There is one exception to the unpredictability of escalations in violence. In the middle of an argument, when the batterer wants to continue arguing and the woman tries to retreat, his violence inevitably escalates. Ruth tried to get away from Gene, and his emotional abuse escalated to physical abuse. This is quite common. When batterers want to leave the house, there is nothing their wives can do to stop them. When women try to leave, even to go to the bathroom, they put themselves in greater peril.

We can further refine the differences between violent and nonviolent couples by comparing nonviolent couples with Cobra couples and with Pit Bull couples. There are some interesting parallels between the things that abusive and nonabusive couples fight about: the themes are sometimes quite similar, and at other times quite different from the themes that underlie the conflicts that other couples have.

To start with, we all live in the same culture, a culture that is permeated by sexism: our cultural practices and political systems have been historically based on either the explicit or implicit assertion that women are inferior to men.[2] "Patriarchy" is the term used to summarize the cultural practices and political system that perpetuates the superiority of men and the inferiority of women.

As we look at contemporary marriage, we still see massive inequality, especially in certain subcultures within the larger society. Men tend to control economic resources and are still considered in many ways to be the head of household. Women have less power in marriage, and the consequences are palpable. No wonder women are primarily the ones who seek couples therapy in marriages.[3] Husbands are often reluctant to enter therapy because they are more satisfied with things as they are. Wives, on the other hand, typically enter therapy wanting change. These changes include more husband involvement in parenting and housework, more intimacy, and greater equality in decision making. Husbands resist giving up power in any of these areas and often try to use therapy as a method of consolidating it.

Thus, one similarity between the arguments of violent and nonviolent couples is that in both cases couples tend to argue about control: who is going to control the level of intimacy in the relationship, who is going to be responsible for particular areas of housework and parenting, and who is going to make the rules? Husbands like to make the rules; they like to be able to come and go as they please. However, the majority do not resort to violence as a means of enforcing their rights in these areas.

In nonviolent marriages, women are commonly in the position of "demanding" more, while men are often "resisting change" in order to avoid having to provide whatever the woman is asking for.[4] This pattern of female demand and husband withdrawal is more common in unhappy than in happy marriages, and not surprisingly, it is also quite common in the marriages between batterers and battered women. As we have seen, it can be a common theme in the arguments of Cobras and their spouses. In the laboratory interactions, as well as the arguments that occurred at home, the recurring theme was wife unhappiness about husband noninvolvement and husband resistance to any rules.

Pit Bulls are different. As we have seen, the most common dynamic among the arguments between Pit Bulls and their spouses is quite different. Pit Bulls are different from both Cobras *and* nonviolent men in that they are "demanding" change from their partners *as well as* resisting their partners' attempts to change them. Because they tend to be emotionally dependent on their wives and terrified of abandonment, they are chronically dissatisfied with the amount of intimacy and emotional involvement from their partners, no matter how much the partner is doing already. They express their demands through emotional and physical abuse.

At the same time, Pit Bulls also resist requests to change from their wives, just as Cobras do. Thus, when demands are made on them, they either ignore their partners' requests or become abusive. In short, they are just as difficult to influence as Cobras are, but they have the additional characteristic of making incessant demands for change from their partners.

When the results of our research first received media attention, the high rates of belligerence and contempt that we found in battered women were inappropriately interpreted by some reporters. In fact, we had to call a press conference in Seattle to counter some of the inappropriate inferences that were being drawn from our findings.

We found that male violence was not predictable from the behavior of battered women. And just because the wife does something that the husband doesn't like doesn't give him the right to beat her. The only justification for male violence would be self-defense, and we never saw battering episodes that could be interpreted as acts of self-defense. The responsibility for behaving nonviolently is the husband's, and the husband's alone.

There were no female batterers in our sample. We found that *only* the men in our sample successfully used violence as a method of control. Consistently, both in the laboratory and the home, only the women were afraid. Fear is the major gender difference between male and female violence. Without fear, there is no control. For us, fear became a barometer of control. The women consistently manifested it in the laboratory during the arguments, whereas the men did not. The women consistently reported fear when describing arguments at home, whereas the men did not. The men were the perpetrators in each and every case. This is not to say that women never batter men. But if it occurs, it is rare.

4

A Closer Look at Cobra Relationships

Cobras taunt their wives by pushing them away. Yet they want their wives to be there for them when they need something: sex, companionship, money, or someone to get high with. Cobras are very frightening to their wives, and yet at the same time captivating. This combination makes Cobras very hard to escape from. Their tactics of control and intimidation are remarkably effective in terrifying their wives into submission.

When we first began our study, we didn't expect to find any Cobras; in fact, the distinction between Cobra and Pit Bull hadn't even occurred to us. We were astonished to discover that *anyone's* heart rate would lower after a shift from rest to arguing. The heart-rate reduction made no intuitive sense. Cobras looked aroused, they acted aroused, they sounded aroused: yet internally, they were getting calmer and calmer. It would have been important just to know that this type of batterer existed. But what made this discovery all the more important were all the factors we found to be associated with being a Cobra. The relationships Cobras had with their wives turned out to be unique.

No matter how reasonable their wives were in discussing an issue, Cobras would begin a discussion of an area of disagreement by immediately becoming belligerent, contemptuous, or defensive. They gave the appearance of being explosive and dangerous. When we play these videotapes for professional audiences, they find these men to be unnerving and frightening. Our analyses of the videotapes showed us that their wives are also frightened. The swift escalation of the Cobra is effective in keeping the wives from becoming angry at their Cobra husbands.

Vicky's and George's Childhoods

Vicky described her childhood as a "war zone." Her father, now deceased, was a highly respected and prominent professional who would one day be absent and disengaged and then suddenly become physically abusive toward Vicky's mother and all of the kids, including Vicky, the protector of her sisters and her father's favorite target. Vicky sees her mom only occasionally now and still feels bitter about the war-zone days when her mother meekly stood by while the father intimidated and beat the kids. Now, none of the siblings are close, and none of the sisters finds it easy to trust other people.

Vicky was different from her siblings in one important way. She refused to let fear run her life. As soon as she could, she ran away from home, believing there was a better life for her somewhere else. On her sixteenth birthday she bought a six-pack of beer, rolled a few joints, and bought a birthday cake with white frosting. Laughing as she lighted and blew out sixteen candles, she ate the whole cake herself and she got high from the beer and pot.

The next day, she found the first big highway headed east, stuck out her thumb and felt her life start for the first time.

She wasn't wild. She had a dream, a dream of a real family, one she had never known. But until she became pregnant by George many years later, she hadn't tried to implement her dream. With George she would finally become a lioness, and build the home she had always wanted with her confident and dashing new husband.

Her new husband, George, had had more than his share of chaos and abuse as a kid, growing up in a small town. His mother was a prostitute who physically abused him. She beat him and his sister each morning, saying, "What's this for? It's just in case you do anything bad today." His father worked on a riverboat, and on those rare occasions when he was home, he also beat the children.

George learned that it was okay to beat and degrade women. He hated his mother. He wished he were big enough to lift weights like his dad and get strong enough to hit her back. Finally that day came, and when she tried to hit him, he saw to it that she would never touch him again. We asked him about his happiest childhood memory. One night at age twelve, he remembers hearing one of his mom's tricks beating her. He grabbed a rifle, pointed it at the customer's head, and told him to "Get the hell out, or I'll blow your head off." That was it. Years later, George expressed regret that he didn't kill the "son-of-a-bitch right then and there."

George became a Cobra early in life. When he was young and his mother hit him he calmed himself down so that he could at least "leave the scene" in his mind. He had developed the power of his mind as he waited for his body to become ready to also grow powerful. And when he finally became physically strong, he did not hesitate to use his strength. Prior to joining the navy, he picked fights and caused trouble whenever he could. Once in the navy, he controlled his outbursts, but he made it a cardinal rule that no one would ever pick on him again. After a few disastrous friendships, he learned never to trust. George enjoyed the company of people and liked a good time as much as his buddies, but deep down he was a loner.

George also refused to allow any woman to penetrate his armor. He could effectively control the women in his life by calming himself down and occasionally threatening them. Over time George's Cobra-like response became automatic. By the time we met him, it was as if his body were wired differently from everyone else's. George had gained control over his own nervous system. He could rail and threaten while focusing his attention so that inside he remained cool.

George and Vicky had this in common: they both ran away from abusive environments at home at sixteen. George went to live with his father, who never checked up on where he was at night. George ran up quite a record as a juvenile delinquent while his father was working on the riverboat. He now thinks back on these as happy times, where "sex, drugs, and rock-n-roll" dominated his life. When he was nineteen, he was engaged to a woman who was later killed in a car he was driving while loaded on drugs and alcohol. George was convicted of involuntary manslaughter, but did no jail time. Instead he joined the navy.

Vicky's Descent into Hell

When George began to reveal his violent side to Vicky, telling her he was planning to kill a few guys who deserved it and suggesting that he had killed before and gotten away with it, he knew he was scaring her. In fact, the whole point was to scare her. Vicky was suddenly seeing a new side of George: George the Cobra was revealing himself to his wife. George's allusions to, threats of, and use of actual violence to intimidate and control Vicky had begun.

George's violence toward Vicky was difficult to predict. Anything could set him off. He reacted to any reasonable request as if it were a threat to his sense of honor. He was hypersensitive to any attempts on Vicky's part to influence his behavior, and reacted to even perfectly reasonable requests with verbal attacks, threats, and violence. When Vicky asked him to do some work around the house, he responded, "I'm not going to follow any damned rules."

Vicky gradually backed off from making these reasonable requests, but George continued being belligerent. His violence also escalated. He constantly blamed her for their financial debts, and she became so frightened of not having money around when he needed it that she avoided paying bills to make sure that he had enough to spend. She trod very lightly and was constantly vigilant. When he drank, his fuse was shorter. He also smoked pot around the house on a daily basis, despite Vicky's concerns about exposing their daughter, Christi, to marijuana smoking.

George was, at least on the surface, a cocky man who bragged that he was superior to other people, and that the rules of society did not apply to him. He had come to the conclusion that human beings were not to be trusted, based on his sense that he had been betrayed by every important person he had encountered in his life. Though he had never hinted at his deep cynicism about humanity during their courtship, he became more open about expressing these views after marriage. "Humans suck," was the phrase that echoed in Vicky's brain, so often did she hear that utterance from George's lips.

In the early stages of their marriage Vicky saw the violence as the "wounded side" of George. She made it her mission to reform his view of people and to bring out the tender, charming, qualities that had initially won her admiration and love. A natural way of building solidarity in any marriage is to support whatever positive view one's partner has of himself or herself, and Vicky tried to ally herself with George's boasting. George enjoyed this. He told Vicky at length how superior he was to other people, what fools they were, and that the rules of society did not apply to him. Vicky at first laughed at his wit when he insulted others and not her. But she encouraged him to see other people in a more positive light, as potential friends, as confidants, as allies in times of stress. No, George countered, this attitude was just weakness. Vicky thought that she needed to be close to George so she could help him heal. She held fast to her dream about what George could become. But her dream was becoming her ticket to hell.

When we met them in our research project, George and Vicky had been married for two years, and their daughter Christi was almost two years old. Vicky had a clerical job at a small company and earned less than $1,000 per month. George enjoyed shocking and scaring people to see the effect he could have. George told us that his job in the navy was "to kill people." This answer, along with much of his behavior throughout the study, teetered on the edge of bravado: like Vicky, we never quite knew how much of this provocative behavior was designed to entertain, impress, or scare us, and how much of it was from the heart.

In the year prior to entering our research project, George had threatened to kill Vicky on numerous occasions, and had been violent toward her about fifteen times. His violence ranged from pushing and shoving to kicking her, choking her, and threatening her with a knife.

Three weeks prior to coming to our research project, they had had a particularly violent argument. George came home late after drinking with his buddies and found Vicky and Christi sharing a pizza. Vicky was angry at him for missing dinner and ignored him when he arrived. Her silence angered him and he shouted, "You got a problem?" When she remained silent, he slammed his fist into the pizza, knocked her off the chair, dragged her across the room by her hair, held her down, and spit pizza in her face. He then beat her up, yelling, "You're a bitch! You've ruined my life!" Vicky described the argument as typical: "powerful, mean, and fast."

Recalling the incident in our laboratory, George characteristically minimized the level of violence, glibly limiting his description to one terse comment: "I just pushed her and threw her around a little bit." He felt as he always did when he beat her, that "she was a bitch and she deserved it." George was perfectly willing to admit to his violence toward Vicky. As he put it, "I don't remember the details because it's not important."

George was also verbally abusive. Despite the fact that Vicky was a classically beautiful woman, he constantly told her how ugly she was. He insulted her religious beliefs, humiliated her in front of other people, and ridiculed her at the drop of a hat. Despite all of the arguments and abuse, George told us that he was happily married. This is what he wanted in a marriage.

Vicky was depressed and openly expressed her unhappiness with her marriage. Her friends told her that she was a battered woman, but she refused to see herself that way. She still believed George would change. She avoided thinking about the violence and passed her time running on instinct, feeling somewhat numb, in a mild state of shock.

George enjoyed the control he had over Vicky. When we videotaped their argument in our laboratory, Vicky calmly tried to reason with George. She said that his life would be better if he were more of a family man, if he didn't go out drinking with his buddies so often. She clearly had not given up her dream of a normal family life with this man, who seemed so poorly suited for the role of husband and father. As she stood her ground and tried to reason with him, he glibly cracked jokes and made fun of her. He was capable of being charming, funny, and entertaining. She laughed and smiled at his humor. He seemed to enjoy being in front of the camera. She scored repeatedly with logic on her side, but he didn't seem to notice or care. The whole conversation seemed like a big joke to George. At one point, George suddenly turned toward Vicky and said, "Don't you see? It's all a game. Life is a game. It's easy, but you make it hard." Vicky responded by asking him, "Then why do you get so mad?" George replied, "Because people suck." When she complained that he had no friends, only drinking buddies, George replied, "What else is there?"

George enjoyed exasperating Vicky. At one point during the conversation, when Vicky sighed, George grinned widely at her and asked, "Are you getting frustrated now?" It was clear that he wanted her answer to be yes. At another point, Vicky said, "It's really hard to talk to you, George." George seized upon that remark and wanted to hear more about it. He asked, "Why?" Without giving her much time to respond, he asked her again. He wanted to hear about her exasperation, his success at controlling her emotions and feelings. He was taunting her, and enjoying himself vastly.

Despite there being no meeting of the minds during this conversation, there was a playful and somewhat flirtatious quality to their interaction. Vicky had clearly not as yet given up on George. There was still chemistry between them, and she wanted him. She wanted more closeness, more involvement, more of his loving side. It seemed as if he played the part of the outlaw who refused to take off his boots and stay awhile, while she played the part of the woman waiting for him at home, ever hopeful that he would come to his senses.

The Dynamics of George and Vicky

It is hard to understand a relationship like the one between Vicky and George. Even for those who have some knowledge of domestic violence, there is much about the relationship between Vicky and George that doesn't fit the stereotype. It is common for batterers to terrorize their intimate partners. But there is something different about the nature of the terror created by Cobras and the way battered women respond to it.

George, a typical Cobra, terrorized Vicky to control her, just as Pit Bulls do. He was also an impulsive man, like most bat-

terers. But unlike Pit Bulls, George was not emotionally dependent on Vicky. He didn't want to be controlled by *anyone*,
including Vicky. Unlike a Pit Bull, George was not worried that
Vicky would flirt with or form relationships with other men.
The attachment between Vicky and George is typical of those
formed between Cobras and the women they batter.

Cobras, we suspect, have learned to choose their partners
very carefully. They are adept at finding women who are vulnerable to their macabre charisma, women whose lives are
guided by a particular kind of dream, women who are down on
their luck, new in town, or susceptible to an apparently attentive listener. George cannily figured out and then preyed on
Vicky's particular vulnerabilities. In a peculiar way, he did need
her. It seemed to us at the time of our first interview with
George that his need for her was infantile, a need to know that
he had the power to control her. Having this power was important to him, perhaps because as a child he was so powerless.

How does a bright, perceptive woman fall for the con job perpetrated by George? The answer to that question is complicated. It is not just the con job that explains the seduction, but
also the life circumstances at the time of the con job. The con
job of the Cobra is persuasive; it can fool therapists, judges,
prosecutors, probation officers, and the police. Thus, it is not
surprising that a young woman in a bar would find George
charming. When you add to the persuasiveness and charisma of
a Cobra the vulnerability of Vicky *at that particular time*, it is
not hard to see why she would be susceptible to George's
charms. She was a lost soul who had just moved back to a place
which had never offered her security or love. Yet it was the only
home she knew. She was also armed with a dream, and George
came along like Prince Charming to rescue her and help her
fulfill this dream. Is it then any wonder that Vicky, despite her
keen intelligence and generally sound instincts about people,
would succumb and enter into this fairy tale with George?

By the time women like Vicky find themselves in abusive relationships, it is much harder to get out of them than it was to get into them. Battered women are afraid of their husbands, afraid of what they might do to them if they tried to leave. For one thing, when violent husbands kill their wives, it is commonly *after* they try to leave the relationship. For another, especially when there are children involved, battered women are often dependent on their husbands for economic survival. Finally, something happens to people who are exposed to chronic terror and trauma. They begin to underestimate themselves, wondering whether they can survive in the outside world without their abusive partners. Cobras are especially good at convincing their partners that they are worthless without them until the battered wives buy into the Cobras' view of themselves and the world.

Cobras and Pit Bulls Are Different

We discovered a number of very interesting and important factors that distinguished Cobras from Pit Bulls.

Cobra Violence is More Severe. Even though the violence was as common among the Pit Bulls as it was among the Cobras, the severity of violence was much greater among the Cobras. For example, 38 percent of the Cobras had threatened their wives with a knife or a gun, compared to only 4 percent of the Pit Bulls. Whereas none of the Pit Bulls had actually *used* a knife or gun in a violent episode, 9 percent of the Cobras had either stabbed or shot their wives. Almost all of the Cobras had beaten up their wives with closed fists, often including choking (91 percent), whereas the percentage was significantly smaller (though still large) in the Pit Bulls (62 percent). George had beaten Vicky up on numerous occasions, and had threatened to kill her (which often included the brandishing of weapons) repeatedly. However, it is important to note that Cobras hold no monopoly on beatings, since the majority of Pit Bulls had also severely beaten their wives.

Cobras Commit More Emotional Abuse. The Cobras were more emotionally abusive than the Pit Bulls, as evidenced by their significantly higher rates of belligerence and contempt, particularly at the very start of the laboratory interaction. George was not as belligerent during the laboratory interaction as a typical Cobra, but he was as contemptuous toward Vicky as they come. He was also contemptuous toward us and toward most other people. Pit Bulls became more emotionally abusive over the course of the conflict discussion, a kind of slow burn in which they became increasingly heated and began to lose control. In contrast, Cobras always stayed in control.

Cobras Have More Chaotic, Traumatic Childhoods. In many ways we were left with the impression that Cobras had come from backgrounds that more seriously crushed something very fragile that every child begins life with, a kind of implicit trust that despite all their limitations, parents have the child's best interest at heart. Our image was that this horrible childhood background had somehow led the Cobras to vow to themselves that no one would ever control them again. Somehow they had all managed to change their normal physiological reactions in the same way, and that change in their physiology was the key that led us to discover them.

Cobras came from more chaotic family backgrounds than Pit Bulls, although the Pit Bulls were more likely to have had batterers as fathers. Specifically, 78 percent of the Cobras in our study came from families where there was some kind of violence in the home when they were children, compared to 51 percent of the Pit Bulls. Even this 51 percent figure is high, since in the population at large (a still alarmingly high) 20 to 25 percent of children grow up in violent homes. So both types of batterers are more likely than members of the general population to have grown up in violent homes.

Twenty-three percent of the Pit Bulls came from families in which their fathers beat up their mothers and the violence went only one way. The Cobras almost invariably came from childhoods that were quite traumatic, with violence manifesting itself in a variety of ways, including having very violent mothers who abused them. George's childhood was a classic example. He was beaten and neglected by both parents, sexually abused by his prostitute mother's male customers, and spent his entire childhood with his parents living apart. He grew up with contempt for his mother, and he hated, but somehow respected, his father.

Women Married to Cobras Are More Depressed and Frightened. The battered women married to Cobras showed less anger, more fear, and more sadness during the laboratory interaction than did women married to Pit Bulls. The first time Vicky and George showed up at the laboratory, Vicky's sadness as well as her fear were much more obvious than her anger. In fact, she was quite gentle with George, still obviously attached to him, yet speaking carefully and deliberately. Women married to Cobras have a lot to be scared about, and every reason to be sad. They also have to work at not expressing whatever anger they might feel because any overt expression of anger could result in a beating.

Cobras and Their Wives Do Not Easily Separate or Divorce. The marriages of the Cobras were less likely to end in separation or divorce, at least over the two-year follow-up period of our study, than the marriages of the Pit Bulls. In fact, at the two-year follow-up not a single couple in the Cobra group had separated, and the one divorced couple (Roy and Helen) were still living together! In contrast, almost half of the couples married to Pit Bulls were separated or divorced at the end of two years.

We think that the relative "stability" of Cobra marriages stems in large part from the terrible fear that these wives have of leaving their husbands. However, based on our final interviews with the women between 1995 and 1996, and our informal observations of the laboratory interactions, these couples also seemed more attached than the Pit Bull couples. As we mentioned in chapter 3, the typical pattern among the Cobra couples was for the wives to be quite committed to the marriages, despite the violence, while the husbands avoided intimacy, demonstrated ambivalence about commitment to the relationship, and engaged in a great deal of provocative, destructive behavior beyond the violence.

Cobras Are More Violent Outside *as Well as Inside the Marriage.* Cobras were much more likely to have a history of violence outside the marriage than Pit Bulls. While 44 percent of the Cobras had histories of violence outside the marriage, only 3 percent of the Pit Bulls had such histories. Virtually all of the Cobras who had been violent outside the marriage were violent with a wide variety of people, including people at work and other family members and acquaintances; most of them had gotten into at least occasional violent altercations with strangers. In contrast, the Pit Bulls were almost never violent toward friends or other family members, and none of those in our sample reported violence directed toward strangers.

Cobras Had More Mental Illness. Cobras were much more likely than the Pit Bulls to qualify for a diagnosis of "personality disorder," specifically "antisocial personality disorder." People with antisocial personality disorders have long histories of impulsive, criminal-like behavior, including but not limited to violence. Typically, these disorders go all the way back to adolescence. Other researchers have found among antisocial youth a history of childhood episodes of lying, stealing, fire setting, and cruelty to animals. They were likely to have few friends as young children, to be rejected by other children because of their violence, to have a history of school failure and depression, and to eventually become connected with a deviant group of children. Their parents were likely not to know where they were at night even when the children were as young as nine years old. While some of the Pit Bulls (about 33 percent) qualified as antisocial, fully 90 percent of the Cobras met the criteria for this classification. Also, even though the two groups of batterers did not differ in their likelihood of abusing alcohol (both abused alcohol at high rates), the Cobras *were* more likely to be dependent on illegal drugs such as cocaine and heroin, and pharmaceutical addictive drugs.

Eighty percent of the women who married Cobras were normal on our personality scales. However, a small proportion of the women married to Cobras also had histories of antisocial behavior. These were the Bonnie and Clyde type of marriages, as if two outlaws had found one another. Despite the battering, these women spoke very freely of how attractive their husbands were to them, how they liked romance "on the edge," how they could never be attracted to a nice guy. Typically, the battered women in these marriages also had extraordinarily traumatic family backgrounds, often including sexual as well as physical abuse. Violence had been so common in their upbringing that they couldn't conceive of a life without it.

One such couple, Helen and Roy, met in the release room of a prison. He was being released after serving a prison term for armed robbery, while she was visiting an ex-boyfriend doing time for child abuse. On the bus ride into town they decided to live together, and after a few weeks they married. When we asked him what his occupation was, he said, "I'm a burglar and a junkie." Like George, he enjoyed taunting us, trying to frighten and shock us with his replies to our questions. Let's look more closely at Helen and Roy.

Romance on the Edge with a Cobra: The Story of Helen and Roy

Roy could not focus. He was often in a drug-induced fog, feeling a bit euphoric, a bit confused, and somewhat groggy. He was even more irritated than usual by an argument he and Helen had had earlier in the day. She was supposed to have brought home some cash, but she forgot. Earlier on this unseasonably warm evening in January 1989, they had been drinking Jack Daniel's, smoking pot, and snorting coke. Not an unusual way for Roy and Helen to spend an evening. Before the evening was over, he had given her one of the worst beatings of her life, and he seemed to be bragging as he told us about it.

Helen was also mad at Roy. No, she was furious at Roy. When they were in the neighborhood bar a couple of hours later, she had threatened to hit on the bartender. She was tired of Roy's promiscuity. Now *she* was going to have an affair with someone, she threatened. Finally, Roy began verbally abusing her at the bar, and she took a swing at him. She began calling him names, kicking him, hitting him, scratching him. Eventually, he lost his temper and beat her up: first in the bar, then outside the bar. He broke her nose, gave her two black eyes, "kicked her up and down the street." The police arrived and carted them both off to jail. However, only Roy was charged with assault, which Roy found outrageous since "I was only fighting in self-defense." Helen didn't press charges, which were eventually dropped. Helen suffered a head injury as a result of this beating, in addition to the cuts, bruises, and contusions. She had headaches for weeks afterwards.

Roy and Helen were living in a trailer park in Oregon at the time. Her family was living with them. It was a very stressful time. They had no money. Helen's mother had cancer. Roy's first wife was demanding child support. Snake, Roy's prison buddy and partner in crime, was pressuring Roy to move back to Seattle, where Snake said they could make some big money dealing drugs. One night during this time, Roy and Helen were in a bar, drinking heavily. Roy was flirting with cocktail waitresses and not paying any attention to Helen. Snake was with them, making sure that Helen noticed each and every unsavory action of Roy's. Helen was getting more and more upset.

Finally, she said: "Look, you want me to just go home? You seem to be having a good time without me."

Helen impulsively walked out into the street, and tried to stand in front of a car that was speeding down the arterial road. Helen was depressed, and the drunken stupor made it worse. Suddenly, suicide seemed like the answer. But Snake and Roy pulled her to safety, and Roy took her home.

Why did Roy save her? Certainly not because he minded her getting physically injured. In fact, as soon as they got home, Roy nearly beat her to death. Helen remembers seeing blood all over the walls and on the bed, but feeling no pain. She was too drunk, and perhaps too numb, to feel the pain. The police arrived because some neighbors had heard the commotion and called. Again, both were taken to jail, and after four hours they were bailed out by her brother Sam.

Later, they were in the car, driving home. Helen had been beaten to a pulp, she was dirty and swollen, and Sam was aghast. He let Roy know in no uncertain terms that he and his brothers were going to mess him up, mess him up good. Astonishingly, Helen defended Roy, and told Sam to stay away. Sam told her she had to choose: it was either Roy, or her family. She said she chose Roy, because unlike her family, he "has been there for me." As she tried to explain to us, "Granted he beat me before that, and he beat me after that, but when push comes to shove he's always there for me when I need him. But I don't count on him being there—that way I don't get disappointed."

Roy and Helen moved to Seattle. Helen was reluctant to follow him, but she did. As a way of celebrating their new start, Helen bought Roy a $75 necklace. They were sitting in a bar when she gave it to him. She had quit drinking, but he was drunk. In walked one of his ex-lovers. Roy disappeared for about half an hour, and when Helen asked him where he had been, he said that he had given this woman the necklace and ten dollars, and in return he received fellatio from her. Helen then dragged him out of the bar and to his mother's house to sober him up. He almost immediately passed out. When he awoke the next morning, she was packing to leave, and he tried to apologize. He begged for one more chance. His mother was yelling at him.

"That's when everything changed," Helen told us a year later. "It scared him when he realized that I was really going to leave. He could tell that I had had enough. He found out how far he could push me. I'm happy to say that that's when he stopped cheating on me. He told me that if we ever broke up, he could be proud to say that he was faithful—he had never done that for any woman, so that makes me feel good."

But the drug use and the battering continued. Her injuries from the incident in April—a broken nose, several broken ribs, numerous bruises, bumps, and contusions—became a distant memory when he promised fidelity. She held on to his fidelity as a sign that he loved her, and for Helen, his "love" was enough to sustain her through his beatings.

Helen's Background

Helen was thirty-two years old when we met her, born into a household which included her parents and eventually a total of seven siblings. Her parents divorced when she was eighteen. Her father made his living as a truck driver, and was away much of the time. But he was there long enough to sexually abuse Helen from the time she was four years old until she turned ten. Although Helen complained to her mother about the incest, her mother didn't believe her. In fact, her mother was physically abusive toward all of the children. She hit them three or four times a day with a belt, a tree branch, or "whatever she could get her hands on." These beatings continued until the parents' divorce, and she was usually in a "blind rage" when she hit them. Often, the children were too bruised to go to school. Her mother would also disappear for days at a time.

When Helen was in second grade, Child Protective Services got involved and placed the children in foster homes. Her father also carried a gun with him at all times and once, when Helen was thirteen, he came home and started shooting the gun inside the house. Helen, who described herself as an obese child, got stuck in a window trying to escape: she was scared to death.

Helen's parents were married for twenty-eight years, and her father beat up her mother two to three times a week. She always had bruises. Sometimes, Helen would try to break up their fights, and her father would throw her against the wall. Helen's mother fought back, and their fights were prolonged as well as frightening to the children. At times, her mother would get him to leave by chasing him out the door brandishing a knife.

Helen was also beaten up by her older sister, and that sister even tried to kill her more than once. For example, when Helen was three years old she was on a ladder about two stories high when her sister tried to trip her off the ladder. Her sister once pushed her out of a second-story window, and on another occasion ran over her with a bicycle.

Helen's first marriage lasted for ten years, and she estimates that she was battered about twenty times a year. During their honeymoon, he gave her a black eye for waking him up too early in the morning. He caused more than one miscarriage by punching her in the abdomen while shouting, "Only the strongest will live! If this one's not strong, you're going to lose it." She did manage to have three strong kids who were eventually taken from her by Child Protective Services. It seems that between husbands, she had a boyfriend who made a videotape of himself molesting her daughter. Helen lost custody of her children.

Helen tried to kill herself by taking an overdose of sleeping pills on two separate occasions, once when she was sixteen, and again at age twenty-eight. She spent time in a psychiatric hospital in 1980 after her first divorce, suffering from alcoholism, severe depression, and cocaine addiction.

Roy's Background

Roy was the same age as Helen. He grew up in a much smaller family, with only one older brother. His father whipped him regularly with a belt, but other than that we know very little about Roy's childhood. He was sparse with details and very secretive about his life. We do know that his father battered his mother, although he refused to provide details. We also know that he was sexually active from age thirteen on. He and his older brother fought all through childhood and now don't speak to one another.

Roy got into lots of fights with peers as well as strangers, from his teenage years on. Usually, the fights occurred at times when he was high on alcohol, cocaine, and other drugs. He even fought with police officers. He was arrested for the first time at age eight, and has a long rap sheet. He was in prison from 1981 to 1986.

But Roy was not just a criminal. He was also quite depressed for much of his life, and much of his drug use was probably a form of self-medication. He tried to kill himself in 1975, and was hospitalized in 1987 for a head injury. He has been in and out of psychiatric settings for twenty years, with arms that are by now completely scarred from self-mutilation and drug abuse. He had a violent, turbulent first marriage, which produced a daughter.

The Dynamics of Roy and Helen

We met Roy and Helen in June 1990, after three years of marriage. Despite all the beatings, her face bore no scars. However, she was in very poor health. She had hepatitis C, ulcers, and arthritis. She seemed intelligent, was highly verbal, and quite friendly and talkative. She told us that if she left Roy, he would probably kill her and then himself. She was clearly quite depressed, despite her friendly, talkative demeanor. Although she had a history of alcoholism and drug addiction, she had been totally clean for nine months. She told us that the violence had been very severe during the past year: Roy had threatened her with a knife, attempted to strangle her, and beaten her repeatedly. Always, he had been drinking whiskey right before the beatings. She had been high on cocaine during many of the incidents until she went straight nine months before we met her. At times, she fought back by biting him, throwing things at him, grabbing him, and pushing him; but usually, she remained passive while she was being beaten, because fighting back just made things worse. The incident in January 1989 was the only time she had struck the first blow. Roy was also quite emotionally abusive, insulting and degrading her in public, calling her a "tramp, slut, no-good whore, rotten mother, no-good wife." He had slept with sixty to seventy other women since they had been together.

Despite it all, Helen rarely considered divorce and almost never regretted marrying Roy. Although the violence made her unhappy, overall she very much wanted the relationship to succeed.

Roy was unemployed when we met him; in fact, Roy and Helen were homeless. Roy was extremely threatening in his demeanor. He was quite candid about his violence, although he blamed Helen for it. He was unkempt, had long, brown hair, and seemed to have a hard time understanding some of our questions. But he considered himself to be happily married and reported that he was very committed to the marriage.

Helen and Roy's laboratory interaction demonstrated their inability to communicate. He was emotionally abusive throughout the interaction, threatening her and giving her menacing looks. It was as if daggers were coming out of his eyes. Helen stared at Roy continuously, whereas Roy looked down except when he was speaking to her. She won the battle of logic, but he conceded nothing. She handled him with kid gloves throughout the fifteen-minute interaction at times when he was threatening or acting very fearful. She talked to him the way one might expect a mother to talk to a ten-year-old child who was misbehaving. He alternated between silence, taunting her, and responding to her gentle verbal challenging by suddenly escalating and lashing out. Some examples of this were his extremely threatening "Don't interrupt me!" (her response was a fearful "I'm not") and "I think you're full of shit!" Roy had a way of turning his head extremely quickly toward her, becoming suddenly and explosively angry, and then retreating, appearing to try to get control of himself, and finally, after a pause, talking to her with a constrained form of anger, as if he were containing a great rage. The total impression was quite unnerving and frightening, even for our trained observers. It was a reminder to her of his past violence, and it effectively controlled her anger. Instead of anger, she expressed primarily tenderness, acting like someone trying to remain calm and rational, but laced with great tension and an enormous sadness.

The content of the laboratory discussion revealed a theme in their relationship. She was prodding him to get back into treatment for his drug and alcohol abuse, and he wanted credit for agreeing to be faithful. He took umbrage with her for interpreting his fidelity as an attempt to avoid catching a sexually transmitted disease, and when she claimed that she had heard him say that, he said, "Well, you heard wrong!" When asked for clarification, he explained his fidelity in a way that completely supported Helen's original claim. But she had to give in. If she had won the battle, she would have lost the war.

Two years later they came back for a follow-up assessment, and Helen held their young infant in her arms during their conversation. They had divorced during that two-year interval, but they were still living together, and they still identified themselves as a couple. They told us that for a year and a half since coming to our laboratory there had been no violent incidents. This was quite a change! Then, about six months before our second visit, he held a knife to her, raped her, and then made her shower so that there would be no evidence of a rape. He then forced her to sit in a corner all night, and said he would kill her if she told his counselor about the incident. He held the knife to her for three hours. After that, they reported to us that there had been three more severe beatings. Astonishingly, both of them reported that they remained happy with and committed to the relationship. As we parted company with Roy and Helen, she confessed to us that she had started shooting heroin again, because, she said, "It was the only thing we can do *together*." She had asked him to give up heroin. His reply was stunning, and perhaps as telling as any of our previous information: "But what you're asking me to do is give up my life. That's all I know, Helen. What else is there?"

In the past year, Helen left Roy and is now remarried and living in another state. Both Roy and Helen have unlisted phone numbers, and have not responded to our letters.

Was Roy a Typical Cobra?

In many ways, Roy was a typical Cobra. He had an antisocial personality disorder, was a chronic drug addict, had a long history of violence outside his marriage to Helen, and came from an abusive, chaotic family. The stability of Roy and Helen's relationship, despite the severity of the violence, fits our profile of the Cobra, as does the perseverance on the part of Helen, despite the abuse. Helen was a sexually and physically abused child who knew nothing but violence throughout her life. She was battered and abused by her mother, her first husband, a boyfriend in between her marriages, and then by Roy. Perhaps by comparison, Roy *was* there for her in a way that her family never was, despite his brutality.

At first glance, her decision to stay with a man who was so

abusive makes her seem crazy. But, given her history of violence and cruelty at the hands of those who supposedly loved
her, the perverse love and attachment between Roy and Helen
may have seemed worth preserving. Who knows how any of us
would have responded under similar life circumstances?

At any rate, Helen was not a typical battered woman, even
among the Cobra subgroup. We presented this case to illustrate the diversity of personalities among both batterer and battered women populations, and to do justice to the complexity
of these relationships. Even though Helen was atypical in
many respects, many of the battered women, especially those
married to Cobras, seemed irrationally attached to men who
treated them with extreme cruelty. It was all too easy to identify psychological problems in women who stayed with such
men and ignore the sense this decision made from the perspective of the victim. Helen looked like a partner in crime:
self-destructive, an abuser of drugs and alcohol, someone with
a criminal background who was judged to be an unfit mother.
Yet, we were moved and impressed by Helen. To us, she
seemed strong for having been through all that she had been
through and surviving. She was a kind, gentle woman who was
dealt a very bad hand throughout her life. She had no reason
to believe that life held anything more for her than men like
Roy. For a woman with Helen's past, Roy's promise of fidelity
seemed like a gift. Her life read like an advertisement for post-
traumatic stress disorder (PTSD): a spiteful, abusive mother,
incest, and many close encounters with death at the hands of
loved ones. There was no doubt that Helen's judgment was
clouded by PTSD, and that she was beyond the reach of the
rational persuasion of psychotherapists. But despite it all there
was a sense of stability about her. She was always able to get
and hold a job. Roy was economically dependent on her. She
was bright, managed to complete two years of college, and was
relentless and focused in her efforts to help Roy with his drug
and alcohol problems—even though she joined him when she

couldn't beat him. As one of our graduate students, Sara Berns, put it, "She's definitely in a different world: but in *her* world, she really has it together."

Finally, Roy once again illustrates that, despite the things that Cobras have in common, there are also important individual differences. On the one hand, Roy was so much the dominant force in the relationship with Helen that he came across as most Cobras do: fiercely independent, avoiding intimacy, unwilling to be controlled or derailed in any way. On the other hand, when faced with the *realistic* prospect of losing Helen, he seemed to need her. We believed Helen when she predicted that if they ever split up for good, he would try to kill both of them. We believed her not just because she was an astute, reliable source, but because we saw much corroborating evidence. On those few occasions when she gave him cause for jealousy, he didn't seem to be any more capable of functioning without her than she was of functioning without him: when he moved back to Seattle with Snake, Roy called her begging her to join them.

Roy and George were similar in some ways, different in others. One obvious difference is that George was more manipulative and seemingly less at the mercy of his moment-by-moment impulses than was Roy. On the other hand, Roy, like George, was hedonistic and self-absorbed. Yet both were capable of a wide range of emotional experiences. For example, both George and Roy went through periods of depression that were quite severe.

We know where Roy and Helen are, and that they are not still together. Somehow, unlike most Cobras and their battered partners—they are not still a couple. The glue that binds Cobras to their partners is one of the most striking characteristics of these relationships. We wish we could talk to them again and find out how Helen got away.

We do know what has happened between George and Vicky, and we will return to them in a later chapter.

5

More About Pit Bull Relationships

Martha was a long way from rural Nebraska. As she got on the bus heading toward the university district, she remembered that when she first used public transportation in Seattle, a few short months ago, she wasn't even sure that she was headed in the right direction. Seattle had seemed huge to her, and was in fact about ten times the size of the largest city she had ever been in. After being raised on a small farm near a tiny hamlet, she was now a freshman psychology major at the University of Washington.

In high school, she was homecoming queen, prom queen, and a very popular, outgoing teenager. But in Seattle, she entered a new world, a world that initially intimidated her. She had a hard time learning the social rules at the University of Washington. The sororities seemed shallow, and the intellectuals seemed pretentious. Martha was enchanted by the natural beauty of the Northwest, and ended up choosing friends who were appreciative of the little things that filled her with wonder, the beautiful vistas of nearby mountains, the songs of birds that were unique to the Northwest, and the political causes that involved preserving the environment. It was funny that having grown up on a farm with parents who were Republicans, she had never thought about the fact that there was an alternative way of looking at the world; yet because of her new beliefs, she registered as a Democrat in Seattle almost instinctively, much to the chagrin of her parents.

She was too busy to date much during her few months at "U-Dub." But today was to be a fateful day. She was about to meet Don, who was to become her husband. Don, who had beaten his two previous girlfriends, and was immediately dumped by both of them after the first violent episode, was about to meet the woman he would still refer to as his "soul mate" even five years after their divorce.

Martha sat down on the bus next to a stranger, who introduced himself to her as Don. Don seemed somewhat delicate for a man. He had sad, vulnerable eyes, and was soft-spoken as he looked into *her* eyes. He was some sort of artist: he wrote songs, played the guitar, dabbled in poetry, and seemed to get an adrenaline rush when he talked about backpacking trips he had taken. He asked her out, and she said yes. She was excited. She had never even met a man on a bus before, let alone one who was ten years older. But Don seemed safe and vulnerable, and she found the artistic side of him sexy.

Just in this initial encounter, we see an important difference between Cobras and Pit Bulls. In chapter 1 we told the story of George's approach to Vicky. His presentation of himself was totally contrived, designed to win her over. He told her what she wanted to hear, and intentionally misrepresented himself in the process. George was trying to win a bet. Don was being himself. There was no bet, no attempt at seduction, but rather an honest attempt at human connection. As Martha would later discover, Don's view of himself was quite distorted, but Don truly believed it, and does to this day. Don's capacity for rewriting history was one of his most striking characteristics. As recently as a few months ago, when we interviewed him five years after he and Martha were divorced, he was no different. He was just as sincere, just as confused, and just as dangerous. But he didn't know that he was dangerous. George and other Cobras know that they are dangerous. They just don't care.

Don, having practically flunked out of high school, was attending a community college. But he saw himself as an artist, and Martha fell for this view of Don hook, line, and sinker. In many ways Don's sincerity and his view of himself as a creative spirit were to make him extremely charismatic for Martha. She fell in love with his passion, his attentiveness, his gentle, soft-spoken manner, and his apparent acceptance of her.

She heard him pour out his heart about the abuse he had suffered as a child. Martha had been happy as a child. Although there was never much money, and she had to compete for attention with seven younger siblings and one older one, she admired the way her parents worked out their problems. Martha's father was quiet and somewhat distant, but gentle with his children. Her mother was the disciplinarian, "strict and controlling."

Martha empathized with Don and tried to help him. She couldn't imagine what it must have been like to grow up in Don's family. Don's father was a minister with a very bad temper, and he lost jobs frequently because of it. If the family was at church listening to another preacher, and Don's father disagreed, he would stand up and start screaming at the presiding pastor. He was so blunt and opinionated that he alienated people quite easily, and Don's parents were left with very few friends. Conversations *with* Don's father inevitably turned into lectures *by* him.

Don was afraid of his father. He remembers being beaten so severely with a belt that he would beg for mercy. Dad's violence was unpredictable, and directed toward Don's brothers as well as toward Don. The father never hit either his wife or daughter. But he humiliated each of his sons, continually challenging them with his belligerent arguments. As a result, his four boys learned how to fight, and they would fight with one another all through their childhood, and even as adults. Most of the family's fights started off as discussions about religion.

Don retreated from his father but he saw his mother as perfect. He viewed his mother as a simple country girl who was dominated by his tyrant of a father. Don was close to no one but his mother, and his mother was totally dependent on his father. She didn't even know how to write a check. As a loner and a poor student, Don's center of gravity as a teenager was the drug and alcohol subculture within his small-town community. He fancied himself a "deep" person with wisdom and insight, and he became his own biggest songwriting and poetry fan. He hated school. He was very shy with women, and an abuser of alcohol. But when Don met Martha he seemed well on the way to overcoming great hurdles in his quest to rebuild his life. Martha was taken with how open Don was about his turbulent past, and she told him that she admired his courage and the degree to which he had struggled. There was an immediate, strong physical attraction between them, and they found that they loved to hike and backpack together.

The first episode of violence occurred one year into their courtship. They were at a party, and while Martha was in the bathroom a drunk man made a pass at her. She told Don about it, he lost his temper, accused her of having an affair, and she uttered the remark that for some reason sent him into a frenzy. She said, "Just leave it." Whenever Martha got mad at Don, she would implore him to leave it alone, whatever the "it" was. Usually, the "it" involved his reaction to something he imagined that she had done, which she had not *actually* done. He felt as dismissed by her requests that he leave things alone as he did by his father's put downs, and thus responded to these remarks like a cornered animal.

Heated and trying to control himself, Don waited until after the party. Don then suddenly grabbed Martha, backed her into a corner, and slapped her so hard she fell to the ground. At the time, Martha did not think of the incident as a physically abusive one. She tried to minimize its importance. When Don finally calmed down afterward he was extremely apologetic, and she basked in the glow of his charm during the month that followed. Then he hit her again.

Don and Martha's Marriage: A Continuation of Battering

Don and Martha dated for two and a half years prior to marriage and never lived together out of wedlock. They didn't want to upset their religious parents by "living in sin." Martha thought, as many battered women do, that marriage would stop the violence. Don suggested as much. He told her that his stress level would be lower if they were married. Martha wanted Don, but not his temper, and he convinced her that marriage would soothe him, make him feel secure and less jealous, and the violence would simply disappear. Don and Martha were wrong but they *both* genuinely believed that marriage would change things, and so they tied the knot.

By the time we met them, Don was hitting Martha about every other day. At first, Martha fought back. If Don slapped her, Martha would return the slap. But as Don's violence escalated, she became too frightened to fight back, although her anger never stopped. She was eventually walking on eggshells, feeling angry, but unable to find an outlet for it. Like most batterers, his violence was hard to predict, so that eventually she was *constantly* walking on eggshells, vigilant, on the lookout for cues that would lead to the ferocious attacks.

Martha told very few people about the battering: she was ashamed of herself for tolerating it, embarrassed by her role as victim, and she felt humiliated after she would tell a friend about what she had to endure. The few friends who did know about the beatings strongly encouraged her to end the relationship.

What was the anatomy of Martha and Don's fights? Don, like so many batterers, subscribed to an honor code that did not allow him to accept influence from women. He constantly attempted to maintain his dominance. He would do this in a variety of ways. Sometimes he would begin by patiently lecturing her in a very condescending way. But if she tried to participate in these lectures of his, even adding such general comments as "for a relationship to work the people have to respect one another," Don would disagree, becoming increasingly belligerent and insulting. He would eventually escalate, insulting Martha's intelligence, calling her a "stupid, dumb bitch." This is common batterer talk. Naturally, these insulting remarks hurt Martha, but they did not succeed in making her *feel* stupid. She began to understand the psyche of the batterer, that his air of superiority came from a position of internal weakness rather than strength.

Don expressed his emotional abuse most clearly in his efforts to isolate her from the rest of the world. He monitored all of her activities, especially when she was late coming home from work. If she said she stopped at the grocery store, he looked for her grocery receipt and scrutinized it. Any attempt on Martha's part to visit family or friends resulted in Don "going bonkers," as Martha called it. Eventually, she quit trying to spend time away from him and resigned herself to being alone when he was working. His abuse had worked.

There was a particularly violent altercation in the winter two years before we first saw them in our laboratory. Martha was severely beaten, the police came and arrested both of them, and her parents had to bail her out of jail. That weekend, having found out for the first time that her daughter was a battered woman, Martha's mother was shocked and extremely upset. She provided her daughter with literature on battered women and begged Martha to stay with her.

Gradually, Don, the creative artist, was becoming an object of contempt and hatred in Martha's family. Martha finished school and began a career as a mental health case worker at a community clinic, while Don drifted between menial jobs and unemployment insurance. She began changing her views of Don. Whereas she once thought of him as "deep and spiritual," now she began to see him as "lazy and unmotivated." Martha had begun giving up her dream about Don and what life with him could be someday.

When we met Don and Martha two years after the first battering incident, they were on the verge of divorce. Although we thought we had seen everything about wife battering by the time we met them, we were stunned by the sheer intensity of Don's temper. There had been at least twenty separate violent episodes within the past year in which Martha was severely beaten. Don's emotional abuse included swearing at Martha and calling her names daily, embarrassing her in public places, making fun of her family, her friends, her religious values, and insulting her physical appearance. Once, he spat in her face and said, "That's what I think of you!" In the middle of love-making, he once commented, "I have more fun with a Playboy magazine than I do with you."

We were also surprised that Don also felt emotionally abused by Martha, even though the incidents that produced these feelings in him were not abusive by any reasonable definition of the term. When Martha attempted to cut off a volatile conversation by asking, "Can't we just drop it for now?" Don saw her question as abusive. In many cases Don put a very different spin on the same events, and even though he reported the events factually in the same way Martha did, he believed his interpretations were the only accurate rendering of the truth. In other cases Don and Martha would disagree, and we would be bewildered by Don's reasoning. For example, Don would argue that Martha provoked a violent altercation by slapping him after he had slapped her. A man who believes that his wife provoked violence by slapping him *after* he had slapped her clearly has "cause" and "effect" mixed up.

We saw them twice, each time making a videotape of them in our laboratory. In the second tape Martha had moved from sadness in response to Don's abuse to resistance, and she showed many facial expressions of disgust and contempt toward him. We recognized this as a familiar pattern indicating that Martha was distancing herself from Don.

The anatomy of their final conversation was fascinating in what it revealed about Pit Bull male batterers, and we tried to understand it. We have watched their videotaped interaction so many times that we practically have the dialogue memorized. There was a mesmerizing quality to their argument. In this conversation Don revealed himself as a batterer, while blaming Martha and avoiding the word "violence." Early in the conversation, he seemed sad, and commented that he never could have imagined that their marriage would have turned out as it had. They then discussed an incident that apparently had resulted in a beating the night before. She drove his car and did not hear a sound indicating a malfunction. He called her "stupid" for not hearing the sound and for not diagnosing the malfunction, and then blamed her for the apparent lack of compassion and empathy she showed when he was sad about his car. She calmly tried to explain that it was hard for her to have compassion for someone who is calling her "stupid," which he apparently did at the beginning of the argument as well as again in front of our cameras. He said that when someone calls him stupid, he tries to learn from them and understand why he was stupid. He argued that she was stupid because she had not shown the little bit of empathy he was asking her for. Whatever Martha said, Don would try to patiently and condescendingly prove to her that her mind was not working very well, and that she had a distorted view of the world. In every instance it seemed as if Don's goal was to show Martha that her thinking was disturbed and disorganized, and that she needed Don even to think straight about what had happened last night.

But Martha was having none of this. Her compassion for Don's abuse in his childhood had given way to her own decision to protect herself. When Martha refuted his interpretations, Don became visibly angry, and his anger intensified as the discussion progressed. In fact, the more diplomatically and gently Martha made the point that insults don't typically lead to compassion, the more he began to mock her, calling her an "airhead" and a "jerk." Although he was meek and mild-mannered when we interviewed him alone, his Dr. Jekyll became Mr. Hyde when he and Martha were in the room together. He squelched her, stifled her, and dominated her during the interaction. Still, any objective judge would determine that he lost the debate.

Perhaps the most striking memory of Don and Martha was the contrast between the way Don saw himself and the way he actually behaved in the relationship. Despite his obvious violence and cruelty, which we observed, he acted like a victim of battering, and we believe he really *saw* himself that way. Don told us that Martha was not afraid of him; on the contrary, she "got off" on making him angry, and the angrier he got, the more antagonistic she became.

About Pit Bull Relationships

In some ways, Pit Bulls form relationships that are more like those of nonviolent couples than of Cobras. However, there are unique qualities to the relationships between Pit Bulls and the battered women they marry. We have also spoken of the complexities in Cobra relationships, and these complexities are also applicable to Pit Bull relationships.

Pit Bulls Demand as Well as Withdraw. Psychologist Andrew Christensen and his colleagues have studied an interaction pattern that is quite common in conflicted marriages. They have labeled it the "demand-withdraw" pattern. In this pattern, one partner requests change, while the other attempts to avoid change. As the conflict intensifies, requests become demands, and avoidance becomes withdrawal. These conflicts are often about closeness and distance. The demanding partner often seeks greater closeness in the relationship, while the withdrawing partner attempts either to maintain the current level of intimacy or create further distance between them.

Dr. Christensen and his colleagues have found that couples who show this demand-withdraw pattern are more likely to describe themselves as unhappily married than couples who do not. They also discovered what many family therapists had already suspected, that women were more often than not in the demanding role, and men were more often in the withdrawing role. This makes sense in light of other research that has been done on differences between men and women in marriage. Women, much more often than men, are the ones who seek therapy. When they do seek therapy, it is usually because they want changes in their husbands, and the women are both unhappy and angry about the current state of the marriage. Husbands tend to be reluctant participants in the therapy process, and when they do participate are less likely to be requesting changes in their wives. Their most frequent refrain is, "Accept me for who I am."

During marital interactions, the wives tend to look angrier, and the husbands look more passive. In fact, it is often tempting for inexperienced therapists to blame the wife for disrupting the conversation, as the husband appears to be friendly and easygoing. But this view is countered when one considers the long history of frustration that the wife has experienced, and the various ways in which the husband has controlled the relationship throughout its history. Naturally, the wife is critical and demanding: *she* is the one who has suffered over the years because of the ways in which the marriage has been structured to suit the husband's needs.

Cobras show this typical demand-withdraw pattern in an extreme form. Even though it is not surprising that a battered woman would want change, it *is* somewhat surprising when she seeks more closeness and intimacy with a man who batters her and tells her so often to go away and get a life independent of him. Women married to Cobras still want a close, loving relationship with a man who has no interest or ability to be loving or to provide intimacy.

The Pit Bull couples are different. Unlike either Cobras or nonbattering husbands, Pit Bulls are often in the *demanding* role. That is, they are demanding changes in their wives' behaviors, even as they are avoiding the changes that their wives request. This demanding behavior on the part of the man reflects a degree of emotional dependency missing in the Cobras, and also in nonviolent men. It is reflected in the incessant demands that Don made of Martha. Everything she did was wrong because nothing she did was ever quite enough for Don. He needed an infinite amount of love and reassurance. Martha had to watch every move she made, she had to avoid his jealousy, she had to try to satisfy what he called his "simple need for just a little empathy," and yet even as she walked on eggshells, she was attacked for being a "stupid bitch."

Don's emotional dependency required that she always be available when he needed her, even though his needs were both unpredictable and unrelenting. Contrary to a Cobra's belligerent demand that he be left alone to do whatever he wants whenever he wants, a Pit Bull wants his wife there for him at all times to meet an excessive need for approval and self-fulfillment. There is a desperate quality in the efforts of a Pit Bull to stifle independence in the battered woman—to know where she is at all times, and to be wary and suspicious of her potential for sexual liaisons. Whereas Cobras want to be left alone except when their hedonism drives them toward seeking contact, Pit Bulls have needs for contact that are insatiable. Yet, they themselves are unable to make the emotional connections they demand. In this inability to make real emotional contact, they are similar to Cobras. In short, Pit Bulls end up blaming their wives for not satisfying needs that can never be satisfied.

Wives of Pit Bulls Seem Angrier and Less Fearful Than Other Battered Women. Martha was somewhat atypical of Pit Bull wives because she was probably just as frightened as the wives of Cobras in our sample. The wife's fear is related to the severity of violence: the more severe the violence, the more fear. Since Cobras generally committed more severe acts of violence than Pit Bulls, Cobra wives were generally more fearful. So Martha's level of fear was extraordinary for the wife of a Pit Bull, but Don was one of the most violent men in our sample.

However, like other wives of Pit Bulls, Martha was also extremely angry. We found that the wife's anger, in contrast to her fear, was independent of the severity of the violence. At first glance this seems strange. But the wives of Pit Bulls felt more trapped, more controlled, and less free to make their life decisions than the wives of Cobras. Martha, for example, had to give up her friends and her family, had to account for all of her time, and was constantly being emotionally abused and degraded when she wasn't being beaten. Because of Don's emotional dependency, he was around all of the time and in Martha's face with his desperate needs. Martha was like Beauty in "Beauty and the Beast," kidnapped because she was needed to reverse a terrible curse. Unfortunately, unlike the Beast, Don was not gentle and loving.

This sense of entrapment, combined with the violence, generates extreme anger on the part of the battered women married to Pit Bulls. At times, these battered women were so angry that they even initiated violent acts, placing themselves at personal risk. Martha learned that fighting back was self-defeating, but her anger remained, and at times it seemed overwhelming.

Other women married to Pit Bulls were more overt in their expressions of anger. Maxine once became so angry at her husband Jim for announcing a fishing trip after her stressful day that she plotted her revenge while he was away. When he walked in the door she threw a pipe wrench at him, aiming for his head. It could have seriously injured him, and she was trying to hit him and hurt him. In the ensuing argument, still enraged, she called him a "fag, just like your father." He ended up beating her so severely that he almost killed her.

When an altercation like this is examined without its broader historical context, it can look as if the woman is asking for trouble, and in fact, Maxine was the perpetrator in this event. But one's analysis changes when the history of chronic abuse is taken into account. Her extreme anger, and the rage reaction that followed, was the outcome of a long history of physical and emotional abuse. Maxine was able to dish out the violence, but she had also taken more than her share of beatings to get her to this point. Yes, she was vengeful, spiteful, and hateful in the way she treated her husband. But Jim was still a batterer, and Maxine was still a battered woman. She had been indoctrinated by Jim and she had entered into the culture of violence.

Why are the wives of Cobras less angry than the wives of Pit Bulls? For one thing, there are often preexisting differences between the life histories of women who marry Cobras and those who marry Pit Bulls. The women who marry Cobras seem to come from childhoods where violence and the degradation of women is routine, and the experience of abuse is familiar to them, although hardly desirable. They seem not to know that women do not deserve to be beaten. When they are beaten, they tolerate it because of the macabre attachment that exists between the partners.

Furthermore, in some ways it is more difficult to be married to a Pit Bull than to a Cobra. Cobras refuse to be controlled, and strike when the wife attempts to have a voice in the relationship. But Cobras also tend to leave their wives alone unless that control is threatened. Pit Bulls constantly scrutinize their wives, and for many that scrutiny is even more oppressive than the violence itself. No amount of reassurance will fill the great emptiness of a Pit Bull. He is sure that he is eventually going to be abandoned. He sets up anger and contempt in his wife that makes this fear come true.

Unlike Cobras, Pit Bulls Are Internally Aroused When Behaving Aggressively. The nervous systems of Pit Bulls appear to work normally. Unlike Cobras, when Pit Bulls enter into marital conflict, they become physiologically aroused. Their heart rates increase, for example. Unlike Cobras, Pit Bulls *do* seem to fly into unintended rages. This does not mean that their violent episodes are characterized by a loss of control. Nor does it belie the fact that Pit Bulls *choose* to be abusive when they act abusively. However, it does mean that Pit Bulls are more prone to fits of rage, and less calculated in their use of violence than most Cobras. Don was an excellent example. He had a terrible temper, and felt so helpless in the wake of his explosions that he didn't consider himself responsible for them.

Unlike Cobras, Pit Bulls Are Seldom Violent Outside Their Marriages. Pit Bulls are no more likely to be violent outside the marriage than nonabusive husbands. Don was somewhat atypical in this regard, since he did fight with his older brothers. But the general pattern of criminal activity associated with Cobras is relatively absent in Pit Bulls. Although Pit Bulls seem to abuse alcohol at a greater rate than the male population at large, they are not more likely to abuse illegal drugs or controlled substances. In contrast, Cobras tended to be serious drug abusers.

We need to add a note of caution, one that is particularly addressed to battered women who read this book. Even though Cobras were generally more violent than Pit Bulls, Pit Bulls are capable of chronic and savage brutality toward their wives. Unfortunately, since we are the first to base a distinction between two subtypes of batterers on physiology, no one knows the percentage of homicides committed by Pit Bulls versus Cobras. But we are convinced that both types are quite capable of murder, even though to date there have been no homicides in our sample. Cobras are more severely violent in ongoing relationships, but once the couple separates, our exit interviews suggest that Pit Bulls may be almost as dangerous.

Pit Bulls are so dependent on their wives that they may respond to separations with stalking, harassment, escalations in battering, and even murder. Indeed, it would be a mistake to conclude that Pit Bulls are safe simply because they are less severely violent than Cobras. Battering is relative. All battering is dangerous.

There are two other important components of the Pit Bull pattern, the role of childhood wounds, and "gaslighting." The story of David and Judy will illustrate the role of wounded childhoods.

David and Judy: The Myth of Healing Childhood Wounds Together

Both David and Judy came from violent, chaotic families.

When they met, they were like two wounded birds, each vulnerable and needy and both with legitimate claims to being victims. David was born in Texas, in 1951, and spent the first twelve years of his life with both of his parents, two brothers, and a sister. His father came from a long line of men who had strong feelings about women's inherent inferiority, and the importance of the husband being "king of the castle." The father was a womanizer who even went so far as to have an affair with a friend of his wife's, a woman who was living with them at the time. Although there was no battering in their marriage, it was not a happy marriage for either parent, and they divorced when Dave was twelve. The father was physically abusive toward all of the children, especially Dave. He beat all of the kids with a belt, as often as every other week, and disowned Dave at the time of the divorce.

By the time of his parents' divorce, Dave had begun to develop a lifelong problem with alcohol. Neither of his parents wanted to live with him, and he ended up spending his teenage years living with the parents of a friend. Although he was in and out of alcohol rehabilitation from his teenage years throughout his twenties, he never could lick the problem.

Judy was born in 1950 in South Africa, and both of her parents were gone from her life by the time she was three years old. Her mother died, and to this day she does not know who her father was. She lived from that time on with adoptive parents, and it was her adoptive mother who did most of the parenting and the discipline. Her adoptive mother was cruel and strict, and spanked Judy repeatedly from the time she was four into her teenage years, using a belt or a hairbrush and often leaving bruises. Judy was also sexually abused by her adoptive father, starting at the age of four and continuing until she was eighteen. He told her that if she ever told anyone, he would kill her, her brother, and her adoptive mother. The abuse was quite brutal. When she was seven years old, during a family vacation, Judy's adoptive father put a knife to her throat and forced her to have intercourse with him.

The legacy passed on to Judy as a result of this childhood was one of depression and a vulnerability to alcohol. When she was twenty years old, she tried to commit suicide by swallowing a bottle of sleeping pills. She almost died. At that point, despite being diagnosed by a psychiatrist as clinically depressed, she didn't pursue any kind of treatment. She did try therapy for depression and anxiety in 1978, and the therapy lasted for twelve sessions. She decided during that period to move to the United States, and ended up in California. After a brief relationship that didn't work, and a pregnancy resulting from that relationship and followed by an abortion, she became severely depressed again and began to drink excessively for the first time. She was in treatment for alcohol abuse when she met Dave, who was also in the treatment program.

These two wounded adults were immediately drawn to one another. There was a strong physical attraction between them. Dave was tall (six feet, two inches), had long hair and a beard, and he reminded her of Peter Fonda in the movie *Easy Rider*. He was very much the California hippie. She had never known anyone who seemed so easygoing, and his lighthearted demeanor was quite a contrast to the austerity and cruelty in her upbringing. He was charming, sang to her (he had a beautiful voice), and essentially swept her off her feet. He found her equally attractive and was mesmerized by what he termed "the whole package": blue eyes that he couldn't stop looking into, long brown hair, and that South African accent. She was witty and bright, and he was equally smitten. Judy was not concerned that Dave was an alcoholic because he was in treatment trying to stop, just like her. She seemed to have found her soul mate, and her dream began: They were kindred spirits who would go through life together, helping one another heal their childhood wounds. The only worrisome aspect of his personality was a cynicism that was reflected in his lack of interest in the "sob stories of others."

Perhaps warning signals should have gone off on their first date, when Dave tried to have sex with Judy. She explained that she couldn't because she had just had an abortion. Suddenly Dave wasn't so easygoing. "Oh, God," he said. "Don't tell me your troubles. Do you think anybody gives a fuck about anybody else's troubles?" Despite his insensitivity, he seemed so helpless in those early years that Judy was willing to take care of him, to help him "get his wings to heal so he could fly." One night, when Dave was drunk out of his mind she put her arms around him, turned toward one of Dave's friends and said, "I'm going to take care of this dude."

The Sober Reality Two Wounded People Create

Dave and Judy immediately moved in together, and were married within three months of their meeting. It didn't take long for the violence to begin. Dave was drinking heavily again and was unemployed. Judy was supporting him with her job as a secretary. One night, she confronted him about his drinking and his apparent unwillingness to do housework while she was out in the world supporting him. He told her to "shut up and stop nagging." Then he wanted to make love. When she told him to "get lost," he called her a "frigid bitch." She didn't make it out of the bed before he took a swing at her, although he was too drunk to connect with a moving target. She hit him back and connected with his jaw. When he passed out, she slept in the living room.

The next day, as she was leaving for work, he apologized for his drinking, and praised her for her courage in fighting back. They made love, and for a few days she had her dream back. But something was nagging at her: After her childhood, she remembered having promised herself that she would never let anyone get away with hurting her again, and now here she was, staying with Dave after he had tried to hit her.

Dave and Judy began to have ongoing conflicts about sex. From Judy's point of view, sex with Dave was somehow more voyeuristic than intimate. She often felt degraded and humiliated as she performed acts that made her uncomfortable. Dave, for example, loved pornography, but Judy was repulsed by it.

In 1982, they moved to South Africa and had their first child, a daughter. Three years later, they had a boy. Dave and Judy were both in and out of therapy. She was coping with depression, anxiety, and confronting her history as an incest survivor. He was trying unsuccessfully to kick the booze habit. About three times a year, Dave was violent, always under the influence of alcohol.

• • •

In July 1985, the relationship took a critical turn for the worse. Judy opened a letter from a doctor documenting that Dave had been tested for sexually transmitted diseases. When she confronted him about it, Dave taunted her: "Why do you think? Because I fucked some other chicks." She began to sob, and yelled, "How could you?" He kept taunting her: "Don't you get it? I'm bored!" She pressed him for details, and he finally admitted that he had slept with "some chick in the back of my truck." Judy lost her temper. She began yelling and swearing at him. She was enraged and flooded by feelings of being betrayed, unappreciated, and unloved. He apologized, but for several days she avoided him. Although their routine resumed, she decided at that point, eleven years before actually ending their relationship, that one day she would leave him.

She might have been harder on him if she hadn't viewed him as "sick" with the "disease" of alcoholism. Her dream assumed that there was a good man underneath this disease, and if the disease would go away, her dream could be realized. Her pessimism about his recovery made her decide to leave; the fact that she thought it would be cruel to leave a sick man kept her from doing it immediately after this betrayal.

Judy's Heroic Journey: Our First Meeting

When we met Dave and Judy in October 1990, they both had jobs. He was counseling developmentally disabled children, and she continued her clerical work. Their daughter was now ten, their son seven. The pattern of violence had been remarkably stable during their twelve years together, about three incidents per year, most of them characterized by pushing, shoving, restraining, grabbing, and slapping. About half the time, Judy fought back; the other half, she left the scene as quickly as she could. Dave's emotional abuse was more constant.

Judy shifted back and forth between minimizing the violence

("He's not really as bad as a lot of other guys who only see women as sluts") and a more accurate assessment of her situation ("I refuse to be treated with the cruelty that Dave shows"). This wavering was frequent during our initial interview with her. At one point, she said that she was determined to leave him. Later on, she was much more ambivalent about leaving him. She was worried about finances, she was worried about the "devastating" effects a divorce would have on the children, and she insisted that there was still a great deal of love and affection between them.

Her ambivalence was a clear example of our earlier point that it is much easier to get into an abusive relationship than to get out of one. This is particularly true when there are children involved. Even though Judy could have escaped without serious violence from Dave (he may have been self-destructive because of a divorce, but he would not have stopped Judy), her life would have been extremely difficult: she would become a single parent with two kids deprived of a father whom they both loved. Furthermore, her dream had not died. There was love, and attachment, and a desire by Judy to take care of Dave.

On the other hand, she was in the middle of that classic shift from fear and sadness to contempt and disgust, a shift that we found signals a future separation—and eventually a divorce. Her pity about his sickness was turning into revulsion, and his childlike helplessness was sporadically becoming disgusting and annoying to her. We caught her right in the middle of this ambivalence and her transition to getting out of this abusive marriage.

Perhaps if she had seen Dave as a mean, vicious person who hated women, Judy would have given up her dream sooner. But instead she saw him as sick, and therefore she hadn't lost her faith that he could be redeemed. However, in her moments of more realistic thinking, she knew that it was only a matter of time before she would leave.

Judy confided in us that she had a vision of what life would be like without Dave. She said that she wouldn't have to "hide herself" anymore. She had been so severely criticized by Dave over the years that she had kept her desirable qualities hidden, like the butterfly she would become once she had shed this iron cocoon of a marriage.

Dave was bland, quiet, and, in contrast to Judy, expressed little emotion during the interview. He admitted to a long string of affairs between 1981 and 1984, only one of which Judy knew about. He minimized his emotional abuse, insisting that he was trying to "improve" Judy, and implying that the ends justified the means. He didn't view himself as a batterer, although he acknowledged "a few shoving matches." Like Don, he minimized the severity of his abuse, denied responsibility for it, and made his wife out to be the difficult person in the relationship. A true Pit Bull, he thought of himself as the victim in this marriage.

Judy Gives Up Her Dream: Our Second Meeting

We saw them again in March 1993. In the interim, the physical and emotional abuse had declined, and they both seemed somewhat happier. Dave had stopped drinking, they were both in therapy, and their communication had improved. Unfortunately, without alcohol, Dave was chronically tense, and this tension produced the same violence that used to accompany his heavy drinking. Nevertheless, Judy encouraged Dave to stay sober. Couples therapy broke down when the therapist confronted Dave by telling him that he was "in denial" about his battering. Dave refused to continue couples therapy, telling us that it was a "big joke" to call him a batterer. He told Judy that she was paranoid because of her traumatic childhood, and Judy thought, "Is this man trying to tell me that I have not been abused, or that I should just learn to accept it? or that I am too sensitive? or that I asked for it?" She knew the reality of her situation.

Judy had to confront great forces that opposed her leaving Dave. For example, when she discussed the possibility of divorce with her son, he said, "If you leave Dad then I may as well be an orphan. You may as well send me to an orphanage." Judy, an orphan herself, was quite upset by her son's response.

Needless to say, the conversation with her son didn't give Judy the courage to resolve her ambivalence. But another series of events did. Her emotionally disturbed brother came from South Africa to live with them. Dave treated him badly, so badly that in May 1993 Judy moved into a separate bedroom for the first time. In recalling the night that she moved out of the room, she told us about a funeral they had just been to, following the suicide of a close friend. Dave mocked her for crying: "I don't care how depressed you are, *you* can go ahead and kill yourself for all I care." Somehow, this incident spoke quite loudly to her. His response was similar to what he said when they first met, when she told him about her abortion.

Dave, like Don and other Pit Bulls, expressed unrelenting contempt for women, and yet both were extremely dependent on *their* women. Neither seemed capable of forming a true emotional connection, despite a tremendous need to have such a connection. Both had been brutalized and humiliated by their fathers. Both were depressed and very introverted, and neither really had a life apart from his abused partner. Unable to make any emotional connection with people, their only way of creating an emotional connection comes from the fighting and abuse they heap on their wives.

A tactic of emotional abuse that is common among Pit Bulls, but not Cobras, is the phenomenon known as "gaslighting." (The term comes from the film *Gaslight*, in which Charles Boyer convinces Ingrid Bergman that she is going insane.) We gave an example of this phenomenon with Dave and Judy, in which he blatantly denied that he was a batterer. Gaslighting is a systematic attack on the wife's perception of reality. Sometimes it is a small part of the abuse of the Pit Bull. In the case of Randy and Cheryl it was central.

Pit Bulls Gaslight Their Wives: The Case of Cheryl and Randy

One sunny afternoon, Cheryl and her husband Randy were talking to their neighbor, Sam. Sam said he and his wife were in counseling because of his wife's extramarital affairs, and their counselor said that Sam should stand up to his wife. Cheryl said, "Why does she have all those affairs? If she's frustrated let her use a vibrator." Randy didn't like Cheryl saying that, so he turned toward her, glared at her, and slapped her hard across the face. She turned to Sam and said, "Did you see that?" Sam said, "I didn't see anything." Cheryl walked slowly into the house, dazed and confused. Her face hurt, but then again maybe she had made it all up. Maybe she really was crazy. Randy said she made everything up, that all her troubles were in her mind, that he never hit her.

"No," said Cheryl during our exit interview, "Randy did not like that comment, so he hit me on the head, just slapped me on the side of the head right in front of Sam. Except then Sam claims that he didn't see it, he didn't hear it, or anything, so it was all in my mind. Randy denied that he had done it, like I was crazy." Randy had told Cheryl that this kind of behavior was just inconsistent with his personality, with what he could do or what he was capable of doing. He told Cheryl that her crazy notions came from her own disturbed mind, that she was self-destructively making a mess of her marriage, projecting her awful childhood onto their marriage, ruining everything.

He was so persuasive that Cheryl wasn't ever sure what had really happened. It was a struggle for her to work on improving the clarity of her memory. In the incident with the neighbor she made herself recall being slapped on the side of the head, she made herself recall the crying, she actively remembered going upstairs and trying to finish getting the dinner together, trying to get her composure together so she could get dinner for the kids: Randy had said that he was going to go out drinking at a bar with Sam. She wrote all this down later, so she could have a documentation that she was not really crazy, that she had not imagined all this.

Cheryl was married to a Pit Bull who was a master of mind control. Randy was an attractive, charismatic, and powerful man who held a respected place in the eyes of his community. He was also known and respected as a civic activist and an amateur athlete. Randy was very conscious of his public appearance. He was a terrific dresser, and he had several wardrobes in the couple's house. Although Cheryl worked and had a respected profession, her income was no match for Randy's. Randy frequently let Cheryl know that she and her children were financially dependent on him.

As usual in abusive marriages, Cheryl had no influence. Batterers so strongly resist influence that we rarely heard a batterer say to his wife, "Good point. I never thought of that before," or "You are beginning to persuade me," or "Yeah, I can see that now."

But the ultimate form of abuse is to gain control of the victim's mind, to make her doubt herself so that she believes the abuser's view of reality. She will then rely on her abuser to interpret every event and to explain to her that the abuse never actually occurred, or if it did occur, that it was minimal, that she was the cause of it and should apologize, or that she should try harder to sympathize with her batterer. Then she will never leave him, and, perfect in her subjugation, she will worship him for the positive qualities that he sees in himself.

Everything Cheryl complained about was denied by Randy, and denied so effectively that Cheryl believed him. But secretly Cheryl was at work on herself, assuring herself that Randy was lying to her, developing confidence in her own perceptions of reality, and making preparations to get out and save herself and her children from this monster she had married. Eventually Cheryl told herself to expect nothing of Randy. She discovered her own rules for survival; Cheryl started dismantling her dream. She built her armor against Randy in secret.

We first met Cheryl when she was deeply imprisoned in hell with Randy, as she still was when we interviewed her again two years later. One skill that helped Cheryl hold on to her dignity was that she was very handy around the house. Randy pretended to be, but was actually completely incompetent. Cheryl observed his incompetence and she secretly laughed at him and nourished a growing pride in herself. Cheryl eventually learned how to fix everything and then taught herself to remodel homes and build furniture.

Then there was the strangling incident.

The Last Straw Incident

For most of the wives who leave, there is a critical last straw incident. "Started off we had had a disagreement," she said. "It was over the bathroom downstairs."

Randy was not a very handy man, and the bathroom became his Achilles' heel, his undoing. He had said that if Cheryl left him to his own time line, he would complete the task of remodeling the bathroom. And so Cheryl did. In her secret notebook about Randy she saw him as a liar, and an incompetent one at that. Randy had said he would skip a seminar so he could come home early and try to complete this project, which had been going on for months. The bathroom was unusable and even hazardous.

Randy and another manager decided to cut out of the seminar, and they went golfing. Randy came home an hour later than he would have come home had he gone to work. Cheryl made a comment about the bathroom project, and he just ignored her. She made sure that she wasn't using a complaining tone, that she was just asking a question. Randy told Cheryl that she was using her "nicey-nice voice" and that voice irritated him.

Suddenly Randy was angry. Then the phone rang and Cheryl asked him not to get it, to let the answering machine pick it up, but Randy answered the phone anyway and he was jovial and quite a different person than he had been with Cheryl. So totally exasperated was Cheryl that she hung up the phone.

Randy took the phone and he threw it down. He picked it up again and threw it wildly. It just missed their son. Both the five-year-old and the three-year-old were crying. Randy picked the phone up and threw it down a third time, but then it rang. He tried to answer it, and it didn't work. He had broken the phone.

At this point Cheryl picked up both kids and tried to get out of the house. To get his older son, Jack, to stop crying, Randy took him to the kitchen and brandished a meat cleaver. Randy told him that if he didn't stop crying he was going to cut off his lip. Jack believed him and he stopped crying.

Randy then grabbed Cheryl, pulled her down the stairs, and started hitting her. She said, "I remember my mouth was all cut up and my head ached and my glasses were all bent out of shape, and I couldn't walk, my ankle got hurt, and he took both kids out of my arms and just threw them on their beds. I'm so stupid, I am still thinking I am going to go into work, and meanwhile their heads are flopping and arms flopping from where he just threw them. I could see their bodies. I was very scared and then he picked me up by the neck and carried me by the head with his fingers around my throat, and he slammed me down on the bed and I remember not saying anything. I was totally blacked out and when I came to again there he was still there with his hands on my throat. I didn't say anything. I just got out and got the kids out that night, I'm not certain. The police came and told me that one of us would have to leave, and I told them that I would leave because I had to leave."

This was not the first strangling incident in their marriage. But it was to be the last because it enabled Cheryl to realize that he could kill her, and the children would then be at his mercy. This man had terrorized their crying son with a meat cleaver. When we talked to Cheryl about this incident she was already divorced and in a new, loving relationship. She had a new baby, and she felt very good about herself. We asked her if her self-esteem had to improve before she was able to leave Randy. No, she told us. After she left Randy she still blamed herself for years. Only later, and very gradually, did her self-esteem improve, and only later did she realize that the violence was not her fault. She wanted to make sure we told all the women who might read this book that "the violence is not their fault, that nobody deserves to be hit, and that you don't have to feel great about yourself to get you and your children out of hell. Just go."

All three of the battered women in this chapter—Martha, Judy, and Cheryl—initially saw their husbands as damaged little boys whom they would support, take care of, and heal until they became the great husbands and fathers the women were sure they could become. This was the dream. Don, Dave, and Randy were all perceived as men who with a little more loving and a little more kindness would blossom into upstanding family men. Until the women gave up that dream, they were unable to leave.

Pit Bulls all have the slow burn and then the quick temper. They all expect to be abandoned. They all have the emotional dependency that leads them to insist on total control. They all seem to act much better in the outside world than they do with their wives, this kind of Jekyll and Hyde, public versus private personality.

Eventually, in all three of these cases, the women had to work actively to overcome the sympathy and the compassion they initially felt so they could escape from their abusive partners.

How do battered women change their minds and decide to escape? In the next chapter, we will tell you who tends to escape, what kinds of men they escape from, and how they do it.

6

When Do Battered Women Leave Abusive Relationships?

When we first started our research one question we heard frequently was, Why do battered women stay in these abusive relationships? This question implies an accusation, namely, What is wrong with these crazy women for staying with these awful men? Often what the questioner really means is, "They are not like me. I would never stay. It's their own fault, and don't ask me to care about them. Serves them right for not getting out."

We have learned that, first of all, battered women *do* get out, and they do so at a very high rate indeed. John Gottman's research on marriage[1] shows that the divorce rate in the general population is typically from 2 to 5 percent over a two-year period. But in our study, the divorce rate was much higher among batterers and their spouses. So the real answer to the question of why battered women stay is that they do not stay. They are much more likely to leave than women in other unhappy marriages.

But what we wanted to know was, What are the stories of the women who manage to leave? How do women get out of these abusive marriages? What we discovered when we interviewed these women was that this leave-taking was in every case an heroic struggle. These women had emerged from hell, and the journey in every case had required them to overcome major obstacles and make psychological transformations. The first step in their transformation was giving up the dream that kept them loyal to their husbands despite the abuse.

We first realized the enormous transformation these women went through by studying our videotapes. Some of the women in our study had shifted dramatically in their attitudes toward their husbands from the first videotapes to the ones we made two years later. As it turned out, these were the women who got out.

Shifting from Fear and Sadness to Contempt

We have discussed Vicky and George, the Cobra couple, in previous chapters. Two years after we met Vicky and George, they came back for their second visit to our laboratory. During that time, Vicky had given up her dream of having a normal marriage, and she had decided to divorce George. Although she was still afraid of him, she now treated him with some of the contempt that he had directed at her two years earlier. Now when he got in her face and threatened her, she told him to get out of the house if he was going to act like a bully. And amazingly, once the battering and threatening failed to control Vicky, the violence toward her stopped. He continued with the threats and the verbal tirades, but he stopped beating her once she decided to leave him.

How did this shift come about? Earlier in that second year, George had been gone for several weeks on navy business. Shortly after he returned, he exploded over some minor incident and started destroying property in their house. He beat up

Vicky, gave her a black eye, and then, as he stomped out of the house, she yelled, "And don't you ever come back." He replied, "You try to keep me out of my house and I'll kill you." This last straw incident was the turning point for Vicky. A lightbulb went on inside of her and she at last realized her dream was just a fantasy.

We heard similar stories from other battered women. They often remembered the incident where, instantaneously, they decided, *I don't care what happens—eventually, I am going to leave him!* Sometimes it took a series of incidents, occurring closely together, but whether it was one or several, the incidents dramatized the battered woman's helplessness. She then used the event to turn the tables around, to exorcise whatever rationalizations were keeping her in the relationship.

• Katherine, another battered woman in our sample, extracted a promise from her husband Paul that he would not stay out all night drinking and gambling because it seemed to her that those occasions were the ones when he was most likely to come back in a foul mood and beat her. When he broke the promise less than two weeks later, she thought to herself, "I'm out of here." She then began a journey of self-change that eventually culminated in her leaving him three years later.

• Annie, the mother of four children, all of whom were battered and abused by her husband, Jack, put up with five years of abuse hoping Jack would change. After he punched their twelve-year-old son in the mouth, it occurred to her that Jack might kill one of the children someday. She took her son to the emergency room, and for the first time told a third party—the attending physician—about the abuse. The physician asked her, "Have you considered leaving your husband?" She answered yes. Her answer was a lie, but only because the question had been put in the past tense. She had been telling herself right up until that moment that Jack would become the responsible father he claimed to be, but when the doctor posed the question, she remembers instantly recognizing that she had been deluding herself, and at that moment she shattered her dream and decided to leave. With enormous determination and courage, the next day she took all four children and slipped away while the husband was at work. Annie never looked back.

- With Virginia, the day of reckoning came while James was cleaning his gun. It had no bullets in it, but when he pointed it at her after it was clean, she did not know it was empty. He said, "Do you realize how easy it would be for me to accidentally use this on you some day?" He was in a relatively good mood, or so it seemed. Somehow, his concrete threat, said in a joking manner, crystallized the danger she was in better than all the serious threats he had made in a bad mood. She took those earlier threats seriously, but she remembers thinking, "Even when he's happy he still likes to torment me." At the moment he pointed the gun at her, Virginia began her countdown to escape.

In Vicky's case, a public, visible bruise and George's volcanic destruction of property gave her the opportunity for the external validation she needed that she was indeed a battered woman. The black eye was there for all to see: so was the broken furniture. Perhaps more important, it was there for *her* to see, especially when she looked in the mirror. As she looked at that black eye she took a hammer to her dream of what she pretended George might someday be.

On our videotapes the women's moods changed from fearful and sad to disgusted and contemptuous of their husbands. We call this "the shift from fear to contempt." This shift often comes about when a battered woman recognizes that her partner is actually a paper tiger. Yes, he is stronger than she is. Yes, he can beat her up, even kill her if he wants to. But he is also a big, strong child, a coward and a loser, not an undiscovered genius. His actions ultimately give him away. This shift from anger to contempt, combined with the perception of danger to themselves or to the children often is what battered women need to gather up their courage and escape. They know that the road to escape is fraught with risk, but it is their determination to escape anyway, whatever the risks, that makes their journey heroic.

Moving from Thought to Action: The Heroic Preparation to Leave

Battered women typically take time to get out of an abusive relationship. There is usually an interval between the decision to leave and the act of leaving. The move is seldom permanent if it is impulsive. They have to plan for their safety, both for themselves and for their children. They have to make plans for their economic security. They have to get used to the idea of leaving. And they have to do a lot of work on themselves, telling themselves that they do not deserve to be beaten.

Vicky moved deliberately. She knew that she would leave George, but not until she was financially able. She told the navy about her black eye and got a restraining order preventing George from reentering the house. That turned out to be an important move. Involving the navy helped Vicky feel bolder, stronger, and less ashamed. She finally got some validation that she did not deserve to be beaten, and she got it from an outside, objective source.

We cannot overemphasize the importance of external validation, no matter where it comes from. During Vicky's long, arduous escape, the navy punished George numerous times: by issuing a restraining order, by ordering him to stay away from her, and finally by confining him to quarters. Vicky was so isolated that the punishment to George provided by the navy contained the message she needed to hear: You don't deserve to be battered. She began to stand up to him from that point on.

Vicky and George looked like a very different couple when they made their second visit to our laboratory. They were still living together, but leading parallel lives. She had told him that she was going to divorce him as soon as she was economically independent. Although George was still critical of Vicky, there was none of his old playfulness, none of his old taunting. His swagger was gone. He seemed bored and even a bit depressed. Vicky defended herself against his verbal attacks, and showed contempt and anger rather than using rational persuasion. She was disgusted with him. At one point, she asked, "Why are you such an asshole?" At another point, she said, "Marrying you was my first mistake." She accused him of being "ignorant and uneducated." So much for the undiscovered genius. She said she was on to him now.

By the end of that year, Vicky had saved enough money to look for a place of her own. She was feeling better about herself than she had in years. When George tried to ridicule or threaten her, she told him to "get the hell out of the house." Instead of beating her, he would leave, but on the way out the door he would beat up their dog.

As Vicky's life improved, George became noticeably depressed. He sat and brooded about how humans were ruining the world, and that most humans had no right to live. His life was going nowhere. As Vicky moved forward into sales and computer graphics, George was losing control of her. Vicky's heroism was about to receive its sternest test.

"He got out of bed at four A.M. one morning," Vicky later recalled, "and I thought that he had left to go to work, so I got up about seven, and I was getting ready for the day. I didn't notice him at first. And then I saw him, sitting in the dark fully clothed, just standing there with his sunglasses on. He already was late to work. And my blood froze." Vicky's heroism was in setting up her own life. She remembers the terror of that moment, wondering whether she would even have a life to set up.

"He came up to me with his sunglasses on and said, 'I told you this before and I'm telling you again. You need to get out of here.' And despite my terror I was really angry and was just about to lay into him when he said, 'And I'm checking myself into the mental hospital today.' And I said, 'My God, George, what did you do?' And he said, 'It's not what I did, it's what I will do if I don't.'

"My daughter and I immediately left. I was terrified. Instantly I thought, 'I have to get out of here or he's gonna kill me.' He did check himself into the hospital. I was calling there all day trying to get information. I was very, very scared. Finally, I got hold of the doctor, and she said that he was very dangerous and that he was threatening to kill our daughter. And he really felt that it was his duty to kill himself and her because the world was cruel. I did not deserve to be killed because I'm just as screwed up and ugly as the world and the best thing for me would be to stay here and suffer.

"Her advice was to take my daughter out of the state and hide her. Her advice was to consider leaving permanently and consider changing my name and my identity. Then three days later they changed his doctor to a man who said it was just stress, and he wasn't dangerous after all. A week later, he was out of the hospital. The second doctor said that George was taunting the first doctor because she was a woman."

Why did George check himself into a mental hospital that day? Was it really to protect himself from killing his daughter? Or was it simply another attempt at power and control? The psychiatrists couldn't decide. The navy couldn't decide. Vicky was getting contradictory messages.

If the plan was designed to scare Vicky so that she would not act, it failed. It only made her more determined. She gathered whatever courage she had left and acted swiftly. She filed for divorce immediately, obtained a civil restraining order, and then went about her business, which was to make sure that she and her daughter were safe and secure.

Vicky's actions in the face of George's threats took tremendous courage. But George did not give up. He just switched tactics. He violated the restraining order by calling her and writing to her, at times turning on his charm, at other times writing threatening poetry in blood.

Vicky was frightened but determined throughout this transition phase. After the divorce was final, George tried to convince Vicky that he was changing and that he should be allowed to see Christi. For the next six months, George and Vicky continued a struggle, with him even trying to convince her that they should be a family again, and Vicky saying no. On two occasions, George kidnapped Christi for a day or so. Then Vicky took another step in her heroic struggle. She began to confront the massive machine of the navy single-handedly.

"That's when I went to his unit, straight to the commanding officer," she said, "and I told him everything: 'He has lost all rights in the divorce. I've tried to be fair. I've actually violated the restraining order by letting him write to me and talk to my daughter, but I did it because I wanted to give George an opportunity not to lose everything that was important to him. But this is the second time he tried to kidnap Christi, and I am not jeopardizing her safety again.' I said, 'He's not gonna see her. I want you to keep him away from me and her.'" The navy did just as she requested.

Vicky knew that George would be discharged soon, and that the navy would be no help once George was a civilian. It is easy to give other people advice to hide forever, to sever all their ties with family and friends, change their name and their identity. However, it is very difficult to do these things. No one wants to spend the rest of her life running or hiding. Besides, even this is no guarantee of safety. Vicky needed to strike a balance. She needed to continue moving forward with her life, creating a semblance of normalcy. She needed to strike a balance between protecting herself and providing her daughter with a normal life. Every battered woman who is threatened by a former spouse has to find this balance under conditions where lives are at stake.

Vicky decided to get a place to live, but with an unlisted phone number, to continue with her job, to reenroll Christi in preschool, and to plan for George's eventual discharge. She came up with a plan to ensure her own and her daughter's safety. As a first step she began to enforce her restraining order. For the next three months, Vicky would hold George accountable for any violation of the order, which legally forbade him from making any kind of contact—by letter, by phone, or in person—with either Vicky or Christi. Despite her embarrassment, she informed her coworkers that if he called, the call should not be put through to her. If he did manage to reach her by phone, she said to him, "You're in violation of the restraining order. I'm going to report it." Then she hung up on him. His letters were returned unopened, and each time he wrote a letter to her she informed both the military and the local police. Within a week of Vicky starting this powerful strategy, all letters and phone calls ceased.

Then Vicky began to prepare for George's discharge. She informed Christi's school that any sign of George on or near the school should be reported to her. During the two weeks following the discharge, Vicky took Christi out of school, the two of them left town, and she told all friends and family members to report any sign of George at the workplace or school. This two-week period came and went without incident, and they resumed their lives. It gradually became clear that George was not going to come after them. At the time of his discharge, George informed his commanding officer that he was going to leave the state. Apparently he did. Perhaps he decided that disappearing was better than paying child support. Vicky has since taken the offensive and mobilized the institutional resources at her disposal, including the navy, to go after George for child support.

As this book is being written, Vicky feels safe from George

for the first time since his initial violent outburst. However, she is not out of the woods. She is depressed, poor, understandably mistrustful of men, and extremely cautious about the possibility of marriage in the future. On the other hand, she is safe, and she has made the transition to a new life. George's desire to terrorize her was ultimately replaced by a different method of control, the only one he still had: keeping her indigent, and refusing to provide an income that would allow her to support her child.

A year has now passed since George's discharge. The next step in Vicky's heroic struggle has begun. She is starting to shake off the trauma of this abusive relationship. She is exploring new career options, making overtures to reconcile with certain members of her family, and gradually attempting to improve her economic situation. She has done most of this alone, without the concrete support of family, friends, and community.

No one would argue that Vicky is lucky. But she is rid of George, and is gradually resuming a normal life. She now believes that it is possible for her to have a father for Christi and a partner for herself. She gets up every morning, drives her daughter to school, and goes to work. She spends her free time taking courses, developing new skills, and exploring her own victimization. She feels on the upswing, and more in control of her life.

Vicky now realizes that she was not to blame for having chosen George, that she had no way of knowing that he was a batterer, and that falling for him during their courtship does not make her stupid. She has come a long way in a year.

Who Are the Women Who Leave? Who Are the Men They Are Married To?

Vicky is one of the many women in our sample who left their abusive husbands. A whopping 38 percent of the women in abusive marriages left within our two-year follow-up period. Vicky was not counted as one of these women because she left after the follow-up period, although her plans were in place by the time we saw Vicky and George for the second time. Vicky was one of the few women married to a Cobra who left. Recall that by our two-year follow-up, *all* of the Cobras were still living with their abused partners. However, by 1995, five years after initial contact with us, at least 25 percent of the battered women married to Cobras had left them. This was a smaller percentage than the women married to Pit Bulls, but a substantial change from our two-year follow-up. So it is not that wives of Cobras *never* leave their husbands, just that *fewer* of them do, and it takes a longer period of time.

We did not study why wives of Pit Bulls leave their partners more often, and more quickly, than the wives of Cobras. But we can offer speculations that are consistent with our findings. The intent to leave a relationship is not the same as the ability to leave the relationship. Leaving takes a lot of courage and planning. It is a long, hard road from wanting to leave to actual leaving.

Wives of Pit Bulls are more eager to leave their husbands, but that does not mean that Pit Bulls are easier to leave. We think that there are two reasons for the higher separation and divorce rate in Pit Bull couples. One has to do with the ability to leave, and the other has to do with the desire to leave.

First, the wives of Cobras *perceived* themselves as less free to get out of the relationships than the wives of Pit Bulls did. They were frightened by the ferocity of their husbands and assumed that they were putting themselves at great risk by an attempt to escape. In relative terms, the path to escape seemed less fraught with peril for the wives of Pit Bulls than for the wives of Cobras.

Second, the wives of Pit Bulls, with their every movement controlled and watched, were generally more eager to get away from their husbands than the wives of Cobras were.

Simply put, the Pit Bulls were harder to live with. Although this may seem counterintuitive, our findings will clear up this confusion.

If you were a battered woman living with a Cobra, you could create conditions for parallel lives that might minimize the horrible contact you had to have. But if you lived with a Pit Bull, he would be "in your face" constantly. There would be no escape other than getting out of the marriage. The Pit Bull would not leave you alone; the Cobra generally would.

While in constant terror, the battered woman married to a Cobra has to avoid trying to control him and making even reasonable demands. With the Pit Bulls' insatiable needs, this adjustment is almost impossible. There is so much emotional dependency on the part of the Pit Bulls that their wives usually have no peace, even between violent episodes. Under such circumstances, it is not hard to understand why the wives of Pit Bulls would have the will to leave, despite the risks. Nor is it hard to understand how the wives of Cobras could adjust to daily living, despite the fear.

We have learned a great deal from our research about the types of men who drive battered women out of relationships, and the types of women who escape. In fact, with our data we were able to identify with over 90 percent accuracy which women would leave within a two-year period.

As we examine the factors which tell us that the woman is on the verge of leaving, it is important to remember that these factors do not necessarily "cause" their departure. They are simply signs that the relationship is falling apart, and that the woman is about to embark on the heroic struggle that will take her out of this hell once and for all. Just because we can identify what happens prior to the woman's departure doesn't mean that if you *make* it happen, then you will be able to leave. It does not mean that an attempt to leave will be safe. The risk of severe assault, and even homicide, often *increases* when women try to get out of abusive relationships. It may be that the same factors that predict departure also put women at increased risk—at least in the short-term. Although there is much we still do not know, we think we know which women leave abusive relationships, as well as which kinds of men they are married to.

Emotional Abuse Helps Women Escape

One of our most interesting findings is that severe emotional abuse is more likely to drive women away than severe physical abuse. This is not to minimize the role of the beatings and the physical assault in any way. Nevertheless, when women are subjected to a physically abusive relationship, it is the severity of the emotional abuse that is most effective in getting the women to make a plan to leave. Virtually all batterers are also guilty of emotional abuse. But when that emotional abuse is particularly severe, and when it is of a particular type, battered women move to extricate themselves from the relationship.

What do we mean by emotional abuse? All partners in close relationships become angry at, criticize, and disagree with one another. In the heat of arguments, even happily married couples may insult each other, or behave in a way that looks like emotional abuse. But what makes emotional abuse different is the function it serves within a physically abusive relationship. By emotional abuse we mean the use of verbal and other non-physical forms of aggression to intimidate, subjugate, and control another human being. It is not only mean and cruel behavior on the face of it, but behavior that serves to consolidate power and maintain fear. It gains its strength through past and present violence and the ever-present threat of further violence.

In our research, we concentrated on four categories of emotional abuse. Our statistical analyses indicated that these categories were distinct, and our interviews suggested that each category told us something different about the relationship:

- Destruction of pets and property
- Sexual coercion
- Attempts to isolate the woman
- Degradation

Destruction of Pets and Property

We have seen how the destruction of property and the cruelty to animals played a role in Vicky's relationship with George. Long after their decision to divorce, long after the violence toward Vicky had ended, George had fits of rage where he would destroy property and, right before his breakdown, beat up the dog. These fits not only maintained Vicky's fear even in the absence of violence toward her, but his beating of the dog created vivid images of his capacity for disregarding the pain of living beings. Similarly, some of the most violent episodes between Don, the Pit Bull, and his wife Martha involved the destruction of property. Martha also remembers the night that she heard Don beating up the cat as the night she decided to leave him. This was her last straw incident. Her immediate thought was, "What will this man do to my children?" And she instantly knew that she could not spend her life with him.

The most violent batterers in our sample also tended to behave sadistically toward pets and relied heavily on destruction of property as an intimidation tactic.

Sexual Coercion and Marital Rape

Sexual assault and coercion go hand in hand with battering. They have not been studied nearly to the same degree as physical aggression outside the bedroom.[2] We still put sex in a different category in our culture. We know that rape is about power, and that it is a violent crime against women, not a matter of sex. But somehow that hasn't been understood with marital rape. A high percentage of batterers rape their wives, but until recently marital rape was considered an oxymoron. The law applied a marital rape exemption in most states, which stated that a husband could not rape his wife, because—by implication—he was entitled to sex as part of the marriage contract. Although this barbaric legal exemption has been abolished in most states, many citizens have lagged behind the law in their attitudes, and many law enforcement officials and prosecutors don't spend much time either arresting people or prosecuting them for marital rape. Unfortunately, women still often feel guilty enough to submit to sex when they don't want it, even under coercive conditions. Even more unfortunately, many wives don't consider the sexual coercion as rape. Jacobson recently asked a female client if her husband had ever forced her to have sex, and she said no. A week later, she said: "I've thought about that question you asked me last week, you know, the one about forced sex. Would choking me until I give him a blow job count?" This woman had minimized this extremely violent act because she also subscribed to the belief that her husband was entitled to sex whenever and however he wanted it.

But sexual coercion can occur without physical force, and when it does, its effects can be equally insidious. This type of sexual coercion is what we would call emotional abuse. David and Judy had a relationship in which sexual humiliation was a dominant theme. David would ask Judy to do things which she found degrading and disgusting and threaten to have affairs when she would refuse. The cumulative effect of this degrading sex was to make Judy feel ashamed and guilty. She was afraid to say no, yet dreaded saying yes.

Roy was actively promiscuous, with dozens of extramarital affairs during the early years of his marriage to Helen. He created such a legacy of infidelity that when he stopped being promiscuous, she accepted it gratefully as a sign that he loved her and stayed with him despite his beatings and his drug addictions. Promiscuity, or the threat of infidelity, is a powerful method of sexual coercion in a great many marriages between batterers and battered women.

George didn't even need to use infidelity or propose degrading sex to maintain his sexually coercive relationship with Vicky. He simply reminded her constantly how ugly she was, flirted with women when they went out at night, and showed little sexual interest in her.

Experts have long believed that sexual assault, when combined with battering, is associated with a high risk of potentially lethal violence at some point in the future.[3] Although the research needed to confirm this opinion has not been undertaken, we believe that the safety of battered women who are also sexually assaulted is especially precarious.

Our other two categories of emotional abuse—isolation and degradation—were like our last straw incidents: these were the forms of emotional abuse most likely to drive women away.

Attempts to Isolate the Woman

This tactic of robbing battered women of their independence is primarily used by Pit Bulls. Women's freedom is restricted to the point where they often feel as if they are in prison. They are deprived of their freedom of movement, and often even their right to be a person separate from their partner. These restrictions are experienced as quite severe, and they help motivate the women to get out of the relationship. It was Don who provided the most striking and consistent example. Martha was on a time clock. Don needed to know where she was at all times, and when she was not at work, she was to be either at home by herself, or with him. He tried to keep her from her friends and her family, monitored her every movement, and used jealousy as a weapon of vigilance and control. He frequently accused her of having affairs; in fact, as we reported in chapter 5, thi is what their first violent episode was about. The claustrop obia that results from these tactics for battered women contributes to their ultimate decision to escape. Women consistently told us that the monitoring drove them crazy. It literally made them feel like they had to account for every moment. The isolation also led to extreme loneliness, often reaching intolerable proportions. Here are some examples:

• One woman in our sample was locked in to her house by her husband each day before he left for work. In this case, she was *literally* imprisoned on a daily basis.

• Another battered woman described the effects of having her friends constantly disparaged by her husband, even to the point of gaslighting. She said, "I began to believe that all of my girlfriends, people that I had been close to or trusted as confidants for years, were either sluts, evil, or stupid. I gradually took on these opinions as if they were my own, and after a while lost all of my friends. He never really told me that I couldn't see them, but he was so effective at convincing me that they were slime that I didn't want to see them. So, soon I had no friends, and I didn't feel that I could directly blame my husband for that. But I came to feel like it was just the two of us, alone on a desert island. I was as lonely as I would have been if we were the only two people on the planet."

• Still another woman from our sample was constantly accused by her husband of flirting with other men. On one occasion, he slapped her at a party because he said a man was looking her up and down, as if she had been encouraging him. It got to the point where she dreaded going out with him at all. But even when she suggested that they not go to a particular event, he would get suspicious: "Why don't you want to go?" he once asked. "Is your lover going to be there?" Ultimately, she was afraid to go out—with or without him—but equally afraid to suggest that they stay home. She was now an accomplice in her own isolation.

But the isolation had other consequences as well, which may have been equally important in helping the women decide to get out of the relationship. he isolation was often so thorough that when the women ma aged to break through and make contact with the world, the stood in awe of the contrast. They moved from claustrophobi and loneliness to a sense of possibility and external validati n. In Vicky's case, she went to the navy to restrain George, a d when they actually did discipline him, she felt exhilarated. T e external validation often contains within it a message that t e husband has shielded her from. That message is: *You don't eserve to be beaten.* This seemingly obvious observation beco es a revelation to someone whose world has shrunk to nothing after years of beatings, emotional abuse, and the loneliness a d claustrophobia inherent in isolation. We are convinced tha the contrast effect of experiencing the "other world," the wor d without the batterer, makes that world seem irresistible, and helps motivate the battered woman to plan her escape.

Table 1 shows the item on the Isolation subscale of our Emotional Abuse Question aire. If a married woman completing this questionnaire score greater than 51, she is being emotionally abused through th husband's attempts to isolate her. If her score is 68 or greate , the emotional abuse is so severe that she is like the wome who were so tyrannized by their husbands that they got o t of the relationships within two years of the time they met s.

Table 1. Emotional Abuse Isolation

Read each statement, and circ e the word that best describes the frequency with which each beha or occurs.

1. I have to do things to av id my partner's jealousy.

   NEVER   RARELY   OCCASI NALLY   VERY OFTEN

2. My partner tries to contr l whom I spend my time with.

   NEVER   RARELY   OCCASI NALLY   VERY OFTEN

3. My partner disapproves o my friends.

   NEVER   RARELY   OCCASI NALLY   VERY OFTEN

4. My partner does not believe me when I talk about where I have been.

NEVER   RARELY   OCCASIONALLY   VERY OFTEN

5. My partner complains that I spend too much time with other people.

NEVER   RARELY   OCCASIONALLY   VERY OFTEN

6. My partner accuses me of flirting with other people.

NEVER   RARELY   OCCASIONALLY   VERY OFTEN

7. In social situations my partner complains that I ignore him.

NEVER   RARELY   OCCASIONALLY   VERY OFTEN

8. My partner is suspicious that I am unfaithful.

NEVER   RARELY   OCCASIONALLY   VERY OFTEN

9. My partner acts like a detective, looking for clues that I've done something wrong.

NEVER   RARELY   OCCASIONALLY   VERY OFTEN

10. My partner checks up on me.

NEVER   RARELY   OCCASIONALLY   VERY OFTEN

11. My partner keeps me from going places I want to go.

NEVER   RARELY   OCCASIONALLY   VERY OFTEN

12. My partner keeps me from doing things I want to do.

NEVER   RARELY   OCCASIONALLY   VERY OFTEN

13. My partner says I act too seductively.

NEVER   RARELY   OCCASIONALLY   VERY OFTEN

14. My partner keeps me from spending time at the things I enjoy.

NEVER   RARELY   OCCASIONALLY   VERY OFTEN

15. My partner threatens to take the car keys if I don't do as I am told.

NEVER   RARELY   OCCASIONALLY   VERY OFTEN

16. My partner threatens to take the money if I don't do as I am told.

NEVER   RARELY   OCCASIONALLY   VERY OFTEN

17. My partner threatens to take the checkbook if I don't do as I am told.

NEVER   RARELY   OCCASIONALLY   VERY OFTEN

18. My partner prevents me from leaving the house when I want to.

NEVER   RARELY   OCCASIONALLY   VERY OFTEN

19. My partner disables the phone to prevent my using it.

NEVER   RARELY   OCCASIONALLY   VERY OFTEN

20. My partner disables the ar to prevent my using it.

   NEVER   RARELY   OCCASI NALLY   VERY OFTEN

21. My partner threatens to ull the phone out of the wall.

   NEVER   RARELY   OCCASI NALLY   VERY OFTEN

22. My partner forcibly tries o restrict my movements.

   NEVER   RARELY   OCCASI NALLY   VERY OFTEN

23. My partner acts jealous.

   NEVER   RARELY   OCCASI NALLY   VERY OFTEN

24. My partner keeps me fro spending time with the people I choose.

   NEVER   RARELY   OCCASI NALLY   VERY OFTEN

We believe that no one sh uld have to live under conditions of degradation or coercion, even o a small degree. The scores from this questionnaire and the ones th t follow are suggested only as a rough guide. It is your own judgmen whether these conditions are intolerable.

Here's how to find out whe her you are being emotionally abused through isolation:

Give yourself 1 point for e ery "Never" circled, 2 points for every "Rarely" circled, 4 points fo every "Occasionally" circled, and 5 points for every "Very Often" ircled.

If you scored between 51– 7, you are being emotionally abused through isolation.

If you scored 68 or highe the emotional abuse is more severe than the typical battered wom n in our sample.

Degradation

Perhaps the most commo type of severe emotional abuse involves both public and private insults, humiliation, and attempts to degrade. We s w it in practically all of our wife-battering husbands. It wa unrelenting, overwhelming, and seemed to be an ineluctable characteristic of the batterers in our sample. Long after eorge stopped hitting Vicky, he insulted her, often in front f their daughter, and even in public situations. In an inexpli ably perverse act of sadism, even for Roy, he publicly—in Helen's presence—gave a gift of hers to a former girlfriend in return for sexual favors. Don was constantly calling Martha a bitch, a stupid jerk, a slut. Martha never believed herself to be any of those things, and gradually became so angry because of the name-calling that she said it bothered her even more than the beatings did. Her overwhelming anger at the constant attempts at degradation helped drive her away.

Table 2 contains the items from the Degradation subscale of our Emotional Abuse Questionnaire. Like the other subscales, it can be scored by battered women. The lower cutoff indicates as much emotional abuse as the average battered woman in our sample. The higher cutoff score is the average score of women who left their abusive partners.

Table 2. Emotional Abuse—Degradation

Read each statement, and circle the word that best describes the frequency with which each behavior occurs.

1. My partner tries to catch me at inconsistencies to show that I'm lying.

    NEVER   RARELY   OCCASIONALLY   VERY OFTEN

2. My partner tries to convince other people that I'm crazy.

    NEVER   RARELY   OCCASIONALLY   VERY OFTEN

3. My partner tells other people that there is something wrong with me.

    NEVER   RARELY   OCCASIONALLY   VERY OFTEN

4. My partner says things to hurt me out of spite.

    NEVER   RARELY   OCCASIONALLY   VERY OFTEN

5. My partner has told me that I am sexually unattractive.

    NEVER   RARELY   OCCASIONALLY   VERY OFTEN

6. My partner tells me that I am sexually inadequate.

    NEVER   RARELY   OCCASIONALLY   VERY OFTEN

7. My partner insults my religious background or beliefs.

    NEVER   RARELY   OCCASIONALLY   VERY OFTEN

8. My partner insults my et nic background.

NEVER   RARELY   OCCASI NALLY   VERY OFTEN

9. My partner insults my fa ily.

NEVER   RARELY   OCCASI NALLY   VERY OFTEN

10. My partner talks me into doing things that make me feel bad.

NEVER   RARELY   OCCASI NALLY   VERY OFTEN

11. My partner tells me that o one else would ever want me.

NEVER   RARELY   OCCASI NALLY   VERY OFTEN

12. My partner humiliates m in front of others.

NEVER   RARELY   OCCASI NALLY   VERY OFTEN

13. My partner makes me do degrading things.

NEVER   RARELY   OCCASI NALLY   VERY OFTEN

14. My partner questions my sanity.

NEVER   RARELY   OCCASI NALLY   VERY OFTEN

15. My partner tells other pe ple personal information or secrets about me.

NEVER   RARELY   OCCASI NALLY   VERY OFTEN

16. My partner swears at me.

NEVER   RARELY   OCCASI NALLY   VERY OFTEN

17. My partner verbally attac s my personality.

NEVER   RARELY   OCCASI NALLY   VERY OFTEN

18. My partner has insulted e by telling me that I am incompetent.

NEVER   RARELY   OCCASI NALLY   VERY OFTEN

19. My partner ridicules me.

NEVER   RARELY   OCCASI NALLY   VERY OFTEN

20. My partner forces me to o things that are against my values.

NEVER   RARELY   OCCASIONALLY   VERY OFTEN

21. My partner questions whether my love is true.

NEVER   RARELY   OCCASIONALLY   VERY OFTEN

22. My partner compares me unfavorably to other partners.

NEVER   RARELY   OCCASIONALLY   VERY OFTEN

23. My partner intentionally does things to scare me.

NEVER   RARELY   OCCASIONALLY   VERY OFTEN

24. My partner threatens me physically during arguments.

NEVER   RARELY   OCCASIONALLY   VERY OFTEN

25. My partner warns me that if I keep doing something violence will follow.

   NEVER   RARELY   OCCASIONALLY   VERY OFTEN

26. Our arguments escalate out of control.

   NEVER   RARELY   OCCASIONALLY   VERY OFTEN

27. I'm worried most when my partner is quiet.

   NEVER   RARELY   OCCASIONALLY   VERY OFTEN

28. My partner drives recklessly or too fast when he is angry.

   NEVER   RARELY   OCCASIONALLY   VERY OFTEN

Here's how to find out whether you are being emotionally abused through degradation:

Give yourself 1 point for every "Never" circled, 2 points for every "Rarely" circled, 4 points for every "Occasionally" circled, and 5 points for every "Very Often" circled.

If you scored between 73–94, you are being emotionally abused through degradation.

If you scored 95 or higher, you are being more severely emotionally abused than the average battered woman in our sample.

Verbal Threats and Continued Emotional Abuse

Verbal threats of physical abuse often continue even when the physical abuse has stopped. There is a complicated relationship between emotional and physical abuse. We have said that emotional abuse is more important in driving women to make the first moves to escape from their attackers than the attacks themselves. Does this mean that the verbal onslaughts hurt more? Not at all. The key point to remember is that *emotional abuse would not have the power that it does in the absence of physical abuse.* We must always remember that no matter how important emotional abuse is in getting women to leave abusive relationships, it occurs in the context of battering. But the central importance of emotional abuse in creating psychological torture cannot be overstated. Emotional abuse convinces battered women that their husbands are unlikely to change, and that they must give up their dream of a normal relationship.

When considering the central importance of emotional abuse, we must remember that because emotional and physical abuse often occur together, emotional abuse is not only traumatic in its own right. It also reminds women of the physical abuse they are experiencing. After a period of time, some batterers decrease their use of physical violence and rely primarily on emotional abuse for this very reason: because it scares battered women as much as physical abuse does, it helps to maintain power and control without potentially subjecting batterers to trouble with the law. The marriage then moves into another circle of hell. Emotional abuse is not against the law, whereas physical and sexual assault are. Therefore, when considering whether any battering relationship has changed for the better, emotional abuse must be considered as well as physical abuse. One could easily be misled into thinking that because the violence has stopped there is no battering going on. In fact, with Vicky and George the emotional abuse continued long after the physical violence had stopped.

Emotional abuse can be a powerful reminder of and substitute for physical abuse, and can be at least as effective in controlling women. That is why it is useful for batterers. When all of these issues are taken into account, it is hardly surprising that emotional abuse has the power that it does to drive battered women away.

Other Predictors That the Woman Will Leave

The more emotionally dependent the Pit Bulls are, the more active their methods of control. The more the batterer "needs" his partner, the more vigilant he will be of her actions, social contacts, and independent activities. We have already seen that in general Pit Bulls are more emotionally dependent than Cobras, who are often fiercely *independent*. The control exerted by Cobras tends to look different, driven by their need for immediate gratification and their determination to remain uninfluenced by their wives.

Along with this emotional dependency comes a tendency to blame the violence on the woman, to be hypersensitive to the wife's words and actions, and to be easily threatened by behaviors that would ordinarily not be threatening. Batterers, especially Pit Bulls, tend to view their wives as causing the violence, or even to label their wives' nonviolent behavior as violent if it provokes in them a violent response. The hypersensitivity can be seen in the batterer's exquisite awareness of the partner's verbal and nonverbal behavior, which we saw throughout the study in various forms: Don's monitoring of Martha's grocery receipts to check the time of departure from the store; the tendency on the part of men to confuse violence with nonviolent but seemingly threatening remarks; and an edginess exuded by some batterers that maintains a high level of fear in the women, along with a justified apprehension that they are never far away from a beating.

In our study, we found that the more often the husbands viewed their wives as violent, the more likely the women were to separate or divorce their husbands. But the closer we looked, the more complicated it became. In fact, women who *did* fight back *were* more likely to leave their battering husbands. Here are some examples:

• One woman, after a five-year history of beatings and emotional abuse, became so angry at her husband that she frequently fantasized about revenge. One night, in the wake of a beating, she punched him in the face while he was asleep. He woke up and beat her again. But she smiled the next morning when he wasn't looking, because she liked the way he looked with a black eye. Shortly thereafter, she left him.

• Greta, after being slapped in the face in front of their friends, taunted her husband for his cowardice in having to beat women. Among her taunts was a challenge: "You know,

Max, you never really hurt me. You're such a weakling that you can't even hurt a woman." He was extremely embarrassed by what he perceived to be a public humiliation. Max told himself that he would settle the score later. But Greta, sensing his embarrassment, began to push him harder, shouting, "See? Look everyone. He's a sissy." Greta was severely beaten later that night. But she looked back on this episode as a fight that she had won. She may have been beaten up, but she had stood up to him publicly and not allowed him to control her. She was willing to accept the beating in order to show the world that she could stand up to him.

• Whenever Tim and Amanda fought, she tried her best to hurt him while at the same time attempting to ward off his blows. Although she rarely succeeded in warding off his blows, she often succeeded in hurting him. In between violent episodes, she frequently vowed to herself that she would never let him walk away from a beating unscathed. Her ability to hurt him, whether it came from scratching, biting, or kicking, took some of the sting out of her own wounds. One night the police came and *she* was arrested. She later expressed fond memories of being arrested: "It made him look like a wimp," she explained. "He was scared to death of spending a night in jail. I couldn't have cared less. He even tried to post bail for me, and I said no. I told the officer, 'I would rather be in jail than be bailed out by that jackass.'" Tim laughed at her when she finally accepted the bail the next day, when it was posted by her mother. But Amanda didn't care. She knew that he had come across as a coward the night before, and he knew it as well.

The tendency to fight fire with fire is characteristic of women who leave. These women are more violent than those who stay in abusive relationships.

It was not just physically violent acts on the part of the women that resulted in the batterers perceiving the women as violent:

often the men would consider actions "violent" when in fact the women were simply criticizing them, insulting them, or directly expressing anger. Some batterers labeled any verbal challenge from their wives as "violent." In other words, a large component of what these men labeled violent was a perceptual distortion. Men who were threatened by verbal challenges from their wives were most likely to perceive such challenges as violent. They would claim to be justified in squelching these perceived challenges by both physical and emotional abuse.

What we discovered was that the men who were so easily threatened that they saw provocation or "violence" everywhere in their wives' behavior were also the men who were more likely to be left. The emotional dependency that may have been motivated by a fear of abandonment then becomes self-fulfilling. The men who feared abandonment were more likely to be abandoned, because they saw the threat of abandonment everywhere, and struck out in ways that produced the exact outcome that they were trying so hard to prevent.

These men also showed alarm at the physiological level. We think that this alarm "leaks out," and is something that the women are constantly aware of. That is, their husbands are easily threatened, the threat produces an extreme emotional response, and the emotional response reminds the women that the men are on the verge of being abusive. Even if the abuse is not constant, the alarm is nearly always present. The battered women live with the alarm, find it oppressive, and it contributes to driving them away.

The Batterer's Antisocial Personality

When clinicians use the term "antisocial," it can have multiple meanings. For example, when someone is said to have an "antisocial personality disorder," that means he has a history of wide-ranging nonconformity and criminal behavior that is so much a part of his character that it has been going on at least since adolescence. General resistance to authority, violation of society's rules, breaking the law, and behaving impulsively are all characteristics of being antisocial. During courtship, the less severe forms of antisocial behavior present in batterers can be a source of attraction. He may look like a rebel and present himself as an undiscovered genius, one whom society has scorned. He may express a great deal of contempt for the conventions—either legal or moral—defined by the larger culture. These characteristics can be especially appealing to women who have been raised in very conventional, conforming families, or to those women who are themselves comfortable in an antisocial world. During courtship, when even batterers are usually on their best behavior, their partners perceive the attractive side of this antisocial streak.

However, in the end, antisocial behavior is a factor that contributes to the battered woman giving up her dream as she changes her view of this previously charismatic man and starts seeing him as a loser. Women who are first attracted to the antisocial charisma eventually get tired of living on the edge. They often describe the experience in terms of maturity: they grow up, but their partners never do. Instead of idealizing the good old days of innocence, women begin to show contempt for the irresponsible and adolescent behavior of their battering Peter Pans.

Having children is one responsibility that exacerbates the growing disenchantment. The batterers in our sample were generally unwilling to modify their lifestyles after their children were born, and were usually (but not always) either absent, abusive, or indifferent fathers. Although there were exceptions, most of the batterers we studied showed a striking insensitivity to their children, expecting them to act like adults and having little appreciation for the limitations that their age and life experience imposed upon them. When George got annoyed at the crying of his baby Christi, he expected Christi to stop, and he punished both mother and daughter when the crying continued.

Not all of the batterers in our sample were antisocial. Some who beat their wives were quite conforming in other ways. But when the batterers were antisocial, their wives were more likely eventually to leave them.

The Wives' Assertive Self-Defense

The battered women who left their abusive husbands tended also to be those who vigorously defended themselves, as we mentioned earlier. During the laboratory interaction, this assertive self-defense was quite apparent. Those women who eventually left defended themselves without belligerence, usually without contempt, but with firm and appropriate anger. Although they were afraid, they showed a great deal of courage in standing up to their husbands. Even at the risk of being beaten, they were not submissive. It may have been risky as well as heroic, but it also provided us with a clue that these women would not tolerate such relationships forever. We could see it in George and Vicky from the beginning. Even when Vicky was getting nowhere and George was taunting her, she would stay calm and continue to state her point of view. As time went on and she started to separate from George, this assertive self-defense turned to contempt. Thus, two years after their first visit to the lab, her defense was much more steady and assertive. But that was already after she had decided to leave, and it was public knowledge that they were getting a divorce.

The Wife's Level of Dissatisfaction with the Marriage

Not all women were equally affected by the physical and emotional abuse. At one extreme were women who described themselves as happily married, despite the violence. They didn't like the violence and wished it would stop. We see this as evidence that they viewed the marriage through the script of their dream. They claimed that they didn't see the violence toward them as a reason to end the relationship. Viewing the marriage through this dream, they would point to their husbands' other virtues and put the violence in perspective.

Generally, we found that these women had grown up in a climate of violence and saw stronger people beating up weaker people as one of the grim realities of life. At the other extreme were those women who were extremely unhappy because of the physical and emotional abuse.

Not surprisingly, the more dissatisfied the women were with the marriage as a whole, the more likely they were to end it. It *did* surprise us that the frequency of assaultive acts was not associated with overall relationship satisfaction. Husbands could be violent without losing their wives when their wives were still holding on to their dream, because then the husbands were perceived as having redeeming virtues, and the emotional abuse was seen as not excessive beyond some critical threshold.

The Deterrents to Leaving

All of this discussion about separation and divorce must be viewed within a context of fear, economic dependency, and at times continued love and commitment to a dream that things will change.

Fear. If it weren't for the justifiable fears that leaving would put them at even greater risk, and the more general fear of their husbands that pervaded their lives, many more women would have left much sooner. Fear fails to predict divorce or separation because it is such a constant in abusive relationships. Women who leave do so despite the fear. Women who stay have good reasons for being afraid to leave, and in their own ways survive heroically in ongoing abusive relationships.

Economic Dependency. Economic dependency is another strong deterrent. In fact, it was cited by women in our sample more frequently than fear as a deterrent to leaving. Batterers often systematically use financial resources as yet another vehicle for control. We have seen how dependent Vicky was on George's child support payments from the navy. Since she knew that he would not pay child support after his discharge, she had to delay her divorce for over a year to put herself in a state of financial readiness to leave. The need to control does not end for batterers just because the couple is no longer married. Batterers will fight fiercely to avoid sharing community property with their former wives, even when children are involved. At times, as in the case of George and Vicky, the only mechanism of control that remains is keeping the ex-wife poor.

Continuing Love and Traumatic Bonding. Despite the centrality of fear and economic security as deterrents to leaving, we would be remiss if we did not mention the strength of love and attachment between many of the couples in our sample, and the lengths to which battered women would go to find ways of justifying their continuance in a violent relationship. We have spoken many times in earlier chapters of battered women holding on to a dream, a fantasy of a loving marriage, rationalizing the violence in various ways. For example, it is attributed to alcohol, or a difficult childhood. Time and again, we heard about the lightbulb going on, the end to rationalization, the giving up of the dream. Along with that, we saw a shift from fear to contempt.

Traumatic Bonding. Another part of what makes it difficult to leave these marriages is what psychologist Donald Dutton has called "traumatic bonding." [4] This is a bizarre phenomenon that happens when love and violence are combined. It turns out that if dogs are trained with a mixture of love and violence, they become more attached to their trainers than if only love is used. This appears to be true in many other species as well. There is a very strong bond created by the violence being paired with love that we do not understand very well, but it is likely to be operating in some of these marriages, and it makes leaving very difficult.

Two Stories of Heroic Escape

The day after Don beat up their cat Martha started to look for an apartment. She moved out one week later. She presented it to Don as a trial separation, but she secretly knew that she would never be back. She had to get away, and fast. Don seemed willing to tolerate a trial separation, but she worried that a final break would be too much for him. She was right. Although he allowed her to move out, he stalked her and beat her repeatedly during the separation. On one occasion, he called and asked her to come to his apartment. When she showed up, they argued over whether or not to divorce. Don started to choke Martha, and she thought she was going to die this time. Now he had nothing to lose. Miraculously, he stopped, but when she left he yelled at her on the way out, "I'm coming over there to kill you." She remembers thinking on the way home, "I'm going to have to file and if he kills me, he kills me. If I don't, he'll kill me for sure. Even death would be better than this." She filed for divorce a week later.

Martha risked her life by filing for divorce. But by this time she saw only three possible outcomes, regardless of what she did. She could return to Don, she could be dead, or she could be rid of him. Of the three, returning to Don seemed worse than death. Once she came to that conclusion, her heroism took over, and she took that final step.

Don escalated his threats as well as his violence after Martha filed for divorce. He continued to stalk her, following her everywhere she went: when she left her apartment, he was always there. One night he came over unexpectedly with a gun.

He kept talking to her, all the while holding a loaded gun and acting as though it was not there. Even idle conversation is completely bizarre when one person, a very violent person, is holding a loaded gun. He then threatened suicide unless she returned to him. Even after the divorce was final, Don kept following her, kept calling her, kept threatening to kill her and himself—depending on his mood. In the past, she had tried to pacify him by following his immediate orders and coming to his house. One night she said, "Fuck you!" instead, and slammed the phone down. He called back and said, "I'm going to kill you. I'm going to slit your throat." But it was as if all the years of anger had turned Martha into an erupting volcano. She said, "Try it, you asshole. I'm not scared of you anymore. Death would be better than dealing with you. Blow yourself away instead. A whole lot of people would be happier."

This language was not typical of Martha. Standing up to him had unleashed a seething cauldron of rage, and she suddenly wanted him to die. She was no longer afraid. She had been living in hell. What did she have to lose? She also began to sense his fragility and was on to him. She had called his bluff. It was more of a turning point than the filing for divorce itself.

From this point on, there was no way she was going to let him get to her. He continued to send her threatening cards and came to her apartment on occasion trying to break the door down. But she obtained a restraining order and the stalking gradually decreased. Martha started dating a new man. She filed the restraining order as much to protect the new relationship as she did to protect herself. A restraining order does not always work, but in this case it put an end to the harassment.

Martha married Jesse in the summer of 1995. They had been dating since late 1992. It was hard for Martha to trust a man again, and she took things slowly with Jesse. She told Jesse all about the abuse she had suffered, and early on was hypersensitive to his apparent mood changes. But Jesse was supportive, understanding, and patient. He seems like a gentle man, as different from Don as a man can be.

Martha ran into Don during her engagement to Jesse and told him about it. Don wept briefly, but was nice to her during this encounter on the street. He tried one last time to coax her back, but she could see that he hadn't changed. She felt nothing but contempt for him.

Don has been celibate since his breakup with Martha, at least as of April 1996. For five years he has mourned the demise of this abusive relationship. When we interviewed him at that time he made clear to us what had been clear to Martha: he hadn't changed. He had been a loner before Martha, and he had reverted to being a loner after Martha. He took backpacking trips by himself and seemed happy only when he was alone in the wilderness. Mostly, he was depressed and lonely. People were too much for him, though. Being alone was lonely, but it was easier. Don still minimized his role in the violence, saw himself as a victim, and rewrote history in a way that made him out to be a saint who had tried unsuccessfully to reform the crazy woman that he was married to.

We could tell that he knew it was best for him to stay away from women. He was no altruist, but he suffered profoundly in his relationship with Martha and didn't want to subject himself to the pain of being out of control, the worries, the obsessive jealousy, and the constant experience of being a victim.

Don and Martha were a classic example of a relationship between a batterer and a battered woman where the woman catches on and leaves. As marriages go, this was a short one. And although Martha was beaten for many years, she got out immediately when she gave up the dream. At first she thought marriage would change him, and she cut him some slack for his traumatic childhood. When she stopped believing that, she left.

Don's emotional abuse was extremely intense, especially his

tendency to degrade and isolate Martha. We have seen that these factors, probably more than the multiple acts of violence, drove Martha away. Don was also extremely dependent on Martha, which is also typical of the batterers whose wives left them. He had a history of delinquency, drug abuse, and excessive drinking, which also put him in the high-risk category for getting dumped.

What about Martha? Although she was not a typical "leaver" in that she was not overtly assertive with Don and tried to placate him often until she decided to leave him, she did share the extreme emotional discomfort of battered women who leave. As a woman who grew up in a family that provided support and security but taught little about emotional expression, Martha was overwhelmingly angry, and she did not know what to do with the anger. She was in control of herself enough to know that she shouldn't try to antagonize him, but once she had, and he began to beat her, she would yell and scream. This constant state of negative emotional arousal and dissatisfaction seemed to be common among battered women who left. The danger signs were there. Martha escaped, but Don did not. His demons were, and may always remain, internal.

David and Judy

Judy finally left David, but as we have already seen in chapter 5, there were many false starts before the final breakup. One night during an argument, Judy said, "You're not my god!" Dave replied, "For all intents and purposes, I am. You're stupid, you're nuts, you're crazy, and you're sick." He then knocked her down with a slap in the face, and caused a concussion. In her woozy state, she decided, "This is it." He continued to come toward her, but she was more angry now than scared. She was ready to die rather than submit to him. She called the police, but Dave left the house before they arrived. That night, she slept in a shelter for battered women for the first time. They had been together for seventeen years.

Dave was convicted of assault, and paroled contingent upon joining a therapy group for batterers. He violated his parole by not attending the sessions. He continued drinking, and started having an affair with Judy's work associate. Judy felt humiliated. She wanted to die. However, instead of trying to kill herself, she divorced Dave. He had pushed beyond her level of tolerance, and that last argument was her last straw incident. By prosecuting him she changed her life. Lying there with a concussion, her life flashed before her and she saw it as a never-ending cycle of violence. Somehow, she dredged up the courage to recognize that she had to save herself. The dream was gone forever.

It probably helped that she now had the blessing of her children. Both had started to hate their father. Their daughter was now a teenager. Dave tried to control her in any way he could, especially by insulting her friends and in particular her boyfriends. He also began to beat up his teenage son. The son's teacher called Judy in to school and told her that her son's viability as a human being depended on the father being out of the picture. Strong words! This was external validation.

Dave tried to talk Judy into taking him back. But now she saw him as a coward and a loser. In 1995, Judy divorced Dave. She hadn't given up on men, especially if she could find one who would be a good role model for her children. She was not depressed. She couldn't remember feeling this good—ever!

Judy had this to say to other battered women:

"It doesn't change. You can't put your problems away. He's a loser and an abuser. That's what he was when we first met, and I was hopeful enough and in denial enough that it would be different because it was me. I lived with my parents' impression of me for years. I have just recently, not magically, but through introspection, reading, prayer, and meditation, come to have my own opinion of myself. I said, 'No, if I'm stupid I need to be educated. If I'm nuts I need an asylum. If I'm evil I need to be incarcerated. But I don't ever need to be hit by anybody and especially not by the man who has vowed to love me forever.'"

7

When Does the Abuse Stop?

Every day in this country, thousands of chronically battered women ask, How do I avoid getting hit? How do I get through the day? Should I be in this relationship at all? Might he change? Do I dare leave him?

As we have said, it is much easier to get into an abusive relationship than it is to get out of one. In chapter 6, we described the characteristics of women who tend to leave abusive relationships and the characteristics of batterers that help impel the women on the courageous course of leaving them. But we didn't discuss one of the most salient questions on the minds of battered women who are contemplating escape: Will he ever change? The hope that a violent partner will change keeps many battered women in abusive relationships. This hope is usually misplaced. When battered women realize that their husbands aren't going to change, some of them begin the heroic struggle to escape.

However, our research data reveal that often the violence

declines, and sometimes the violence *does* stop. Sometimes even the emotional abuse stops along with the physical abuse. In this chapter, we'll attempt to pinpoint how often the abuse stops, why it does, and how a woman may be able to determine whether the violence will stop in *her* relationship.

Violence Now *Usually* Means Violence Later

In the absence of treatment or criminal sanctions, men who batter usually continue to do so, at least for the next few years. The more severe the violence, the less likely it is to stop. When there is violence before marriage, it usually continues after marriage. And when the violence before marriage is severe, it almost never stops any time soon.

Dr. Kenneth E. Leonard and his associates[1] began to report their findings on newlyweds where the husband was violent during the year prior to marriage. This research group divided the abusive husbands into three categories: mild, moderate, and severe. These categories were derived from the Conflict Tactics Scale (CTS),[2] the most widely used questionnaire for measuring domestic violence. The CTS is reprinted in Table 3.

As the table shows, the items on the CTS vary according to how severe the husband's response to conflict is. According to Dr. Leonard and his colleagues, "mild" violence was defined as one occurrence during the previous year of "pushing, grabbing, or shoving." "Moderate" violence was defined as more than one episode within the past year of "pushing, grabbing, or shoving," but no instances of severe violence. "Severe" violence was defined as at least one episode of hitting with a fist or beating up the partner. Despite the use of these terms for research purposes, no violence in a marriage, even "pushing, grabbing, or shoving," is mild. These scientists did not ask couples about the most severe forms of violence, those involving the use or threatened use of weapons. Recall that Cobras

Table 3. Conflict Tactics Scale

No matter how well a couple gets along, there are times when they disagree on major decisions, get annoyed about something the other person does, or have spats or fights because they're in a bad mood or for some other reason. A couple may also use many different ways to settle their differences. Listed below are some things that you or your spouse may have done when you had a dispute. First, rate how many times you have done any of these things in the last year. Second, rate how many times your spouse has done any of these things in the last year. Then rate whether you or your spouse has ever done any of these things.

	You in the Past Year								Spouse in the Past Year								Ever Happened		
	Never	Once	Twice	3-5 times	6-10 times	11-20 times	More than 20	Don't know	Never	Once	Twice	3-5 times	6-10 times	11-20 times	More than 20	Don't know	Yes	No	Don't know
a. Discussed the issue calmly	0	1	2	3	4	5	6	X	0	1	2	3	4	5	6	X	1	2	X
b. Got information to back up (your/his or her) side of things	0	1	2	3	4	5	6	X	0	1	2	3	4	5	6	X	1	2	X
c. Brought in or tried to bring in help to settle things	0	1	2	3	4	5	6	X	0	1	2	3	4	5	6	X	1	2	X
d. Insulted or swore at the other one	0	1	2	3	4	5	6	X	0	1	2	3	4	5	6	X	1	2	X
e. Sulked and/or refused to talk about it	0	1	2	3	4	5	6	X	0	1	2	3	4	5	6	X	1	2	X
f. Stomped out of the room or house (or yard)	0	1	2	3	4	5	6	X	0	1	2	3	4	5	6	X	1	2	X

(continued next page)

Table 3. (Continued)

	You in the Past Year								Spouse in the Past Year								Ever Happened		
	Never	Once	Twice	3-5 times	6-10 times	11-20 times	More than 20	Don't know	Never	Once	Twice	3-5 times	6-10 times	11-20 times	More than 20	Don't know	Yes	No	Don't know
g. Cried	0	1	2	3	4	5	6	X	0	1	2	3	4	5	6	X	1	2	X
h. Did or said something to spite the other one	0	1	2	3	4	5	6	X	0	1	2	3	4	5	6	X	1	2	X
i. Threatened to hit or throw something at the other one	0	1	2	3	4	5	6	X	0	1	2	3	4	5	6	X	1	2	X
j. Threw or smashed or hit or kicked something	0	1	2	3	4	5	6	X	0	1	2	3	4	5	6	X	1	2	X
k. Threw something at the other one	0	1	2	3	4	5	6	X	0	1	2	3	4	5	6	X	1	2	X
l. Pushed, grabbed or shoved the other one	0	1	2	3	4	5	6	X	0	1	2	3	4	5	6	X	1	2	X
m. Slapped the other one	0	1	2	3	4	5	6	X	0	1	2	3	4	5	6	X	1	2	X
n. Kicked, bit, or hit with a fist	0	1	2	3	4	5	6	X	0	1	2	3	4	5	6	X	1	2	X
o. Hit or tried to hit with something	0	1	2	3	4	5	6	X	0	1	2	3	4	5	6	X	1	2	X
p. Beat up the other one	0	1	2	3	4	5	6	X	0	1	2	3	4	5	6	X	1	2	X
q. Threatened with a knife or gun	0	1	2	3	4	5	6	X	0	1	2	3	4	5	6	X	1	2	X
r. Used a knife or gun	0	1	2	3	4	5	6	X	0	1	2	3	4	5	6	X	1	2	X
s. Other	0	1	2	3	4	5	6	X	0	1	2	3	4	5	6	X	1	2	X

were more likely than Pit Bulls to threaten their wives with a knife or a gun.

How often did men who were violent prior to marriage continue to be violent during the first two years following marriage? Among couples where the violence prior to marriage was categorized as "mild," 65 percent of the husbands continued to be violent. When the violence rate was moderate, 75 percent of the husbands continued their violence. And, when the violence during the year prior to marriage was severe, 87 percent were still violent two years later. Thus, for newlywed couples, violence before marriage usually means violence after marriage, and even one episode of severe violence before marriage practically guarantees that the violence will continue for at least the first two years after marriage.

Dr. Leonard and his colleagues also discovered that at the time of marriage, female victims of physical aggression were depressed, and that the depression continued if the violence did. However, when violence stopped, so did the depression. This is not surprising. But it *was* somewhat surprising that a wife's overall satisfaction with the marriage did not increase when the violence stopped. Our research suggests that this is because emotional abuse continued.

But what if you're not a newlywed? A recent study by Dr. Etiony Aldarondo[3] examined a broader sample of couples, not just newlyweds. Though he used the CTS, Dr. Aldarondo used a somewhat different classification scheme, where he included in his definition of "severe" "kicked, bit, or hit her with a fist," as well as Dr. Leonard's criteria of punching or beating up the partner. Also, unlike Dr. Leonard, Dr. Aldarondo included the items from the CTS involving the use or threatened use of weapons. Dr. Aldarondo's research revealed that if husbands had been violent in the previous year, about two-thirds of them continued their violence over the next two years. These findings support those of Dr. Leonard in showing that the majority of violent men continue to be violent. In addition, Dr. Aldarondo found emotional abuse to be much higher in the men who continued to be violent than in those who did not. Thus, once again we find the connection between emotional and physical abuse: the more emotionally abusive, the more likely they were to continue their violence. However, even the men who stopped their physical aggression continued to display at least some emotional abuse, as we think occurred in the Leonard study.

Violence Often Decreases, but It Seldom Stops

Our study is quite different from those we just talked about. For one thing, although we collected these data, we did not have to rely on people's reports of emotional abuse. Ours was the first study to actually observe *real* marital conflict with severely violent husbands. We also collected data that provided us with more information about what was happening physiologically to people as they became emotionally aroused. As we mentioned in chapter 1, in order to be selected for our study, husbands had to have pushed, grabbed, or shoved their wives six or more times within the past year; kicked, hit, or slapped them at least twice; or committed at least one more severe act (hitting with a closed fist, beating up, threatening with a weapon, using a weapon). Because of our criteria, we were able to recruit a sample of severely violent men. Furthermore, by directly measuring observable behavior as well as recording physiological responses, we were able to avoid the biases of previous studies and objectively determine how the partners were feeling and acting during arguments.

We were interested in how often violence decreased, how often it did not, how often violence stopped, how often emotional abuse stopped, and whether we could identify factors that contributed to changes in violence over time.

One thing we do not yet know is whether the short-term changes in violence in our study are a sign that the violence will stop completely at some later date. However, we were surprised to find that in our sample a whopping 54 percent of the men showed decreases in violence during the second of our two follow-up years. The other 46 percent either continued battering at current rates or increased their frequency of violence. In fact, not only did some men decrease in physical violence, but they no longer met our standards for being included in our violent group. The drop in violence was dramatic. Of the batterers who showed decreases in violence, 86 percent did nothing more severe than a single push or shove during that year. Another 7 percent of the "decreasers" had one more serious episode of slapping or hitting. However, only 7 percent stopped their physical abuse altogether.

There were no significant differences between Pit Bulls and Cobras in the course of their violence over time. Even though the Cobras were both more physically and emotionally abusive than the Pit Bulls, they were just as likely to decrease their violence over time as the Pit Bulls were, and just as unlikely to stop the violence altogether.

On the surface, these data appear to be good news for women who are caught in an abusive marriage. However, we have cause for concern about how these results are interpreted. First, the fact that there is still *at least some violence in 93 percent of the batterers* is alarming. Any violence in a marriage is a violation of the marriage contract: husbands as well as wives are supposed to be loving and nurturing to one another, not violent. Also, the decrease in violence shown by both our groups of violent men, in the absence of total cessation of violence, may be misleading. Once control is established over a woman through battering, perhaps it can be maintained by continued emotional abuse with intermittent battering used as a terrifying reminder of what is possible in this marriage. In fact, the Cobras' violence was so severe that it may have been easier for them than for the Pit Bulls to maintain control through emotional abuse alone. Thus, perhaps it is not that surprising that many of the Cobras showed decreased violence over time.

In our view, unless the batterer totally ceases both physical and emotional abuse, he is still a batterer. The systematic use of intimidation to control the woman is the basis of our definition. So we are not as encouraged by the dramatic decreases in violence in our data as we might be if there had been high proportions of complete cessation of violence.

Although batterers in our sample rarely stopped their violence, we thought that it would be of interest to examine factors that led to substantial decreases in violence. We reasoned that perhaps such factors, if continued, might eventually result in the ending of abuse.

Characteristics of Batterers Who Decreased Their Violence

What were the characteristics of men who substantially decreased their levels of violence over time? Here is what we found:

• Husbands who decreased their violence were *younger* than those who continued. This finding contradicts previous research, which suggests that younger men are more likely to be batterers than older men.[4] However, none of those previous studies had followed the same batterers over time. Our research suggests that although in general younger men may be more likely to batter, they are also more likely to decrease their frequency of violence.

• We found that the happier batterers were with their marriages, the more likely they were to decrease their battering.

• Emotional abuse, especially the type we referred to as "degradation," was related to decreases in violence. The less emotionally abusive husbands were, the more likely they were to decrease the frequency and severity of battering. In other words, the least emotionally abusive husbands were most likely to be the ones who decreased their high levels of physical violence.

• Batterers who were less domineering, belligerent, and contemptuous during the laboratory marital interaction were more likely to decrease their levels of physical abuse. Continued violence was especially likely when men were extremely domineering during the laboratory interactions. Domineering behavior in the laboratory did not bode well for the battered women. This behavior was exquisitely sensitive to predicting subsequent physical abuse.

• Batterers who maintained high levels of violence were more aroused at the physiological level during the laboratory arguments than those who decreased their levels of violence. Their heart rates were higher, they perspired more, and they were more physically active. For most of our batterers, this physiological arousal reflected general emotional upset. Physical arousal takes measures other than heart rate into account. It is the "change" in arousal that defines a Cobra, not absolute levels.

• Neither the frequency nor the severity of prior physical abuse predicted whether the violence would continue at those rates. In other words, it is impossible to tell, based on the amount of violence itself, whether it will continue. Although this appears to contradict the results of the study by Dr. Leonard, it is important to remember that, unlike the men in Leonard's study, in our sample all of the husbands were quite violent to begin with.

• When husband violence decreased, wife violence did as well. However, wife violence did not affect husband violence. In other words, husbands were not becoming less violent *because* of anything their wives were doing. It was quite the reverse. When husbands became less violent, so did their wives. This finding is consistent with our analyses of arguments presented in chapter 3. Husband violence is the determining factor and is difficult to predict. In contrast, wife violence is lawful, and can be viewed almost in toto as a *reaction* to husband violence.

• Those battered women whose husbands decreased their violence showed an increase in their own marital happiness.

To summarize, those men who dramatically decreased their high level of violence were younger, more happily married, less likely to degrade their wives verbally, were less domineering, contemptuous, and belligerent in the videotaped marital interaction and less physiologically aroused during that interaction. These patterns may be a helpful guide for battered women in assessing whether the violence they are living through is likely to substantially decrease over time.

However, we need to express some caution about our findings. Are these findings indicative of other good long-term outcomes? Possibly. But they may also be signs that the abuse has simply gone "underground" and been replaced by emotional abuse. At this point in our research, we simply don't know. Hence, we would caution anyone reading our results to *separately* evaluate both the physical and emotional abuse in the marriage.

No amount of violence ought to be considered acceptable by battered women, and only total cessation of violence and emotional abuse ought to be considered a true positive outcome. Our sample reflects the types of batterers who come into contact with the criminal justice system, who injure their wives repeatedly, and for whom the risk for homicide is high. It is therefore quite relevant to know how rarely the violence stops over a two-year period in an ongoing battering relationship. Unfortunately, in our data this kind of positive outcome rarely occurred. Severe battering rarely went away.

Here is another concern that we have about the potential ambiguity in our findings. When we examined the marital interaction, we found some evidence that the men who dramatically decreased their physical violence had also become *more* belligerent during the laboratory interaction than those whose violence continued at high levels. Belligerence is a very provocative and threatening form of intimidation. This makes us wonder whether there might be a "seesaw effect" between physical and emotional abuse. There was some evidence that as physical violence decreased, it was replaced by emotional abuse. This worries us. We know that with at least some couples, as physical abuse went down, emotional abuse went up. Is it the case in these instances that as emotional abuse and physical abuse become closely linked in time over a period of years, intermittent threats of violence coupled with some emotional abuse are enough to maintain control over the women? Maybe in this way batterers maintain control without subjecting themselves to legal sanctions, since emotional abuse is not illegal. Hence, these two dimensions, physical and emotional abuse, have to be evaluated together for people to make a good guess about what the long-term fate of any battering relationship might be.

Sadly, all of the factors that led to decreases in violence were characteristics of the batterers themselves. In other words, there was nothing battered women could do to stop the abuse except get out of the relationship. This is consistent with findings we reported in chapter 3: there is little battered women can do, either to stop the violence while it is occurring or stop husbands from being violent in the future.

Since the cessation of violence was so rare in our sample, it was impossible to predict it using statistical techniques. This is the nature of scientific methods. It is extremely difficult to predict things that don't occur very often. However, rarely does not mean never. We were determined to understand as much about the cessation of violence as we could, despite the limitations of our scientific methods.

Therefore, we moved to our second-line strategy, our exit interviews. With these interviews, we tried to put the problem under a microscope. Every battered woman has to assess—based on all the information she has available—how likely it is that the violence and the emotional abuse will stop. Perhaps by examining examples of violence stopping, and simultaneously looking at the kinds of men who decrease their violence over a two-year period, we can make some guesses as to the batterers who have the potential for change. To engage in such speculation we must make a leap of faith that may or may not be warranted: that the types of men who show decreases in violence may be the types of men most likely to stop eventually. In the interests of this speculation, we will now examine a couple, Karen and Derek, where the violence did stop, and see what we can learn. We must caution the reader that Karen and Derek may not be typical of couples in which all battering and emotional abuse eventually ceases. However, they did transform their relationship from an abusive to a nonabusive one, and few other couples in our sample demonstrated such a dramatic transformation. Thus, we offer them not necessarily as a *typical* example, but as one of the few positive ones we could find in our study.

Karen and Derek

"You shouldn't take that kind of crap from her," John advised his friend. "If she were my wife, I would show her who's boss." Derek was confiding in his friend, *complaining* really. Karen was a handful for him. All he wanted was a little respect and a little tenderness, but Karen was always putting him down. She could outtalk him whenever she wanted, and he was always feeling stupid. But somehow, John's advice didn't seem right to Derek.

John and Derek worked together as dockworkers, and it was a macho culture at the workplace. There were no women, and John was Derek's mentor when it came to women. Derek thought to himself, "Maybe John *is* right! Karen's got the upper hand." But they had had this conversation, or ones like it, many times before. He'd go home after one of these conversations, and when he got angry he would beat Karen. But he would feel very wrong about what he was doing, and also his violence didn't work at all. Her verbal tirades kept right on coming.

Karen's History

Karen was born in September 1950, and spent the first twelve years of her life living with her mother. Karen's childhood was a horror. Her father disappeared before she was born, and the little information she has on him is that he was "sleeping with five other women at the time that he was sleeping with my mother." He paid no child support, so her mother was forced to raise her on a meager army salary. Karen's mother was an alcoholic, and Karen never felt loved or accepted by her. When Karen was eleven, a friend of her mother's tried to rape Karen. Karen remembers yelling at her mom for not being able to tell that the guy was a pervert. Her mother responded by pushing her against the wall. A year later, her mother remarried, and when Karen turned fifteen her birthday present was a baby sister. During these teenage years, Karen's stepfather often kissed Karen, fondled her, and even attempted to have sexual intercourse with her on one occasion. Karen told her mom, and called the police, but he was acquitted. Her stepfather also battered her mother. Karen's mother hit him back when she was battered.

Somehow, Karen got through all of this and became a very accomplished person. She went to college and eventually earned a master's degree in psychology in 1977. Despite her own background of having been sexually abused, she spent several years counseling sex offenders in San Francisco.

But her life was extremely troubled. She was married two times prior to Derek, from 1968 to 1973 and from 1975 to 1984. One of her former husbands battered her. She got a restraining order against him, and spent time in shelters for battered women. In 1973, shortly after the breakup of her first marriage, Karen spent time in a psychiatric hospital for a nervous breakdown. She also tried to kill herself twice between 1966 and 1975, and periodically fought battles against alcohol and marijuana dependence.

Derek's History

Derek was born in 1957 (he is seven years Karen's junior), and grew up with his mother, stepfather, two younger brothers and one younger sister. Derek also knows very little about his biological father, who left the family when Derek was only six months old. From what he knew, his father had served time in military prison. Like Karen's father, Derek's father never paid child support. Derek referred to him as an "asshole." As a young child, Derek was spanked weekly, and recalls being hit once by his stepfather with a willow branch when he was six years old. However, he remembers being very close to his mother, and told us that he could talk to her about anything.

His stepfather was a domineering man with a short fuse, and there were frequent arguments between the stepfather and Derek's mother. Both were strong-willed people, and although the stepfather was not a batterer, his mother frequently hit her husband. She drank heavily, and approximately once a year she'd put on her cowboy boots and, as Derek put it, she would "kick the shit out of him." During these incidents Derek's mother would yell and scream for help and protection. Yet when Derek would arrive on the scene, it was his stepfather who was being beaten, not his mother. His stepfather was violent to Derek a few times, mainly when Derek was caught using drugs and alcohol as a teenager.

Derek turned out to be a violent teenager, and hung out with a motorcycle gang. At age eighteen, he joined the army. It was during his stint in the army that he developed an alcohol problem. He was also sexually harassed and abused by a number of senior military officers during these years. He joined Alcoholics Anonymous in 1985.

Karen and Derek's Courtship

When Derek and Karen met in February 1987, she was working as a waitress, and he was working for a pet-food manufacturer. Karen was burned out from working with sex offenders and saw waitressing as a kind of "sabbatical." One day she came into work and saw a couple sitting in her section. Derek was having breakfast with his girlfriend. They were having an argument about sex. Karen could not help but overhear the argument. Derek's girlfriend was saying, "Stop talking about sex! You are obsessed. I'll sleep with you if and when I'm good and ready."

Derek courted Karen by hanging out at her restaurant. She resisted for months, but Derek was very persistent. Finally, she half-jokingly said to him, "Fine, you can be my lover if I can tie you up and torture you sexually." He replied, "Where can I buy the rope?" And in this way, Karen and Derek became an item.

The Onset of Battering

Problems erupted about four months after they started dating. They started living together almost immediately, had very little money, and Derek changed fairly dramatically. In the throes of seduction, he had been an attentive listener, but he became moody, brooding, and uninterested once the seduction had succeeded.

On that first violent night, four months after Karen surrendered to Derek's advances, she had gone downstairs to pay the rent and had taken a little too long to suit Derek. When she returned Derek accused her—out of the blue—of having an affair with the landlord. He had just finished his third beer, and the alcohol was clearly contributing to his belligerence.

Karen tried to take his fourth from him, saying, "I think you've just had a little too much beer." He asserted his right to drink as much as he pleased, and continued to taunt her about the alleged affair. Karen grabbed Derek's beer and his wallet and said he could have them back when he sobered up. Suddenly, Derek punched her with a closed fist in the eye, breaking her glasses and giving her a black eye. He then grabbed his car keys, and with just his slacks on ran to the car to buy more beer. He yelled to her on his way out that he was going to call the police and charge her with theft.

Karen actually *did* call the police, and about two hours later they arrived. Derek was arrested. Karen thought seriously about breaking up with him right then and there. But she didn't. A year later, Derek and Karen separated. It was to be the first of their two separations. The major conflict area was sex. After much discussion and arguing about how to overcome sexual incompatibilities, they agreed on how he was to approach her sexually. In the past, she had objected to his obsession with his own satisfaction, as well as his insensitivity to her desires. Derek said he would go along, but secretly it enraged him. It usually did no good to express anger verbally because she could win any argument between them. But he was so angry about the agreement that he left home for a number of days. While he was away, he went on a drinking binge and was found hanging out among homeless people in downtown Seattle.

Karen thought about leaving him again, but instead she took him back. However, this time she insisted that he enter a treatment program for batterers. He did, but dropped out after six weeks. As he put it, "I had nothing in common with those psychos." She agreed: "It was one of those Mickey Mouse, bleeding heart programs by feminist do-gooders who don't understand the first thing about the psyche of the batterer."

In December 1988, Karen had her fourth child, and Derek became a father. Even though he was used to children (the other three lived with them) and was generally a devoted stepfather, his becoming a father precipitated their second separation. Derek had stayed out all night drinking. When he came home he beat her, two days after she had given birth. She left with the baby for a shelter, where she stayed for four days. During this period they met daily to negotiate, and made a contract that he would not come home when he had been drinking (even one beer) within the last twenty-four hours.

In May 1990 Karen and Derek had the worst violent argument they were ever to have. Karen had been trying to sleep, and was annoyed that Derek was wandering around the house making noise. When he entered the bedroom, she made him an offer: "Since you're not going to let me get any sleep, just get your damn pants down and I'll let you get your rocks off." He immediately punched her in the nose, breaking her glasses. Then he picked up her glasses, smashed them into smaller pieces, and threw them out the window. They sat on the couch together, stunned, and after a breather they began to calmly discuss the conflict-laden topic of sex. Karen thought that the argument was over. But uncharacteristically, Derek told her that *he* was too angry to have sex, which struck Karen as the irony of ironies, since his chronic complaint was that there was not enough sex. She had had enough for one evening: "Well," she sighed, "I've had enough of this, I'm going back to bed. Kindly be quiet, and let me get some sleep."

As she began to walk away, he grabbed her arm and twisted it, saying, "You're not leaving until I tell you you can." He dislocated her arm. Karen had to walk to the hospital with Derek beside her. She didn't want him with her and told him so. Even in the midst of her pain, she was enraged. She screamed that she was going to leave him and take their son as they walked to the hospital, and Derek beat her up again. By the time they arrived at the hospital, Karen's face was black and blue from his punches.

As they were arguing outside the hospital entrance, someone

called the police. Karen tried to talk the police out of arresting him, but to no avail. Derek was already on probation for previous arrests for battering, and the police took him away.

Derek received probation and was ordered to attend a state-certified treatment program for batterers. Once again, he stopped going to the group shortly after sentencing. The probation officer did not report this violation of his parole. Instead, life went on as before. Karen and Derek went back to their chronic disputes about sex. He was constantly making advances, and she was usually rebuffing him, while insulting him for being a bad lover at the same time.

When we met Derek and Karen in November 1990, Karen was writing mystery novels, and Derek was doing odd jobs (painting, plumbing, repairing). Karen's new career had taken off, and she took it seriously. During her interview with us in 1990 she was quite demonstrative, and spoke in a loud, booming voice. In contrast, Derek was soft-spoken. Although articulate, he took long pauses to think carefully before responding to almost all of the questions. He was honest and accepted full responsibility for the violence.

Derek had beaten Karen more than twenty times in the year before we met them. There was also a great deal of marital rape, and she was frequently physically hurt during sex. Her violence was totally in the service of defending herself: she had punched him in the stomach, wrestled with him, strangled him, and physically hurt *him* during sex. Derek was in several therapy groups at that time, including Emotions Anonymous, and Men Working Against Abuse. He was also being treated for his alcohol abuse.

Despite all of the abuse, both Karen and Derek reported that they were, for the most part, happily married. This surprised us. At the same time, both acknowledged the possibility of divorce. Karen glibly predicted that, "He'd be on skid row, but I'd be fine. I'd have more time to write, I'd be better off financially. He'd be begging me to come back." With the same glibness, Karen could only give "perversity" as the reason for them still being together, whereas Derek felt that he was hanging on for the sake of his son. There was a clear and enormous intellectual discrepancy between them, which they both acknowledged. In addition to the intellectual discrepancy, Karen knew how to handle herself in the world of interpersonal relationships, while Derek was shy, diffident, and had a great deal of trouble forming attachments.

The laboratory interaction between Derek and Karen was unlike any we had ever seen. When we first watched it, we knew nothing else about them. Based on the interaction itself, Karen looked like the first female batterer either of us had ever seen. She looked bigger, stronger, meaner, and braver than Derek did. She put him down, yelled at him, taunted him, and totally dominated the conversation. Derek seemed harmless, meek, almost gentle. Who would have guessed from this verbal beating delivered by Karen that she was a battered woman?

The topic of the laboratory interaction was sex. Karen was expressing her frustration that Derek seemed incapable of pleasing her. Derek was on the defensive. Her piercing glare did not abate during the entire argument—she reeked of anger and contempt. She accused him of "only caring about your next squirt," and not her pleasure. He denied the accusations as best he could, quietly insisting that he was willing to give her whatever she needed during lovemaking. She practically spat, "You fool, I was faking it, I'm always faking the orgasm." She expressed outrage for Derek "dumping on me just because I won't spread my legs." He pleaded: "I don't like hitting you, it's just that you keep hollering at me."

Based on everything we knew, Derek and Karen did not strike us as a couple where the violence was likely to stop. However, when they came back two years later, their relationship had changed dramatically. There had been only one incident of pushing, and no beatings, in the past year. Both rated their marriage as "extremely happy." There was also very little emotional abuse. By 1995, when we conducted our exit interviews, both the violence and the emotional abuse had stopped completely. Derek had stopped both physical and emotional abuse for four years.

Derek's changes were gradual. They may have begun with their 1990 encounter with us: at least, both Derek and Karen attributed the beginning of their improved marriage to their experience with us. But eventually these gradual changes led to a revelation and a turning point for Derek. For the first time, he confronted the unavoidable conclusion that he was a batterer. Being in a research study may have helped with this process. As he was completing one questionnaire at home, he turned to Karen and asked, "God, how could you put up with me for so long? I'm a jerk."

Clearly this "facing up" to being a batterer is very rare in this population: most of the men excuse themselves for the violence and rationalize away their violent actions. The experience of being a research subject provided Derek with a wake-up call. It led him subsequently to try to stay calm when he was angry. He went on to invent his own version of time-out: when he felt like arguing, he stopped himself and asked for a break before he lost his temper. Psychologist Donald Dutton has suggested that batterers often see the light when they are asked to write down the instances in which they think violence is acceptable, and then to subsequently see the ways in which they violate their own moral code.[5] While they may be able to shrug off society's ethics, it is much harder for them to disregard their own.

Another turning point in Derek's stopping the violence was a third arrest for domestic violence. This time, he spent a few weeks in jail. Derek told us that the arrest caused him to reflect on the impact his violence had on the children, as well as on Karen. He mentioned the financial hardship created by fines and jail terms. He mentioned the impact on the children of him being away. He thought of his behavior as literally taking food off the table of his family.

Derek not only concluded that battering was wrong, but that it wasn't getting him what he wanted. Consider the sexual problems that Karen and Derek had. Most of their arguments revolved around sex. Violence simply made it less likely that he would get what he wanted. But even if it had, Derek never really felt that violence against Karen was okay: "I didn't like it even when I was doing it."

By 1995, both Derek and Karen reported that their marriage was much, much better, and both were convinced that the violence was gone for good. Karen commented that they'd reached a point in their marriage when their arguments were no longer attempts to win: rather, it was "us against the problem—the problem is the enemy, not each other." They had both started going to church, and both were working very hard at their jobs. Derek had greatly cut down on his drinking.

Occasionally, Derek still threatens to leave Karen, but when he does she just smiles and says "good-bye." She knows that he doesn't really mean it. He appreciates the changes she has made as well, especially that she's now willing to put forth effort into making him happy. He also commented that he has learned to trust her a lot more than he ever did. He used to be jealous when she would look at a man, but now he is not. In fact, he volunteered that, "She is an independent woman. I have no right to stop her from doing as she pleases, I never did have that right. I just thought I did."

Derek and Karen now say that they have weathered their hard times because they have always shared similar values and interests: they love to garden, create a home, and are committed to having a family life. They also expressed a shared love of nature and of spiritual values.

Finally, their sex life took a dramatic change for the better: now Derek "always takes care of me first," according to Karen.

He is also more receptive to the word "no," since there are times when she's just not interested in sex. Their disagreements are much less hostile, and there is a sense of compromise and mutual accommodation. They each get what they want, some of the time. And they each insisted that "sometime" was enough.

Reflecting on their previous violent episodes, Derek recognized that he was often frustrated: Karen was so good at "outtalking" him, that he underestimated his own verbal proficiency. She thought quickly and talked quickly. He was slower off the block, but when he eventually had a chance to develop his position, he could hold his own. When he was given that room, he became less frustrated. He believes that he was often violent because he was tired of always losing arguments.

A Possible Formula for Stopping Abuse

Scientists have a hard time trying to chart the course of any phenomenon that occurs at a very low rate among the population. Our statistical methods of prediction simply don't do well when it comes to helping us understand rare events. We couldn't predict the ending of abuse because it was so rare.

We are going to try to be both speculative and cautious in what we conclude from cases like Karen and Derek's. The stakes are high in this decision-making process: the wrong prediction, and subsequently mistaken action, could mean more brutal beatings, continued emotional abuse, or even murder. Furthermore, even if we can make good guesses about the kinds of men who will eventually stop, this does not mean that women *should* wait instead of getting out of the relationship. Getting out still may be the best decision, even if the man is a good bet for stopping someday. Why should a battered woman put up with even one beating, let alone a series of beatings because she believes that someday the batterer will stop?

Given these caveats, why even proceed with our speculations? Because, in fact, women often *do* stay in abusive relationships hoping that they will change. We *do* have some
opinions about factors that may lead to the ending of abuse.
We will offer them as guesses, or hypotheses to be tested, at
this point. We will be testing them in the future.

The following is our list of speculations about what *may* be
related to the violence and the emotional abuse eventually
stopping altogether:

• *If the man does not minimize, deny, or distort his responsibility for the violence.* Most batterers are skillful at minimizing the severity of the violence, blaming their partners for it,
and at times even denying that it has occurred. By minimizing the severity of violence ("I was just pushing her around a
little bit"), denying that it has occurred at all ("I didn't touch
you last night. You're crazy, woman!"), and by distorting
responsibility for the violence ("I was simply retaliating and
standing up for myself, just like any man would do"), batterers keep legal and moral sanctions at a distance, and perhaps
at times even fool themselves into avoiding a confrontation
with a potentially unforgiving conscience. When batterers
avoid these rationalizations, we think they are likely to eventually stop the abuse. For example, it is clear that Derek
never felt right about his violence toward Karen. He knew
that it was wrong from the start, felt perpetually guilty about
it, and never found an effective way of rationalizing it. Ultimately, he couldn't live with himself, let alone show his face
in public, until he no longer saw himself as a batterer. This
unwillingness to minimize, deny, and distort should not be
confused with the temporary remorse expressed by batterers
right after an abusive episode. Nor should it be mistaken for
the brief periods of contrition when confronted with potential
legal sanctions. It is not uncommon for batterers to express
remorse; however, the remorse is usually temporary, and

when pressed, they ultimately shift back to the familiar rationalizations. Derek was different: he *never* felt right about being a batterer.

• *His own ethics do not justify hitting.* If the batterer's violence violates his own code of ethics, and he is able to state this in his own words.

• *If the battering is unsuccessful as a method of control.* Battering is first and foremost a method of control, and a very effective one. But in those instances where it is unsuccessful, it is likely to stop. This observation was not directly tested in our study, but has been indirectly supported by interviews with women who have left abusive relationships. Dr. Diane Follingstad and her colleagues found that battered women vary dramatically in their response to the first few instances of domestic violence, and that their initial responses affect subsequent abuse as well as the longevity of the relationship.[6] Karen was a very unusual woman. As far as we could tell, no matter how often she was beaten, she continued to do as she pleased. She resisted having sex when she didn't want it, even though she was frequently beaten as a result. She expressed her anger openly and—in our laboratory—contemptuously. And she didn't hesitate to prod Derek into getting help for his alcohol problems, despite the possibility of yet another beating. Derek acknowledged to us in his exit interview that it did no good to hit Karen. She continued to do what she wanted, when she wanted to.

We are on a slippery slope by even pointing out that Karen's unwillingness to be controlled contributed to the ending of her victimization. It is all too easy to infer from Karen's determination not to be controlled that it is up to battered women to resist control. Such an inference would be totally erroneous, another form of blaming the victim. It is the batterer's responsibility to stop the violence, and his alone. Battered women should *never* be called upon to accept beatings to prove to their husbands that violence is a waste of time. It is almost inevitable that the threat of abuse, along with a history of it, will successfully subjugate most human beings. However, any voluntary behavior that is unsuccessful in achieving its objective is eventually going to stop: this is a well-established principle of learning. Battering is no exception.

How useful is this information for most battered women? It is unclear. Karen might have gotten herself killed in the process of responding resiliently to the beatings. In our view, not only was her behavior risky, but she was an unusually spunky person and even her tolerance for pain was high. Nevertheless, Karen and Derek ended up staying together, developing a close and loving marriage, despite long personal and relationship histories that stacked the deck against them. We think that one of the secrets to their success was Karen's determination not to be controlled.

• *If there are low levels of emotional abuse.* Derek was one of the least emotionally abusive men in our sample, and a low level of emotional abuse is one of the strongest predictors of decreased violence. In fact, during the laboratory interaction, Karen was considerably more belligerent and contemptuous than Derek was. Keep in mind that when battered women are belligerent and contemptuous that does not typically constitute emotional abuse. The power of emotional abuse is derived from its association with physical abuse, and its ability to control, intimidate, and subjugate depends in large part on that association. Karen was responding naturally, given the rage that she experienced after repeated beatings. Nevertheless, it is striking to us that emotional abuse emerged as a sensitive indicator of changes in violence over time, and—in the case of Karen and Derek—a man who was only mildly abusive ended up stopping the violence altogether.

• *If there are low levels of domineering behavior.* Husbands who were frequently domineering during the laboratory interaction were highly unlikely to decrease their level of violence. In fact, domineering behavior during the laboratory arguments was overwhelmingly predictive of subsequent violence. The batterers who maintained or increased their levels of violence held the floor during conversation for an extraordinary amount of the interaction time, squelching their partners' attempts to express their points of view, lecturing their wives in a condescending manner, and essentially taking away their wives' voices. They could do so by interrupting, by belittling the other person's point of view, or by the sheer force of their assertion of their point of view. This behavior was so predictive of continued violence that we began to see it as a laboratory proxy for chronic violence. That is, when confined to a laboratory interaction, and hooked up to a polygraph, chronic batterers tended to batter through their domineering performance during the arguments. Interestingly, Derek and Karen were one of the few couples in the sample where the battered woman was actually *more* domineering than the batterer. This discrepancy reflected both unusually high levels of dominance (for a battered woman) in Karen, and unusually low levels of dominance (for a batterer) in Derek.

• *If there are higher levels of husband marital satisfaction.* Derek described himself as a happily married man, despite his battering. We found that the husband's level of marital satisfaction was generally associated with decreases in violence. Although it may seem incongruous to imagine either partner in an abusive relationship happy, marital satisfaction varies widely among both batterers and battered women. When batterers are relatively satisfied with the relationship, perhaps there is more hope for the violence eventually stopping. It was certainly true in Derek's case.

• *If there are low levels of drug and alcohol abuse.* The relationship between battering and substance abuse has been a topic of considerable debate within the professional community. Despite routine clinical observations that batterers tend to abuse drugs and alcohol, any causal inference is subject to attack by those who fear the potential consequences of an admission that battering is triggered by the drug-altered state: somehow, if the battering is attributed to the alcohol and drug abuse then the batterer will be seen as sick rather than as responsible for his actions, and he is less likely to be held accountable for the battering. Since there is general agreement that accountability and acceptance of responsibility are prerequisites to stopping the violence, there is no widespread treatment model for battering that includes state-of-the-art drug and alcohol rehabilitation components. In fact, we entered our program of research prepared to see alcohol abuse as an important and widespread characteristic of batterers, but not as an element that figured prominently in the causal chain. Yet again and again, we saw examples of battering cycles that were clearly triggered by alcohol. A substantial proportion of the batterers in our sample were *always* under the influence of drugs or alcohol when they were violent. We think that substance abuse influences battering in two ways: first, by lowering inhibitions; and second, by providing men with an excuse to batter that they would not otherwise have. Furthermore, we see no reason to view the batterer as sick rather than responsible because he takes alcohol or drugs when he batters. We suspect that when substance-abusing men stop their violence, it often follows their learning to successfully control their substance abuse. This was certainly true with Derek.

• *If the husband has been held accountable for his violence.* Here we will simply echo the prevailing paradigm within the professional advocacy community. Derek was arrested three times, and eventually punished with criminal sanctions for being a batterer. He attributes his greater self-control to the experience of being held accountable. He claims to have gotten nothing out of psychotherapy, a claim which Karen, despite being trained as a therapist, echoes. But the humiliation, loss of freedom, and economic consequences of jail had a major impact on Derek. We think that for the violence to end completely, there must be negative consequences for battering. The deterrents must be made so powerful that they are more punishing than the obtained control is rewarding. We believe that this is the most basic prerequisite for stopping the violence: the batterer must pay, and pay dearly. In our sample, the batterers were rarely punished for the violence except by having their wives leave them. This hurt many batterers, but there was little reason to doubt their potential for battering in subsequent relationships. In fact, battering was a way of life for most of the batterers in our sample—part of what it means to them to be in an intimate relationship. For many, violence was the only way that they could build an emotional connection. Changing that is not easy. Finding consequences that outweigh the rewards of power and control is not easy. But we suspect that such consequences are necessary for the violence to stop.

To summarize, if we were going to look for signs that the violence and emotional abuse might someday stop altogether, at this stage of knowledge we would want to know: 1) Has the husband been held accountable for the battering and been forced to pay a steep price for it? 2) How successful has the violence been in controlling, subjugating, and intimidating the battered woman? 3) How emotionally abusive is he? 4) Does he show high levels of conversational dominance during our structured interaction tasks? 5) Was the husband's overall level of marital satisfaction high? 6) Does the husband minimize, deny, and distort the abuse? and 7) To the extent that the batterer is dependent on drugs and alcohol, how successful has he been at stopping the substance abuse?

Let us reiterate a point that we made at the beginning of this section. To the extent that future research allows us to determine the conditions under which abuse will end in a particular relationship, does that mean that battered women should stay in the relationship if the husband has the right credentials? The answer is a resounding no. No woman deserves to be beaten by her partner, even once. The decision about whether or not to stay in an abusive relationship must be made based on a variety of considerations. We already know what some of the factors are that influence women's decisions to leave. Where the battering is severe, physical and emotional abuse rarely stops on its own. Some battered women stay in abusive relationships despite the severity and frequency of abusive episodes. It would be useful to have better data than we have at the moment that would help women know when the violence is likely to stop. We see that as an important avenue for future research.

In the meantime, we are left with one unanswered question: does rehabilitation make a difference? Thus far, we have talked about violence stopping without considering education and rehabilitation programs. Given the amount of time and money that goes into developing and staffing such programs for batterers, it would seem important to know whether or not they are successful in achieving the complete cessation of the physical violence and the emotional abuse in a reasonable proportion of the men who participate. In chapter 8, we explore current options in detail, along with existing criminal sanctions.

8

Rehabilitating Batterers

Our study put the phenomenon of battering under a microscope to obtain some basic information about the interaction patterns between batterers and battered women. We closely examined some common myths about domestic violence and described the dynamics of violent altercations. We distinguished between two types of batterers: Cobras and Pit Bulls. We profiled the types of batterers who drive battered women out of their relationships, and the kinds of battered women most inclined to leave. Finally, we examined the information that we and others have gathered on the conditions under which violence stops.

In this chapter we want to examine available options for rehabilitating batterers, including sanctions within the criminal justice system. When a battered woman is trying to decide whether or not to get out of an abusive relationship, one important consideration is the availability of remedies that can stop the battering. The good news is that, at least in our sample, a substantial number of women did get out of their abusive relationships, and did so safely. The bad news is that all too often the escape was risky and dangerous, with women subjected to stalking, further beatings, and in some cases an escalation of those beatings. We also know from other research findings that the escape process can put the battered woman at greater risk than she is in during the abusive relationship. In particular, the risk of homicide *increases* when women try to leave.[1] Even though there were no homicides in our sample, it is clear both from previous research and from the reports that appear all too frequently in the media that leaving an abusive relationship can be lethal.

Given these risks, it is natural for battered women to turn to the culture at large for solutions. Can they count on the criminal justice system to protect them? Can they reasonably hope that education programs for batterers will have a successful outcome? If the criminal justice system can protect them, they might be more willing to risk the attempted escape. If criminal sanctions are effective in rehabilitating the batterer, perhaps there is hope for the relationship. If education programs are successful in stopping the abuse, there is further reason to be hopeful. When women consider whether or not to end an abusive relationship, they want as much information as possible about the protections that society offers them, and the likelihood that legal or psychotherapeutic remedies will end the abuse. As we've discussed, most battered women cling to a dream that somehow the violence will stop, if not on its own then through legal or educational interventions.

Legal Remedies: Part of the Solution or Part of the Problem?

Tracy Thurman was twenty-one years old, and for two years had been married to a batterer.[2] In the fall of 1982, she tried to leave her battering husband, Charles "Buck" Thurman in

Virginia. She went home to her roots, to a small town in Connecticut where she had grown up, hoping for the peace she could never find in her two-year marriage to Buck. She figured that if there was any such thing as a safe environment for her and her son C.J., it was where family and friends abounded.

Buck followed her, found her, and nearly killed her. He stabbed her thirteen times and left her partially paralyzed and permanently disabled. He was very vocal about his intentions. He stalked Tracy for eight months and told virtually everyone who would listen what he was going to do to his battered wife. The local police had a file listing his threats, but did nothing about them. Buck would taunt Tracy with these facts. "See," he laughed, "they ain't goin' to do nothin'."

Buck's persistence and desperation suggest that he was a Pit Bull. As a result of his stalking and threatening behavior, and after smashing the windshield of Tracy's car, Buck was sentenced to six months in jail. But instead of serving the sentence, he was placed on probation. Even though a restraining order was already in effect, he was allowed to return to Virginia.

Soon, he was back in Tracy's home town. On New Year's Eve, as 1982 became 1983, a neighbor called Tracy to warn her that Buck was standing outside her home. Tracy called the police. They took no action. A week later, Buck told a friend of Tracy's that he was going to "hurt Tracy real bad." Tracy called the police again, but again no action was taken.

The police made records of every phone call, but claimed that they could take no action until he actually committed a crime. In fact, this was not true, since obeying the restraining order was one of the terms of his probation. He should have immediately begun serving the six-month jail sentence that had been suspended. Tracy was told by one police officer that, "It would be easier for us to act if the two of you were not married." Statements such as this helped establish grounds for her subsequent lawsuit.

Buck continued to stalk Tracy, and she was terrified. She filed for divorce, and Buck escalated. He threatened to kill both her and her son. On May 6, Tracy filed for an order of protection, which specified that Buck was to be arrested. She went to the police station on three separate occasions to see whether or not the order had been carried out; on the first occasion, the file had not been completed; on the second occasion, it had been misplaced; on the third occasion, she was told that the official handling her case was on vacation, and that no action could be taken until he returned.

Meanwhile, Buck was publicly bragging that he was going to kill his wife and even brandished the murder weapon, a knife. Many people later testified to this public display. Finally, on June 10, he went to Tracy's house with the intent of murdering her. Tracy called the police. She tried to stall for as long as possible, hoping to time their confrontation with the arrival of the police. But the police were slow in arriving. Eventually, Tracy became worried that, as Buck waited and became more angry, things could only get worse—she was especially worried about their son. She came down to face him. As she did, a police officer named Petrovich arrived and parked near the house. Buck asked Tracy if she had called the police. After two denials, she saw him reach for his knife. She ran for the backyard.

Buck caught up with Tracy in the backyard and began to stab her. She described in court how she had struggled to ward off his stabs, but to no avail. She described the feeling of the knife entering her in various parts of her body. Her roommate, Judy, witnessed the stabbing. At some point, Officer Petrovich entered the backyard. He said that he had stopped on the way to the house because he had to go to the bathroom. He got to the house and saw the couple arguing, and he watched. After hearing Judy scream and seeing the couple run to the backyard, Petrovich drove to the backyard, but then he inexplicably knocked on the front door of the house. When Petrovich finally approached the couple, he took the bloody knife, but did not arrest Buck. Instead, he walked away from Buck to lock the knife in his trunk. He later testified that, "For all I knew, since I hadn't seen the body, the man had stabbed a dog or a chicken."

Buck came at Tracy again, stepped on her head, and broke her neck. By then a crowd had gathered at the scene. Twenty-seven minutes after Petrovich had arrived at the scene, he discovered Tracy, called an ambulance, and requested additional police officers. He still didn't arrest Buck. Eventually, Petrovich attempted to tackle Buck but Buck got away. Petrovich then tried again, but this time tackled the wrong man. Buck went back and kicked Tracy in the head a few times.

Five additional police officers arrived, and they attempted to bandage Tracy's wounds. But none of them arrested Buck. When the ambulance arrived, bystanders described the cops as being in a state of panic. They were in such a hurry to get Tracy to the hospital that they threw her onto the stretcher like a slab of meat and tossed the stretcher into the back of the ambulance. It was then that Buck approached the ambulance for an incredible *third* attack, all of which had occurred under police surveillance!

Tracy screamed, "Get him away from me!" At that point, forty minutes after Officer Petrovich first arrived at the scene, Buck Thurman was finally subdued and arrested by four police officers. Tracy was in the hospital for the next eight months. It took two years for Tracy to get her day in court, but on June 4, 1985, she pled her case against twenty-nine police officers working for the Torrington, Connecticut, Police Department. The police denied that they were negligent in this case. But the judge ruled that the police must treat batterers the same way they would treat criminals whose victims were strangers, and that Tracy Thurman's civil rights were violated. In short, Tracy Thurman won her suit, and the judge agreed that her civil rights were violated *because* the case was one of domestic abuse. Twenty-four of the twenty-nine police officers were found to have been negligent. Tracy received $2.3 million in compensatory damages.

This case was a watershed in the fight for justice on the part of advocates for battered women. Partly as a result of this case and others like it, training programs were set up by advocates to help police officers learn how to intervene in domestic violence cases. This was also one of the cases that contributed to the rise in mandatory arrest laws, those laws that require police officers to arrest the perpetrator if there is probable cause to believe that a crime has been committed. If Torrington had had a mandatory arrest law at the time that Tracy Thurman had been fleeing from Buck, and the law had been enforced properly, Buck would have been arrested the first night he showed up.

Today, it is against the law to physically assault one's spouse. Unfortunately, the crime that those who assault their partner are charged with varies dramatically from state to state. Even within the same state enforcement varies from county to county, and even from police precinct to police precinct. Thus, a battered woman seeking to protect herself through the criminal justice system cannot count on consistent protection. As the Tracy Thurman case illustrates, law enforcement can break down at various stages in the process: police may not do what the law expects of them, which is to arrest the perpetrator; once an arrest is made, there is no obligation to seek an indictment; if an indictment is obtained, usually a judge is called upon to decide on guilt or innocence, and if the verdict is guilty, the appropriate sanctions. These sanctions could be a fine, jail time, a mandate that the batterer enroll in an education group for batterers, or probation with no requirement other than future avoidance of violence. In the case of Tracy Thurman, the original judge's decision to suspend Buck's prison sentence almost proved lethal for the victim.

At some point in the process, unless the charges are dropped, probation officers become an important source of differential law enforcement. They are the ones who report to judges whether or not probation or parole has been violated. Despite guidelines designed to ensure uniformity in their response, probation officers exercise considerable discretion: some simply don't keep track of convicted batterers assigned to them; others keep track of their batterer caseloads, but are lenient in their enforcement of violations such as refusing to enter education groups for batterers. Still others are committed to holding batterers accountable and sending them to jail if the terms of their probation are violated. It is clear that Buck Thurman violated the terms of his parole, both by returning to Connecticut and by ignoring the restraining order. The system broke down again when these violations did not result in Buck's serving a six-month jail sentence.

A third complex web of legal options involves the various recourses available to women whose husbands may not have been arrested. Depending on state law, battered women are entitled to certain forms of protection if they can convince legal authorities that they need it: there are restraining orders; orders of protection; antiharassment orders; antistalking orders; and various forms of protection during divorce proceedings. Once again, even if the law is clear, enforcement is often discretionary, varying from judge to judge and complicated by bewildering bureaucracies which can be extremely daunting even to a trained advocate, let alone a battered woman with no experience with the criminal justice system.

A final set of factors affecting protection of battered women pertains to public education: the extent to which citizens are aware of what these various agencies have to offer. Many battered women, especially poor women who cannot afford legal counsel, are not aware of their legal options—even at the most basic level. In fact, a high percentage of battered women don't even know that domestic violence is against the law.[3] This factor severely limits the ability of even the most progressive jurisdictions to perform their duties since the criminal justice system can work only when crimes are reported.

The criminal justice system can break down at several points in the enforcement process: the crime might not be reported; if it is reported, an arrest might not be made; if an arrest is made, the state may decide not to prosecute; if prosecution occurs, the batterer may be acquitted even if he is guilty; and even if convicted, the punishment may be too mild to deter future episodes of battering. And the system *does* break down at each stage in the process: not for all battered women, but often enough to cause concern. However, it is important to remember that the trend is in the positive direction in all of these areas: as public education improves, battered women are more likely to report their husbands' crimes; as the laws become more progressive and police are better trained, a much higher percentage of batterers are arrested when the crimes are reported; many counties and jurisdictions have progressive and *aggressive* prosecutors specializing in domestic-violence cases, making it more likely that the state will vigorously pursue defenders; and judges are slowly becoming educated about the importance of punishment as a deterrent.

As we discuss in the next chapter, the criminal justice system is simply one tool for dealing with an abusive relationship. Many women in our sample extricated themselves from abusive relationships without this tool, relying on little more than their own resourcefulness and heroism. However, when battered women are informed about available help and how to access it, they can—in consultation with trained and experienced counselors—make a better, informed decision for *them*. Here are some of the factors to take into account when considering the criminal justice system as a tool.

Accountability for Battering Is the Ultimate Goal. Advocates for battered women believe that the law, and the agencies that enforce the law, must be structured to maximize the batterer's accountability for the violence. The assumption has been that in order for the violence to stop, the batterer must be held totally accountable for it. We wholeheartedly agree with this position. In

chapter 7, we discussed factors that may be related to the cessation of abuse, one of which is holding the batterer accountable.
We believe this factor is crucial. Until this happens, the other
factors may not even come into play. Accountability requires a
responsive criminal justice system. There are many factors that
influence the responsivity of this system and its ability to make
contact with the women who require its services.

*Public Education Results in a Greater Likelihood That Bat-
tering Will Be Reported.* Psychologist Donald Dutton estimated
that only about 15 percent of battered women call the police in
response to battering episodes.[4] If five out of six battered
women never report the crime, the criminal justice system cannot become involved. Why are these reporting rates so low? We
and others can only speculate. We believe that one factor is
fear. Women who report the crime and whose husbands find
out may be putting themselves in even greater danger. A second factor, in our opinion, is trauma. We have already discussed the ways in which physical and emotional abuse make
it difficult for battered women to plan systematically and take
optimal care of themselves. The continuous exposure to a traumatic environment generates symptoms associated with post-
traumatic stress disorder,[5] often including incapacitating
anxiety and depression. A third deterrent is undoubtedly the
negative experiences that many battered women have had in
the past with police, lawyers, probation officers, therapists, and
other officials they associate with the criminal justice system.
There is still a widespread tendency in our culture to blame
the victim, and this tendency can manifest itself at every stage
of the criminal justice system. Given all these reasons, women
who don't report battering are not acting irrationally.

Finally, Dutton has concluded that many battered women do
not know that they have the option of having their husbands
arrested. The fact that battering is a crime is more widely
known among middle- and upper-middle-class, highly educated
communities.

Domestic Violence: A Family Matter? Tracy Thurman was able to prove in her lawsuit that the Torrington police force were muted in their response to her complaints because they viewed her squabble as a family matter. Even since the mid-1980s, when laws were passed in many jurisdictions *requiring* that crimes against spouses be treated the same way as crimes against strangers, the values of the culture have been slow to change. As we traveled throughout the country presenting our research findings and talking to groups of advocates in various states, we frequently heard about continuing difficulties that advocates have in confronting this widespread view: in many circles, including law enforcement, disputes between family members are often minimized as "family matters." This usually translates into a prejudice that family matters fall outside the jurisdiction of the law. The personal beliefs of the policeman called to the home, the prosecutor whose discretion determines whether the case will be tried, and the judge who must decide the case strongly influence the response to battered women's search for protection and justice.

A major job of advocacy groups has been to convince legislators that violence against family members should be taken at least as seriously by the courts as violence against strangers. These efforts have led to major reforms in arrest laws, in the greater access of battered women to protection from the state, and other methods of holding batterers accountable. But the human beings asked to enforce these reforms may have attitudes that are harder to change than we might wish. The goal is to remove the double standard between crimes within families and crimes outside of families. A crime is a crime. A batterer who has assaulted his wife is no less a criminal than a man who has punched a stranger.

This view that violence is a family matter is found even among some battered women. We heard it often from the women in our sample. Some who stayed with their abusive partners felt that it would be violating a family secret to take the problem outside the family. Even when the battered women had had enough and were ready to take action, they often encountered resistance from family members and friends.

- Vicky had trouble getting her family to support her efforts to rid herself of George. They wanted her to settle her problems within the family, and didn't want to get the police involved.

- For many years, Judy felt that she should be able to change Dave. She saw it as her wifely duty to take care of him, regardless of the fact that he was abusing her both physically and emotionally. She finally wised up and left him. But her dream that she could reform him was a manifestation of the view that violence is all in the family.

- There is extensive documentation, by Dutton[6] and others, that police officers saw themselves as family therapists when they intervened in a "domestic" prior to the advent of mandatory arrest laws. Police officers were only trained to "mediate," separate the spouses, and provide counsel.

- The language used by batterers to minimize, deny, and distort the significance of battering episodes contributes to the mystification of battering as a criminal act. Back in 1989, in an interview with ESPN, O. J. Simpson dismissed his recent arrest for battering as a family matter, and said, "We have gotten on with our lives as a family." The implication was that only the media (who barely covered the story) made this story newsworthy. *They* had turned a family squabble ("rassling," as he put it at his civil trial) into an embarrassing public relations scandal for the charming sports analyst and former football star.

- When Warren Moon, the Seattle Seahawks quarterback, was arrested for domestic violence, he appeared on TV with his whole family by his side. The image implied that a mountain had been made out of a molehill. They were presenting a united front as a family. Viewers were supposed to conclude that nothing untoward could happen in this happy-looking, all-American family.

A family matter indeed. Values change slowly in our culture.

Blaming the Victim. There is still a widespread tendency in the culture to blame battered women for their plight. This is especially true when it appears that battered women choose to stay with batterers, despite the beatings. The blaming can affect the relationship between domestic violence and the criminal justice system:

• It can prejudice law enforcement officials against the wives, thus making it less likely that laws will be enforced.

• It can reduce support from family and friends, thus isolating the battered woman further and ultimately making her *more* dependent on her battering husband, and therefore more likely to stay in the relationship.

• It can lead prosecutors not to seek indictments against batterers, because they assume that battered women will not press charges, or will eventually drop them.

Mandatory Arrest. Historically, police officers called to the scene of a domestic assault were allowed to use their judgment regarding how to handle the case. Typically, no arrest was made. Police officers would act based on their own values and experiences, and most often offer little more than advice. Police officers hate intervening in disputes between married partners. Beginning in the mid-1980s, some states began to pass mandatory arrest laws, which removed much of the discretion that police officers used to have. Under mandatory arrest, if a crime has been committed an arrest must be made. During the early years of mandatory arrest laws the confused police officer would often arrest both parties instead of just the batterer. At times, the battered woman would be arrested instead of the perpetrator. This occurred in part because police officers would enter a scene and find an enraged, apparently out-of-control woman, and a calm, rational man. Both Cobras and Pit Bulls learned to calm down by the time the police arrived, whereas their wives, still enraged, often injured, and usually traumatized, seemed much more out of control. Their stories would differ, but the batterer would sound more credible. If he left no marks and the wife in her state of rage was insulting either the husband or the police officer, the police officer might falsely conclude that the wife has perpetrated the crime and arrest her.

Now, some states have rewritten their statutes to prevent such miscarriages of police action. For example, in the state of Washington, the police officer decides who the perpetrator is, and *must* arrest *only* the perpetrator. The advocacy community in Washington State has also been effective in training police officers to detect battering at the scene, and to take appropriate action. Not all counties and jurisdictions are equally committed to carrying out the new laws as they were intended. Nevertheless, arrests of innocent victims are less likely under current law.

Most Acts of Battering Go Unpunished. Dutton has determined that about 15 percent of serious assaults are reported to the police. If, as he has estimated, only 78 percent of these reports lead to police action, this means that police come into contact with approximately 12 percent of all severely violent acts. But only half of these contacts lead to the criminal justice system. So, now we are down to only 6 percent of severely violent episodes leading to the batterer entering the criminal justice system. In other words, in about 94 percent of the cases of severe assault, there are no legal consequences at all for the batterer.

The situation gets even more bleak when one takes into account the likelihood of prosecution, conviction, and punishment. About two-thirds of the cases that enter the criminal justice system end up in court. When cases do go to court, a conviction occurs about half of the time. But quite often the conviction involves either a suspended sentence or probation. When all these factors are taken into account only about one out of every 10,000 acts of battering result in a fine or a jail sentence. And even when punishment does occur, it is rarely severe.

Clearly, in order for batterers to be held accountable arrest rates need to be higher, more incidents of violence need to be identified, and the consequences of conviction need to be much more severe. The response on the part of police officers is particularly crucial since the courts can do nothing unless offenders are arrested.

Pressing Charges versus Dropping Them. Dutton reports a study during the 1980s[7] that looked at the effects of prosecution, therapy, and simple arrest without prosecution on subsequent violence. The study showed, not unexpectedly, that the actions of prosecutors can have a dramatic effect on whether violence continues. Even if the case never went to trial, simply pressing charges and going as far as a pretrial hearing led to less subsequent violence—even if the charges were later dropped. When batterers are arrested, one valuable consequence may be to reinforce the idea that battered women do not deserve to be beaten. As we have discussed, this is an important step in the process of getting out of abusive relationships. This consequence may be quite important, since arrest without prosecution and punishment does not deter future violence, except among highly educated, white-collar batterers.[8] However, violence might be *indirectly* affected by the message arrest sends to victims: that they do not deserve to be beaten, that violence is unacceptable, and that there are consequences for the batterer.

There are numerous reasons why battered women may decide to drop the charges, many of them the same factors that deter women from leaving abusive relationships. When women refuse to press charges, prosecutors have a history of not forcing the issue: usually, the charges are dismissed. However, in some states prosecutors are now mandated to prosecute domestic violence, even if the victim drops the charges. Prosecution is in the best interests of the state even if the battered woman decides not to press charges. Battering is a crime not just against a particular battered woman, but also against all battered women and society at large. When prosecutors bring charges, with or without the support of battered women, a powerful message is sent that battering will not be tolerated. In the long run, this consistent policy has the greatest likelihood of reducing battering.

Restraining Orders Are No Guarantee of Restraint. Courts can also provide protection to battered women by issuing restraining orders (including no-contact orders, orders of protection, antiharassment orders, etc.), which require that the batterer stay away from the battered woman. Violating such restraining orders is a criminal offense, and can lead to incarceration. In one study,[9] it was found that although not all batterers honor restraining orders, such orders *do* reduce violence, at least in the short run. Thirty-four percent of the batterers did not honor the restraining order. If the batterers abused alcohol, the violation rates increased to 47 percent. If the batterer was unemployed, the violation rate was 83 percent. And if the batterer had a prior criminal record, *all* who were served violated the order—100 percent.

The important thing for battered women to know is that the courts *can* order a batterer to stay away. And the orders *do* deter a substantial proportion of men. Therefore, battered women must use all of the information they have, especially their instincts about the man they know better than anyone else. By following the steps that we outline in chapter 9, each battered woman can come to a decision about the best course of action once she has access to all pertinent information: the laws in her state and county; the characteristics of her partner; the advice of a trained advocate; and a comprehensive understanding of her options. The criminal justice system is just one of many tools at the disposal of battered women. Some women find the tool does more harm than good; others find that it helps; still others ignore this tool altogether.

States vary in the particular types of orders that they issue: typically, they depend on the relationship between the batterer and the battered woman (for example, married versus unmarried); the severity and history of violence; and the type of protection the battered woman wants. In the state of Washington, the three most common types of orders are orders of protection, no-contact orders, and restraining orders. Their definition varies from one state to another. All advocates trained by the Washington State Coalition Against Domestic Violence know these forms of protection. In fact, the following information comes from the training manual, revised in 1996 by Tyra Lindquist, used by the state coalition to train advocates.[10]

Orders of Protection

In Washington State, "orders of protection" is the term that most closely corresponds to what people mean when they use the term "restraining order." Any battered woman can apply for an order of protection on behalf of herself or a child, and she can do so without a lawyer. All she has to do is fill out a form at the local courthouse, and a judge rules on whether or not a temporary order will be granted. These orders prohibit the batterer from making any kind of contact with the victim or, if relevant, the victim's children. It is important for battered women to know that these orders can be obtained without a lawyer since batterers often try to convince their partners that they will not be able to afford legal help if they try to get out of the relationship. To obtain a protection order, when filling out the request the battered woman must satisfy a judge that she is in imminent danger. No details should be spared, including the dates, times, locations, and the history of abuse—including present and past injuries and threats made by the batterer. The judge needs details, and it is important that battered women not minimize the danger they are in. The orders can be fairly comprehensive, prohibiting not only physical assault, but living at their residence, and custody of or visitation with the children.

The major weaknesses with protection orders is that they don't go into effect until either a police officer or a process server serves the batterer with papers informing him of the order. In other words, the battered woman is not protected unless the batterer knows about the order. If he knows that an order is on the way, he may try to keep away from those bearers of bad news.

Even poor battered women without financial resources can get protection from the courts, and these orders of protection can become permanent. For a battered woman who is reluctant to apply for civil orders of protection because she mistakenly believes that her husband will have a criminal record—or lose his job—protection orders do not place him at risk for either. There is no criminal proceeding and no public record. Batterers are not prosecuted under this statute. Only when the order is violated does a criminal offense occur.

No-Contact Orders

In Washington State, a no-contact order can be issued immediately, simply by a police officer placing a phone call to a judge. For example, Guy, one of our subjects, was arrested for beating up his wife, Sarah. When the police arrived at the scene, she had a black eye and bruised ribs. Guy tried to show the officers the teeth marks that Sarah had left on Guy's wrist as evidence that Guy was simply defending himself. He was calm, and Sarah was quite agitated. But the police officers recognized that a perpetrator does not approach a victim, bite him, and then receive a black eye and bruised ribs in self-defense. They called a judge, who issued a no-contact order. The judge ordered Guy to leave the house and avoid all further contact with Sarah until a scheduled hearing.

Restraining Orders

Given the language of the law, in Washington State the commonly used catch-all term "restraining order" is issued only as part of a divorce proceeding. Unlike protection and no-contact orders, an attorney *is* usually required to obtain a restraining order. The couple must either be legally married or have a child. The extra advantage of a restraining order is that in addition to protecting women and children from assault, it can safeguard her property—which an order of protection cannot do. Even though divorce is a civil and not a criminal process, violation of a restraining order is a criminal act. Police officers are often confused about this distinction, and therefore reluctant to enforce violations of restraining orders because they typically don't intervene in divorce proceedings.

The Criminal Justice System Does Not Ensure Safety. There are many considerations involved in deciding whether or not to apply for a civil protection order. One is the possibility that this particular tool could backfire with a particular batterer. Jacobson recently counseled a battered woman who was married to a highly visible member of the Seattle community. Her battering husband was served with an order of protection, and was both shamed and embarrassed by the service. It pushed him over the edge. He broke into her house and nearly killed her. As the state coalition training manual says, restraining orders do not stop bullets.[11] The criminal justice system can only enforce orders of protection when the batterers cooperate with them.

Here are some factors that advocates trained by the Washington State Coalition Against Domestic Violence consider when helping battered women make a decision about filing for orders of protection.

- Has the battered woman already made her escape? If she is in hiding, she might be better off staying that way. When a battered woman applies for a protection order, papers are served which indicate the county in which she has filed. This information may help the batterer find the former partner.

- Has the batterer threatened to kill her? If so, she may be in danger if he is in the same room with her, even if others are there as well. Staying out of court may be a safer solution than seeking protection from the state.

- What is the likelihood that battered women will report violations of the order? Often, battered women know themselves well enough to determine whether or not they will report a violation. If they are not prepared to report such violations, then they should not apply for the order in the first place. Why? Because if they have doubts that they will report violations, their husbands probably know that as well. This in-creases the risk that violations will occur.

- How quickly do the police in a community typically respond if the battered woman calls to report a violation? Chapter 9 provides methods for obtaining detailed information about the response time by the community.

- Will the batterer use the legal system to his advantage? If a battered woman goes to court to seek an order of protection in the state of Washington, her battering partner obtains access to her so that he can serve legal papers of his own. He could hire a lawyer and make life extremely difficult for her. Child custody and property could become pawns to be used for retaliation. Court appearances are supposed to protect battered women, but quite often the outcome is to add to their woes.

- What will the batterer's reaction be to being served? We have already seen how hard it is to predict the behavior of batterers using statistical methods. Generally, a battered woman is better than anyone else at predicting her partner's behavior. Nevertheless, making predictions can be risky. No legal solution should be initiated by battered women except in the context of an overall safety plan. In another recent case where Jacobson worked closely with both a battered woman and a lawyer, we all decided that it would be better to obtain an order of protection only after filing for divorce, and thereby circumventing some of the husband's potential for legal maneuvers. Since the battered woman and her daughter were safe and out of town when the divorce papers were served, and the divorce took the husband by surprise, he was unable to hide assets in anticipation of this move.

• How do battered women protect themselves until their partners have been served? Service can take many days, sometimes weeks. Batterers are often adept at avoiding being served. Advocates in Washington State advise women to keep the orders with them at all times since police called to the scene will not be aware of their content, and the order will clarify the nature of protection to which the battered woman is entitled.

The Criminal Justice System Can Be a Useful Tool, but It Is Not a Panacea. The criminal justice system is capable of offering battered women a great deal of protection. In the short run, women can be protected by various types of restraining orders, and in the long run they can be protected by the arrest, prosecution, and punishment of the batterers. However, battered women cannot count on the various officials doing their jobs properly at each step along the way, and the consequences of a mistake can be lethal.

Advocates have worked hard over the past twenty years to prevent violence against women by working through the criminal justice system. Changing laws and better training for police officers give battered women much more protection than they had ten years ago. However, protection is not guaranteed, and the quality of both laws and their enforcement varies dramatically. Perhaps most importantly, the criminal justice system does not typically produce repentant, peaceful men who are rehabilitated and therefore safe. It prevents violence by the deterrent value of arrest and punishment. Arrest in and of itself does not deter most batterers. Punishment is rarely severe enough to deter batterers for very long. But at its best the criminal justice system buys women time, validates them, empowers them, and becomes part of a safety plan. The criminal justice system does not cure batterers. Can they be rehabilitated or educated to stop battering in other ways? Let's take a look.

Education and Rehabilitation of Batterers

Batterers Are Criminals, Not Patients. It is hard to evaluate the effectiveness of existing rehabilitation and education programs for batterers because most have not been subjected to rigorous scientific investigation.12 There are thousands of dedicated counselors who are absolutely convinced that they make a difference, at least with some batterers. We hope that they do. We know that some batterers stop being violent, if not in their current relationship then in subsequent relationships. We have met reformed batterers, who not only become peace-loving, gentle men after completing an education program, but become active in the battered women's movement themselves. Indeed, some of the most articulate spokespeople against the evils of battering are ex-batterers.

If nothing else, counselors who devote their professional lives to rehabilitating batterers gain the benefits of exposure to hundreds if not thousands of cases. The experience alone should make them more effective. It may or may not lead to the counselor becoming more effective at stopping the violence, but at the very least, we have no doubt that experienced counselors learn a great deal about the population they treat, and in the process can help battered women by, for example, advising them about the likelihood that the batterer will change. Here are some things to remember when contemplating the rehabilitation of and education for batterers:

• The vast majority of psychiatrists, psychologists, and social workers in the United States have little or no training in the rehabilitation of batterers. Although batterers are treated every day and all too commonly by counselors without such training, batterers provide unique challenges. There are programs which are certified by some states as offering state-of-the-art methods for rehabilitating batterers. Generally, state certification is no guarantee that the violence will stop, but it does tell the battered woman that the counselors performing the education groups are experienced, and *specialize* with this particular population. Sticking with such programs is far better than going through the Yellow Pages. We will be identifying methods for obtaining information regarding state certification in chapter 9.

• Counseling can, in the worst of all possible worlds, directly lead to escalations in severe battering and even lead to homicide, rather than decreased battering or the ending of abuse. No one knows how often such deplorable outcomes occur, but as Dr. Amy Holtzworth-Munroe and colleagues argued,[13] every shelter in America has documented instances of battered women assuming that because their husbands had entered counseling, it was now safe to return home. Psychotherapy still has positive connotations in our culture, as evidenced by the recent survey in the November 1995 issue of *Consumer Reports*.[14] When "being in therapy" is equated with "cure," battered women put themselves at risk for further beatings. In fact, husbands in our sample often openly admitted to us that their motivation for seeking counseling was to get their wives back. Once the wives returned, they dropped out of therapy, and the battering resumed.

• Judges are under tremendous pressure to find alternatives to prison whenever possible. The prisons are hopelessly overcrowded, and given the predilection to view domestic violence as a family matter, court-mandated counseling provides a tempting alternative to incarceration. Judges who "sentence" batterers to counseling appear to be enlightened and humanistic at first glance. But given the lack of supporting evidence that counseling is effective, this alternative to real punishment may be the opposite of what the batterer really needs. We believe that if anything is going to stop the violence, it is the deterrent value of real punishment: not a referral to court-mandated treatment; not, for example, the slap on the wrist received by O. J. Simpson in 1989 (a nominal fine and a few sessions of "telephone therapy" with a therapist of his choice); and not probation. We would argue that batterers are primarily criminals, not patients. When counseling is offered as an alternative to prison, batterers are not being held accountable. In the absence of demonstrated efficacy, we must face the fact that to batterers, court-mandated treatment is often considered a big joke. Cobras bragged to us how quickly they would learn to "talk the talk." There is a wide body of research evidence suggesting that the worst offenders drop out.[15] Sadly, this same literature suggests that the negative consequences for such early termination are minimal, even though it is a clear violation of the terms of probation. Apparently, all too many probation officers and judges either don't know or don't care whether batterers stay in treatment.

• In fact, if one truly wants to determine how motivated batterers are to stop the violence, we recommend never mandating treatment, or offering it as an alternative to prison. Make it voluntary. We doubt seriously that batterers who are forced into counseling are likely to benefit anyway.[16] We can hold batterers accountable while still not giving up on attempts to rehabilitate them through education and counseling. But treatment would have to be offered on a voluntary basis, in addition to—not instead of—jail time.

Couples Therapy. We have both spent our careers studying couples: Jacobson has been developing and evaluating treatments for couples since 1972;[17] Gottman began his career studying couples therapy,[18] and has come back to it in recent years.[19] Until research proves us wrong, we think that couples therapy is inappropriate for the population we have described in this book.[20] If we ever had any doubts about the *inappropriateness* of couples therapy for battering, the doubts were dispelled during the course of completing this research. Consider this admonition carefully, because couples therapists often attempt therapy with batterers and battered women, and there is no watchdog agency (like the FDA for drugs) protecting consumers from dangerous forms of psychotherapy.

There is a strong temptation in many battered women to try couples therapy. In part this temptation is based on the refusal of their battering partner to enter into any form of individual therapy, thus leaving couples therapy as the only available treatment option. Furthermore, many battered women in the middle of a traumatic stress reaction blame themselves in part for the abuse, and thus see couples therapy as an appropriate course of action. But we have shown in chapter 3 that battering has little if anything to do with the battered woman. Thus, couples therapy doesn't make sense. Generally, the purpose of couples therapy is to solve problems that are caused by the dynamics of the marriage. With battering, the violence is most definitely *not* caused by marital dynamics. Battering is not about the relationship, it is about the batterer.

It is not just illogical to use couples therapy as a treatment for battering, it is dangerous. Battering is often infrequent, and by avoiding conflict, battered women can get temporary respite from physical abuse. But couples therapy is oriented toward facing conflict directly, thus creating the possibility that the avoidance that usually prevents violence from happening on a more regular basis will be difficult if not impossible. The breakdown of avoidance places the woman at increased risk of violence that is both more frequent and more severe.

Finally, there is an even better reason to avoid couples therapy with batterers. Regardless of the structure of couples therapy, regardless of what the therapist *says* about the unacceptability of violence, the fact that the therapist is treating both of them implicates them both in the perpetration of violence. There is no way around the victim-blaming mentality that permeates the therapy environment. If both are being treated, then somehow, in some way, both are part of the problem.

Still, there is a place for couples therapy as a treatment for physical aggression. Remember that battering is not *just* physical aggression, but physical aggression that functions as a method of control, subjugation, and intimidation. It almost always requires the ability to dominate through greater physical strength, and it operates through the induction of fear. However, there are many couples who are in severe conflict where the conflict occasionally gets physical, but never reaches battering proportions. Who are these couples? They are the couples where the woman occasionally hits the man out of frustration, but neither hurts nor instills fear in him. They are the couples where there is an occasional push or shove, but no injury and no fear on the part of the wife. Couples therapy can be an ideal treatment for these types of couples. In fact, if couples therapy were not practiced with such couples, there would be considerably less couples therapy practiced in the United States, since at least half of all couples seeking therapy have at least some history of low-level violence.[21]

When couples therapy is conducted with even low-level violence, the therapist needs to take precautions. Even low-level violence can be dangerous, and if the therapist is competent, the couple will be asked to agree to a "no-violence" contract. This contract is usually initiated by the therapist as a precondition to therapy. The competent couples therapist will put the contract in writing and insist that both spouses agree to accept a referral for individual therapy if they are deemed by the therapist to be responsible for violating the contract. The contract would also include provisions for helping the couple de-escalate if they are in the middle of a high-risk situation. These steps would be spelled out in detail. Both partners would have to agree to the contract in its entirety in order for couples therapy to commence. Following this initial agreement, each week the therapist would check on the contract to make sure it was going well. Any breach of contract would lead to an automatic termination of couples therapy and its replacement by individual therapy for the perpetrator.

The most common procedure used by therapists to help couples de-escalate when they are in potentially dangerous situations is called "time-out." Time-out can mean many different things, but in the context of couples therapy it refers to taking a break from the discussion or argument, so that cooler heads have a chance to prevail, and violence can be avoided. Ideally, a time-out will be called by the person who experiences himself as losing control. If the spouse who is at greatest risk for losing control learns to regulate his emotional expression to the point where he can call a time-out when necessary, he has come a long way toward managing his anger. Unfortunately, many couples, once embroiled in conflict, have trouble putting on the brakes. Winning the argument often takes precedence over obeying the rules of the contract. Another stumbling block to successful implementation of the time-out procedure is that it can be used as a weapon to avoid conflict: "I need a time-out" can mean "I want an excuse to avoid having to talk about this."

In practice, time-outs are often suggested by the person who is calm, because that person can see the other starting to lose control. "You need a time-out," is often not well received by the already angry partner. He experiences it as an accusation, and the likely outcome is the opposite of what was intended. Time-out works only when it is used by the person losing control. It sounds good in theory, but it is very difficult to implement in practice.

Is there ever a place for couples therapy with batterers and battered women? Yes, after the batterer has successfully completed a rehabilitation or education program designed to stop the violence and no instances of violence have occurred either during the course of therapy, or for at least six months after the termination of violence-focused education. We would also recommend that the battered woman talk to the batterer's counselor and make sure that the counselor thinks couples therapy is safe. If the violence has stopped for at least six months following the termination of an education or rehabilitation program for the batterer, couples therapy is worth a try.

So how does the battered woman know whether the couples therapist is competent to deal with physical aggression? The therapist is probably competent:

• If the therapist refuses to treat battering as a marital problem;

• If the therapist recognizes the distinction between battering and physical aggression without battering;

• If the therapist insists upon a no-violence contract as a precondition to couples therapy, even when the physical aggression does not include battering;

• If the therapist includes procedures for de-escalation in the contract, like some form of time-out;

• If the therapist includes in the contract a provision requiring that either spouse, at the discretion of the therapist, enter into an individual or group education or rehabilitation program in the event that the contract is violated;

• If the therapist reviews the contract at the beginning of each session;

• If the therapist follows through on his or her commitments by terminating couples therapy in the event of a contract violation;

• If the therapist waits at least six months following the termination of the education or rehabilitation program for the batterer before beginning couples therapy, and insists on "avoidance of violence" during that period as a prerequisite for couples therapy.

Alternative Education and Rehabilitation Programs for the Batterer. It is perfectly appropriate to inquire about the counselor's training in the rehabilitation and education of batterers. It is also reasonable to ask counselors specific questions about their philosophy of battering as well as their theoretical orientation. Here are some of the things to look for:

• Does the counselor view violence as a problem in its own right and not simply a symptom of some more important problem, like communication or early childhood trauma? The consumer is looking for "yes" as an answer to this question.

• Does the counselor's philosophy include a view of battering as a tactic to achieve power and control, rather than simply out-of-control anger? There should be recognition that battering has a function, and that the function is control. Although batterers are certainly angry when they batter, it is important that the counselor be aware of the function of battering and not see it primarily as an impulse-control problem.

• Does the counselor say or imply that the battered woman bears at least some of the responsibility for the violence? Except in those rare Bonnie and Clyde couples whom we discussed in chapter 2, the counselor should be clear and direct with both partners about where the responsibility for the violence lies: with the batterer. Sexism and victim-blaming occur in subtle as well as not so subtle ways, and we have found that battered women are usually pretty good at detecting attitudes. When the counselor uses words like "provoke" to describe the woman's role in eliciting violence, the battered woman should beware.

• Look for humility on the part of the counselor regarding the likelihood that treatment will help. The counselor should not attempt to sell the consumer on the program. In fact, the counselor should be extremely cautious, should know how little scientific evidence there is about the effectiveness of counseling, and openly acknowledge that stopping the abuse is not likely.

• Beware of the counselor who dismisses as unimportant the lack of scientific evidence in support of current rehabilitation and education programs for batterers. It is a fact that the efficacy of all such programs is unknown.[22] If the therapist either does not know or does not care about this fact, find another counselor!

Coordinated Community Response (CCR) and Other Treatment Options

In Duluth, Minnesota, Ellen Pence, Michael Paymar, and their colleagues developed a concept which is now almost universal among certified treatment programs for batterers: the coordinated-community response (CCR).[23] Although the CCR has not yet been proven to be effective in reducing battering, it makes good sense to us. Remember that just because there is no scientific evidence to support the CCR *doesn't* mean that it is ineffective, simply that it is untested and therefore unproved. Unlike other attempts at rehabilitation and education, the CCR relies on community organization and links together the criminal justice system, advocacy work, and the education of batterers. What appeals to us most about CCR is that it takes the entire social context of battering into account and recognizes the necessity of engaging the social environment in a synchronous effort to punish violence and reward nonabusive behavior. The CCR involves the coordinated efforts of education groups for batterers, support groups for battered women, shelters, police practices, and prosecutorial tendencies. The best CCR programs include probation officers and judges, as well as the groups just named.

For example, once a CCR program is in full swing, there is a consistent philosophy practiced by all officials likely to come into contact with a batterer who has been arrested. The unifying principle is accountability. All of the major players are united in the view that in order for violence to stop, batterers must be held accountable for it. Police are trained to intervene in ways which are sensitive to this principle: instead of blaming the battered woman, police actions support the view that the batterer is solely responsible for the violence. If the batterer enters an education program with a CCR philosophy, probation officers punish him for not showing up for group education sessions by making sure that he goes to jail (if not already in jail). There is regular and systematic communication between counselors and prosecutors so that deferred prosecutions can commence if violence continues or if group education is not being taken seriously.

The education provided for batterers varies from city to city, but usually involves working in groups. The emphasis is on trying to get batterers to accept responsibility for the violence without blaming their partners and changing the attitudes of batterers so that they no longer see violence as an acceptable response in any situation. The various and sundry ways in which batterers wield power and control, through emotional as well as physical abuse, are discussed in a structured format. The connection between battering and our patriarchal culture, which among other things has designed marriage as an institution which benefits men and oppresses women, is emphasized.

Whatever the effectiveness of the CCR in stopping violence, the notion of treating batterers in groups is well established and almost universally accepted. We would question the qualifications of any counselors who claimed to treat batterers but did not at least offer some group education. The group allows batterers to confront one another regarding their tendency to minimize, deny, and distort their abuse. Often, veteran group members are rewarded for pointing out instances of minimization, denial, and distortion in their fellow group members. A culture can be created in the group that provides batterers with an alternative to previous influences by the culture at large. The power of being confronted by a fellow batterer is often much greater than a similar confrontation coming from a counselor.

Before recommending any education program for batterers, we would at least want to know whether or not it endorsed the concept of CCR. If not, we would suggest terminating with that program. If the program were familiar with CCR but did not practice it, we would want to know the reasons for not practicing it. How can you find out whether or not a program is using the CCR concept?

- The program should have a policy on court referrals that failure by the batterer to attend leads to direct communication with their probation officer, and subsequently to jail.
- Counselors offering the education groups should be involved in the training of the police, or be affiliated with advocacy groups that provide training. The training program should be oriented toward enforcing mandatory arrest laws.
- Do criminal justice officials seek the counsel of counselors on a regular basis, and is this counsel institutionalized? We would look for education group leaders to be involved in training police officers, prosecutors, judges and probation officers. We would look for direct lines of communication between counselors and probation officers, and between judges and education groups for batterers. We would also hope that prosecutors regularly consult education groups for batterers when considering whether and how to try a case. Finally, in the best of all possible worlds, we would hope that advocacy was institutionalized within the criminal justice system itself. This would mean that there are special units within major city district attorneys' offices specializing in domestic violence, and that

there are specialists within the police department providing counsel to battered women.

Remember, one can be cautious and skeptical about the effectiveness of a rehabilitation program, and still be optimistic. *We doubt whether any of the current education and rehabilitation programs will ever rehabilitate Cobras. But it is entirely possible that a substantial number of Pit Bulls may benefit from an intervention using a CCR.* We look forward to scientific tests of CCR, and would like to see such tests given highest priority when federal research dollars are allocated for reducing domestic violence.

Anger Management and Social Skills Training. Treatment programs that teach batterers to control their anger and improve their social skills[24] have fallen into disfavor in recent years among much of the advocacy community.[25] It appears to us that most of the negative feelings about such programs are based on political ideology rather than objective evidence regarding the effectiveness of these programs. This is especially true of anger-management programs. The advocacy point is that batterers do not batter because they are angry; they batter to achieve instrumental goals such as power and control. While it is certainly true that most Cobras do not batter because they are angry, and that all batterers continue to batter to the extent that power and control are achieved, the fact is that batterers *are* quite angry when they batter. There is no reason to believe that anger management can't be useful, at least as part of a CCR.

In our opinion, both anger management and social skills training are limited because they don't attempt to deal with the broader social causes of battering: our patriarchal culture; the support for battering that exists among some groups within American culture; the lack of a CCR; and a lack of attention to sexism and other attitudes toward women that justify violence. However, when integrated with a CCR and combined with education around issues related to power and control, these programs might very well have a place in the treatment of batterers. Only time will tell.

Using Drugs to Treat Impulsive Behavior in Batterers. Some physicians have begun to experiment with drugs such as Prozac, Paxil, and Zoloft in the treatment of batterers.[26] These drugs are officially known as Selective Serotonin Reuptake Inhibitors (SSRIs), and all increase the supply of serotonin in the brain. Serotonin is a chemical that aids in the transmission of information from one nerve cell to another. Low rates of serotonin have been shown to be related to impulsive aggression in animals,[27] and to impulsive violence in humans.[28] The scientific community is currently investigating the effectiveness of these medications at curbing violence. No definitive information is available yet, but it is possible that for some batterers who are highly impulsive and prone to fits of rage, SSRIs may be helpful.

A second reason for using these drugs is that they are effective antidepressants, and at least some Pit Bulls, and even some Cobras, have histories of depression. Some therapists have also argued that Prozac and similar drugs control the obsessive preoccupation that Pit Bulls have with their spouses and through this indirect path can lead reductions in violence.

Just as with anger management, there is considerable opposition to the promotion of such drugs on the part of some advocacy groups. The concern is that if batterers are given drugs, it seems the scientific community is saying that they are sick and therefore not responsible for their battering. The objection is similar to the concerns about attributing battering to drug and alcohol abuse. To the extent that the batterer is viewed as having a brain disease, the illness could be used as a defense strategy in criminal court and potentially exonerate the batterer because of "diminished capacity."

We are reluctant to dismiss experimentation with these drugs on political grounds since they may be effective for some batterers. We prefer to experiment with the hope of finding what works.

There have been a number of positive developments with respect to battering over the past twenty years: laws have been passed and increasingly enforced that better protect battered women. The advocacy community has been extremely active in developing concepts such as the CCR, which may contribute to reducing the frequency and severity of domestic violence.

We have more reason to be optimistic about the state of the criminal justice system than ever before. And yet we think it appropriate to maintain an attitude of skepticism. It is not clear as yet that any of these reforms are effective in reducing abuse. We would hate to see battered women misled into staying in an abusive relationship because the batterer has been arrested or entered a rehabilitation program, since the risk of further abuse and even murder may be just as high as it was before the arrest or the entry into treatment.

We hope that battered women will adopt our skepticism until we have evidence that some or all of these approaches are effective. We are particularly skeptical about the rehabilitative potential of Cobras. It may turn out that some or all of the programs mentioned above will work for at least some Pit Bulls, even if not for Cobras. However, even with respect to Pit Bulls, more battered women will get out of abusive relationships if they share our skepticism, and this would be an extremely desirable outcome. Our research has convinced us that once battered women come to terms with the low probability of the violence and emotional abuse ending any time soon, they begin their preparations to end the relationship.

Of course, getting out of an abusive relationship can be even more risky than staying in one, since violence often escalates when women try to leave their battering husbands.[29] A recent study by the Department of Health in New York State examined the women murdered in New York City between

1990 and 1994.[30] More than 50 percent of the women were murdered by husbands, boyfriends, or ex-husbands and ex-boyfriends. At the time of the murder, approximately one-third of the women were in the process of ending the relationship. Attempts to leave must be undertaken with considerable care and only after multiple precautions are taken. Even then the risks are great. But as we have seen, there can be life, often joyous life, after an abusive relationship.

9

When You're Ready to Leave

By now, we hope it's clear that battered women often leave their abusive partners, and that when they stay, many will eventually leave. Those who stay, hoping that the violence and emotional abuse will stop, are usually disappointed. Once women realize that the relationship won't change, they eventually begin the process of escape.

We have also learned that the process of escape is fraught with risk. There is no way to know just how risky that process will be in advance. At times, women in our sample were terrified of leaving, but the act of leaving did not lead to continued or increased abuse. At other times, the abuse did continue even after the woman left, and for a period of time became worse. Batterers often become stalkers and escalate their levels of emotional and physical abuse. In the worst-case scenario, homicides occur. Women and children are killed, some batterers kill themselves and their partners, and at times women have to flee their homes, leave town, change their name and identity, and are still found and murdered. As we discussed, even though most battered women are not murdered when they leave abusive relationships, between 29 and 54 percent of female murder victims are battered women (depending on the state), and many of those murders occur as they try to leave. Even if they escape with their lives, a high percentage of battered women suffer increased abuse for a period of time after they are out of the relationship. Then there are the relatively lucky ones: those battered women whose husbands do not put up much of a fight when the woman leaves.

One of the most striking consistencies in our exit interviews with battered women was the euphoria they reported after getting out. For many, it was not easy. Some were stalked, beaten, and repeatedly threatened. But when they were finally free, the energy and excitement was palpable. Formerly battered women all but glowed with their sense of life's infinite possibilities. It is hard to imagine release from prison being more powerful than the experience they described. All agreed that the outcome of freedom was worth the agony of the escape process. Routinely, formerly battered women told us that if they could have known then what they know now, they would have left much sooner. The vast majority felt no lingering attachment to their former partners, although some continued to express ambivalence and some positive feelings toward them.

In this chapter, we provide practical information on how to get out of abusive relationships. Our advice is based on our own research findings, resources available in the United States for battered women trying to escape from their battering partners, and some conventional wisdom among professionals working with battered women.

We begin with two extremely important warnings. One is that all attempts to escape from abusive relationships are risky. No matter how careful the plan to ensure escape, no matter how expert the advice, no one can predict with anything close to certainty how a batterer will respond. The second caveat was first mentioned in chapter 1, but it bears repeating. We know something about the factors that lead to escape, but these factors do not easily translate into advice.

For example, we know that women in our sample who assertively defended their positions during arguments were more likely to leave during the two years following our initial evaluation. But this does not mean that women who do not defend themselves assertively should be encouraged to do so as a route to successful escape. Why not? Because assertive self-defense is not what *causes* them to successfully escape; rather, it is a characteristic of women who *do* escape. In other words, our research does not provide us with a blueprint for successful escape: all the research tells us is that women who behave in certain ways, when married to men who behave in certain ways, also tend to be the ones to get out of the relationships.

Thus, it would be a mistake to take the findings presented in chapter 7 and say, for example, "If I fight back, that will help me get out of this relationship." We would never advise women who don't fight back to *start* fighting back as part of an escape plan. Fighting back could increase their risk for even more severe, and perhaps lethal, battering. Nevertheless, the characteristics of batterers who are left, and the qualities of women who leave, do provide clues that *may* lead to better decisions about when and how to leave, and what precautions to take. In this chapter, we will offer some of these clues.

Deciding Whether to Leave

The decision whether and when to get out of an abusive relationship is tremendously complicated. If the only relevant factor in this decision is "will the violence and emotional abuse stop?" the decision would be easy. The chances are overwhelming that the violence will continue, especially if there have been multiple episodes, or even *one* episode of *severe* violence. But there are other factors to consider: Will you be safe? What will the economic consequences be? What impact will leaving have on the children? Are there special circumstances which make you think that your partner is an exception, that he is likely to stop despite the fact that the statistics are not on your side? Is your decision making clouded because you have not as yet given up the dream of a normal relationship with a man who cannot or will not give you what you want?

In the early days of the battered women's movement, advocates quickly discovered that despite the wisdom in the advice to get out, battered women in shelters typically returned to their abusive husbands after a period of time. There is general recognition within the battered women's movement that battered women need support, regardless of whether or not they are *ready* to permanently leave the partner. All of the complex deterrents to leaving are well recognized, as is the fact that coming to a final decision is often a long and arduous process. Support can take the forms of legal advice, safety planning, being in a support group, education, and so forth.

No one can make the decision for you, but here are some questions you can ask yourself:

• Are you marching to your own beat? You are the best judge of when and if the time is right to leave. Are you being unduly influenced by the efforts of others to persuade you to leave, despite your own judgment that it is not yet time? If you have been in contact with people who are supposedly experts on helping battered women, you know you are with the right person if that person is understanding and supportive, and if that support remains even if you are not yet ready to leave the relationship. Professionals who are well trained to work with battered women are supposed to be concerned primarily with fostering your safety needs. However, those concerns must be balanced with respect for your autonomy and resourcefulness. After all, the vast majority of battered women who leave do so without the help of so-called experts.

When we work with battered women on the decision to leave, we provide information, support, and recommendations when asked, but we do not expect them to make decisions based on our perceptions of reality. You will decide to leave if and when you have that last straw incident and give up the dream. The job of professionals is not to push you down the road to escape. If you are a battered woman, leaving should be *your* decision.

• Is your partner acting as though the abuse is not as serious as it really is? Is he denying that the events that you know occurred actually took place? Is he blaming you for the violence, even though you are the one who was battered? If so, he is not even close to taking that first step necessary for stopping the abuse: accepting responsibility for it.

• How willing is your partner to seek treatment for the violence? If he insists on couples therapy as opposed to individual therapy for himself, it is a bad sign because he is saying in effect that the violence is a mutual problem, rather than his and his alone. If he is willing to seek therapy for the violence, and sticks with therapy once he finds an appropriate therapist, he has at least taken that first step. If the therapy is based on a philosophy that the violence is his responsibility, then his willingness to stay in treatment, and not drop out, is a sign that he takes the responsibility seriously. If he is willing to seek a violence-stopping treatment, but does not follow through, or appears to be following through but does not attend sessions regularly, he is attempting to con you into thinking he intends to stop when in fact he has no intention of stopping. Such behavior is no better than refusing to go at all.

• Is the emotional abuse continuing, even during periods of relief from physical abuse? If so, the relationship is still abusive and will in all likelihood continue to be.

• Do you feel that you have no voice in the relationship? Are you deprived of an identity, a sense of self, an opportunity to have and express opinions? Such a situation is consistent with continued high rates of battering.

How Safe Is It to Leave?

Although there is no hard evidence we can offer to answer this question, there is considerable clinical consensus that a number of factors contribute to the danger of leaving:

• Are you the center of your partner's life? Does his life revolve around you? Is he obsessed with your comings and goings? If your partner feels close to no one but you, he is particularly likely to commit desperate acts of violence when you leave him. He will experience your leaving as abandonment.

• Has your partner beaten you up, injured you with weapons, or threatened to? The best predictor of future behavior is past behavior. If your partner has severely beaten, stabbed, pointed a knife or a gun at you or choked you, he has engaged in acts which could have been lethal. If he has done so with some frequency, there is every reason to expect him to be even more dangerous if you try to leave. Don beat Martha severely twenty times a year, and almost killed her after she left him. He finally stopped, but some men don't.

• Has he threatened to kill you? Threats to kill should be taken seriously and never seen as idle. In our sample, almost invariably, threats to kill were followed up by harassment, stalking, and continued abuse following divorce or separation.

• Does the violence include rape and other forms of sexual assault? It is commonly believed that batterers who engage in rape of their partners are particularly dangerous following attempts at separation on the part of the woman. There is no hard evidence to support this claim, and sexual assault is quite common among batterers: nevertheless, workers in the field have been reporting this association for many years, and there is a logic to it. Rape is not only violent; it is sadistic. It suggests that you are little more than a toy to your partner, to be used when necessary and dispensed with when unnecessary.

• Has he recently been engaging in high-risk behaviors that at one time he was not doing? Examples would be breaking into your apartment after you have moved out, or violating a restraining order.

• Has the severity of violence been escalating? If he started being violent by pushing or shoving, then began to slap, punch, and hit, and has more recently been beating or threatening to kill you, and has brandished or used weapons, you are in danger.

• Do the worst episodes of violence occur under the influence of drugs or alcohol? Batterers who are violent under the influence of drugs or alcohol are either less inhibited because of the intoxication, or more inclined to be looking for an excuse to *perceive* themselves as not responsible. We view addicted batterers as *particularly* dangerous after they have been left.

• Has he been stalking you, or has he stalked previous partners? Stalking often precedes homicide by a batterer toward an ex-partner.

• Does he have a history of depression, and in particular a history of suicide attempts? Batterers who are depressed and prone to suicide broadcast their low regard for human life. They have already demonstrated that they have felt at times that their own lives were not worth living. It is easy to imagine them transferring that low regard for life to you, especially once you have announced your intention to end the relationship. In New York City, in 25 percent of the cases where a battered woman was murdered by her lover, the batterer killed himself. Many batterers have a low regard for human life.

• Is he a Cobra? We think that the characteristics of Cobras make them particularly dangerous during escape attempts by the battered woman. For Cobras, violence is a way of life. Getting their way is also a way of life. They aren't hampered by guilt or remorse, and thus don't have the inhibitions that most of us do which maintain a semblance of civility, even when we can't get what we want. We believe that Cobra marriages end less often in part because their wives recognize the dangers of leaving.

Should the First Straw be the Last Straw?

Given the accounts of battered women in our sample, in almost every instance where the woman left there was a last straw incident. Unfortunately, all too often the last straw came after years of abuse. We find ourselves wishing that, for all of you, the first straw could become the last straw. If he did it once, he is likely to do it again. If the first time was a slap, a punch, or worse, the likelihood of chronic battering is so high that if we had things our way, the first incident would *always* be the last. The safety planning may as well begin with the first beating: otherwise, there will be more beatings, more degradation, and more suffering. And you do not deserve to be treated this way by anyone, and especially not by someone who claims to love you.

Batterers do not love in the sense that the term is normally used. They certainly have needs, often insatiable ones. But if they loved, they wouldn't hit. And if your partner hits, he does not love.

Getting Help

We have seen that in almost every instance where the battered wife left her husband in our sample, there was a period of time, sometimes lasting months, at other times lasting years, between the time the decision to leave was made and the date of actual separation or divorce. Typically, these heroic women were acting alone, with their own plans and their own strategies. Often, as we have seen, they were subjected to a great deal of abuse on the way out of the relationship. That abuse might have been avoidable if they had used existing resources at every step in the process.

Get professional help as soon as you have decided to leave, or even before. This is *our single most important piece of advice:* the process of leaving should not occur in isolation from a network of community support. No matter how many general statements we can make about how to keep safe, we cannot adjust our advice to your unique circumstances. There are people in every state in the United States who are trained to provide aid and support to battered women. These trained individuals are the only ones whose job it is to meet your individual needs once you decide to leave. Family members and friends may be supportive, but unless they have experience and training in helping battered women escape safely, they are likely to give bad advice. The single most important step in escaping safely from an abusive relationship is getting professional help. But make sure that the helper is trained, experienced, and qualified.

You can begin your search for qualified help by finding the right community support network. No matter where you are in the United States or Canada, battered women can call the toll-free Domestic Violence Hotline. This may be the most important telephone call you will ever make. The number is:

1-800-799-7233

The hot line offers you an invaluable packet of information, including graphs and charts explaining the ways in which power and control operate in abusive relationships, and more important, information regarding safety planning. This information can be sent by mail, or in case there is concern that the husband might intercept it, to a trusted third party. But the most important function of the hot line is that battered women are provided with *local* referrals, referrals which provide legal aid, shelter for battered women, and other services in that geographic area.

For example, if you were a Seattle resident, you would be referred to an agency called New Beginnings. New Beginnings operates both a shelter and a community office. The shelter would be available to interview you to see if you are in the middle of a crisis situation. If you were currently being stalked, threatened, or were in imminent danger, you could go to the shelter and receive food, clothing, support and counseling, legal aid, and assistance in finding a job. Otherwise, you would have access to the community program. This program would offer you support groups, individual counseling, legal aid, and provide access to a family-law clinic where you could receive free legal consultation. The program also offers education, a prevention program for teenagers, a list of inexpensive therapists who have experience in helping battered women, a treatment program for drug and alcohol abuse, and a parenting program where children can receive counseling along with their mothers. This agency also provides written materials filled with useful information on services for battered women in the region.

This example is not intended to be an advertisement for any particular agency. Rather, we are illustrating how the referral process works, how you can gain access to appropriate aid, and that the services are available even if you are poor. Some similar services are available almost everywhere in the United States.

Every state has a Coalition Against Domestic Violence. Generally, these are *not* direct service agencies. However, they do provide referrals to the nearest shelter. The state coalitions' primary mission is to affect public policy through lobbying for better laws and services for battered women.

We recommend that you utilize these community resources as soon as you have begun to contemplate getting out of an abusive relationship. That way, you are assured of receiving low-cost help. Whether you need emotional support, safety planning, treatment for drugs and alcohol, aid for your children, or suggestions on how to get your partner into treatment, you will no longer feel isolated once you are in contact with these agencies.

Making a Safety Plan

Generally, the most important help available to you is in safety planning, that is, escaping safely. Safety planning is a complex process, and the skills involved in such planning are not easily acquired. There is nothing commonsensical about safety planning. It requires consultation with people who know what they are doing.

• It is safe to assume that those recommended by agencies specializing in helping battered women know what they are doing.

• This is not a safe assumption with typical therapists, whether the referral comes through the Yellow Pages or from a trusted friend or family member. You can only be assured that your safety needs will be safeguarded using state-of-the-art methods if you work through agencies that specialize in assisting battered women.

• Safety planning at its best attempts to strike a delicate balance: it produces a plan of escape, and it tries to help you learn problem-solving skills to gradually assume responsibility for your own safety and the safety of your children. Safety planning requires knowledge of the resources, the agencies, and the legal options that exist in the community which collectively function to provide for safety. The plan usually includes specific strategies for mobilizing whatever informal sources of support exist in your life, including but not necessarily limited to friends, family members, physicians, and spiritual mentors, as well as the more formal sources of support that we have already mentioned: shelters, agencies for battered women, housing placement, ways of getting food stamps, and other necessities in the event that they become necessary after you leave the relationship.

• Shelters often figure prominently in the safety plan. Some battered women are more willing to go to shelters than others; but even if you are reluctant, you may change your mind once safety planning has commenced, especially after a trained advocate has explained the function of shelters and debunked unrealistic concerns that you may have about them. For example, you may be reluctant to enter a shelter because you are concerned that the advocates will attempt to coerce you into a permanent break with your partner, even though *you* don't feel ready to make that break. Advocacy is *not* designed to force decisions on battered women. Rather, advocates are trained to provide support, protection, and help to battered women, whether the shelter is being used as a temporary respite or as the first step toward divorce. Furthermore, shelters generally operate according to a philosophy that emphasizes survival skills: women are helped to learn new skills and use the ones they already have, rather than rely on the directions of advocates. To be sure, advocates do provide direction when such direction is needed, but they do so in such a way as to help battered women assume increasing responsibility for their own safety. They also provide the skills battered women need in order to assume that responsibility.

• Almost invariably, safety plans include some contact with legal officials. For example, the plan may involve the seeking of a restraining order, or aid in filing for divorce. In order to form a sound safety plan, you should receive some advice from trained advocates about certain aspects of the law, such as the difference between civil actions (for example, obtaining an order of protection), and criminal actions (for example, mandatory arrest).

• Your situation is unique, and therefore so is your safety plan. For example, if your partner is violent only while under the influence of cocaine, an element of the plan might include taking particular precautions when he is using cocaine: stay out of the house; avoid arguments; make sure other people are with the two of you whenever possible. More generally, safety plans identify high-risk situations for violence and include strategies for dealing with each of them: specifically, how safety can be maximized when the high-risk situation occurs. If going to a party is a high-risk situation, parties should be avoided. Or perhaps you should try to make sure that you go to parties in groups so that there are other people around after the party as a deterrent to violence. This particular strategy might not deter *your* partner, but may be invaluable for another battered woman. Every situation calls for a plan with unique provisions, and the plans should be discussed with informed advocates for battered women.

• When safety plans involve escaping from the house, either during an argument or permanently, they would include how to get out of the house from various rooms and floors. Safety plans often include the packing of a survival kit, which is then hidden somewhere outside the house. The survival kit might have extra clothes in it, cash, birth certificates and other important documents. The survival kit should be within easy access. It should not be in the house, but rather with a trusted friend, relative, or other support person.

• When advocates and well-trained therapists form safety plans with you, the plan should feel to you like a joint effort, not a lecture from an "expert." You probably have the survival skills, the resourcefulness, and the heroism to do a good deal of the work, and if you feel that the expert is talking down to you and "telling you how to do it," you are likely to be reminded of the situation you are trying to get out of at home. Ultimately, you will use your own problem-solving skills to get out of abusive relationships, not those of the helper.

• However, you are likely to find the external validation provided by a trained helper extremely beneficial, and in many cases essential, to the process of leaving. You may not be functioning at your best when it comes to problem solving and decision making, due to the depression and stress reaction that often coincide with chronic abuse. Both the depression and the stress reaction often go away once you are safe, but in the meantime you may need an experienced helper to deal with reality. This help includes not just designing the original safety plan, but also following up after the plan has been developed and allowing for practice sessions. Sometimes you will find it useful to rehearse the plan in the presence of the helper, by going over each step, imagining what might go wrong, and including contingency plans just in case certain things *do* go wrong.

• Once safety plans are in place, following up repeatedly with a helper is essential. When you leave your abusive partner there may be many false starts, many rehearsals, many changes of plans, and many new year's resolutions that get postponed. You need helpers who stick with you through these stops and starts. The stops and starts are *normal*. They are *expected*. Any experienced professional or helper will stick with you, whatever your state of mind. At times, there may be a number of resources converging to implement the safety plan. Many support people may be involved. But there should always be one *primary* helper, the first among equals—from the beginning of the inquiry into departing from the relationship until the final escape to safety.

If You're Thinking About Leaving a Cobra

1. Cobras are very hard to leave. Based on our sample, fewer women leave Cobras, and when they do, it takes them longer. Why are Cobras so hard to leave? Because they are scary! Battered women have seen them perform violence methodically, without remorse or conscience. If you are married to a Cobra, you know his history of violence and criminal behavior, and can assume—quite correctly—that he will not hesitate to stop you from leaving based on moral considerations. Cobras tend to be amoral.

You have also known your Cobra to be impulsive, and perhaps to abuse drugs. His inhibitions are often lowered by chemical dependencies, and this makes him even more dangerous. In short, you have had plenty of opportunities to observe him and know how dangerous he can be. You also know that he is quick to strike. Finally, you cannot depend on his sympathy.

2. *The period of danger may be shorter for Cobras than it is for Pit Bulls.* On the other hand, women who have left Cobras—like Vicky—discovered that, if they can escape in the short run, the Cobras generally stop trying to pursue them and go on to new pursuits. Cobras are not as obsessed with the women they get involved with. They *are* obsessed with getting what they want when they want it and will go after it if roadblocks are not placed in their way. But Cobras are also fiercely independent and not interested in deep, emotional commitments. Therefore, they will not pursue women who leave them unless it is easy and causes them little hassle to do so. Cobras are not the chronic stalkers, the batterers who follow women and track them down from across the country. Instead, Cobras are men who live from day to day without making long-term plans. If you can get out safely, you can usually stay out. A short-term safety plan may be sufficient to ensure safety, provided that the plan is competently constructed and implemented.

However, this does not mean that there are no exceptions. It is the characteristics of the particular person that matter most, and this is where help from an expert is essential.

3. *Before the escape: responding with caution to Cobra manipulations.* Perhaps the most important decision, short of leaving, that you have to make if you're married to a Cobra is whether to assertively defend yourself when he is trying to control you. We know that, in general, women who defend themselves assertively are more likely to leave. But we also know that the

assertive behavior does not cause or in any way ensure a safe departure. Indeed, assertiveness might put you at increased risk, at least for a period of time. Nevertheless, we observed several examples of husbands becoming less violent, and even stopping the violence, when it was unsuccessful in producing control. Even though George, for example, beat the dog until the day he was hospitalized, he stopped beating Vicky as soon as she responded to his bullying with anger of her own. When violence is unsuccessful as a method of control, it will eventually cease. This is true of all voluntary behavior: when it doesn't work, it gradually stops. The problem is that before it stops, it often increases in frequency and intensity, and this is what makes the strategy dangerous.

One thing we know for sure: conciliatory behavior doesn't work. Attempts to pacify the Cobra do nothing but consolidate his control tactics.

If You're Thinking About Leaving a Pit Bull

1. Pit Bulls might be easier *to leave in the short run, but* harder *to leave in the long run.* As we have emphasized throughout this book, the Pit Bull burns like a slow fuse, and although he may not explode as quickly, his fuse may burn longer. Pit Bulls have consciences and are capable of remorse. This limits their capacity for impulsive and unrepentant murder of a spouse trying to escape. However, because they have a great capacity to minimize, deny, and distort reality, they can often justify their actions to themselves so that they don't have to deal with remorse. Thus, they can easily find rationalizations to justify their stalking, continued abuse, and at times even murder.

The Pit Bulls, unlike the Cobras, are more likely to become obsessed with the battered partner once she is no longer available. She may live on in his mind long after she has divorced him. Hence, the continuing danger. Some experts estimate that this danger can last two years or longer. O. J. Simpson's emotional dependency on Nicole Brown Simpson, his jealousy and possessiveness, and his lack of violence outside the relationship are all typical of Pit Bulls. According to his friends and confidants, O. J. Simpson continued to ruminate over the demise of his relationship with Nicole Brown Simpson even though he had a new girlfriend, and even though he and Nicole Brown Simpson had been divorced for a number of years. Significantly, it appears that only in the weeks just prior to her murder did Nicole consistently tell O. J. that it was over and act in a way that was consistent with those beliefs. In fact, it now appears that Simpson's new girlfriend, Paula Barbieri, ended her relationship with him *on* June 12, the day in which Nicole Brown Simpson was murdered, and Barbieri ended it *because* of O. J. Simpson's continuing obsession with his former wife. In other words, Pit Bulls can be so emotionally dependent on their partners that they find the departure of the battered woman intolerable.

2. *The initial escape may be relatively uneventful.* When Martha left Don and called it a trial separation, Don had little problem with it. This was typical of a Pit Bull. Sometimes the separation begins with the woman being kicked out of the house by the batterer.

3. *With Pit Bulls, the period of greatest risk may be after the escape.* When Martha continued the separation for more than a month, Don began to abuse and stalk her. The obsession continued for years. Interestingly, it stopped only when Martha consistently and forcefully asserted her rights. She divorced him. She hung up on him. She refused to talk to him. She ended a definitive conversation with a "Fuck you!" Don threatened to kill her but gave up. Martha was taking her greatest risk, but she got lucky. Don might have killed her, but he did not. Instead, he began to leave her alone when it was clear that she would no longer be responsive to his threats. By that time, Martha had decided that even death was preferable to being under the spell of Don. She acted heroically. We saw many

cases in our sample where the process of breaking up resembled the dynamics between Don and Martha.

Some batterers *do* stop chasing, stalking, and battering once they become convinced that the efforts will not work. On the other hand, the tactics used by Martha to get Don off her back could have backfired: battered women do get killed, and some batterers may be *more* likely to kill when they become convinced that the woman will never come back. Such Pit Bulls decide that if they can't have the partner, then no one else will. Their sense of ownership over the battered woman is so all-encompassing that they convince themselves that such actions are justified. This is why consultation with an expert—located through agencies designed to aid battered women—is so crucial in making the decision about when to say "yes" ("Okay, you can have five minutes. But I'll hang up if you start to abuse me.") and when to say "no" ("Don't *ever* call here again!").

Life After Escape

Once you are truly safe from your former partner, your problems may or may not be over. As psychologist Lenore Walker reported in her book *The Battered Woman Syndrome*,[1] there are certainly instances where battered women get over their post-traumatic stress reactions and depressions quite quickly once an abusive relationship is over. In fact, many of the women in our sample were as happy or happier than they had ever been in their lives after they were truly free of the abusive partner. Depressions lifted, trauma reactions disappeared, and there appeared to be little residual damage to their psyches or their self-esteem.

However, this is not always the case. You may continue to suffer psychologically, most commonly from depression and post-traumatic stress disorder, and less commonly from substance-abuse problems even after you are safe. Luckily, there are currently existing forms of psychotherapy and safe drugs which are known to be at least moderately effective for PTSD and depression.

In addition to the continued depression and PTSD, there are numerous practical problems that you may have to contend with, problems not traditionally dealt with by health care providers. Once again, the battered women's movement has produced a community of trained and experienced professionals who are quite competent at helping with these practical problems. It is important here to distinguish between treatment for your partner and help for yourself. Whereas there are no proven treatments for battering, there are effective treatments for PTSD and depression. Also, the help you may want *after* getting out of an abusive relationship may be different from the help you need *in order to get out*. Before and during your escape from an abusive relationship, you may need someone to help plan for your safety and practical help with legal problems, children, and financial survival. After you escape you may need help in rebuilding your life. You may not need it, but if you need it, it can be found.

The trick is finding the right person, a person who will help when help is indicated, and at the same time aid you in acquiring the kinds of skills that will allow you to help yourself in the future. The following information should help you understand the problems of PTSD and depression and guide your search for a competent therapist.

Post-Traumatic Stress Disorder. We have already discussed the common problem of PTSD among battered women. You may continue to experience the symptoms of PTSD even after you are safely out of the relationship. But you should carefully avoid therapists who *assume* that all women formerly in abusive relationships must have PTSD. It simply isn't true.

There is a great deal of controversy within the mental-health professions about what constitutes effective treatment for PTSD. However, there is one treatment that has been shown to be effective, a treatment developed by Dr. Edna Foa and her colleagues at Temple University.[2] This treatment uses a form of "behavior therapy." We urge you to ask your therapist about his or her approach to PTSD and the techniques used to treat it before entering into treatment. Since Foa's approach has been shown to be effective and others have not, it makes sense to us that consumers experiencing PTSD try to find a therapist who practices these behavioral techniques. It is of course possible that other untested treatments might work better than behavior therapy, but until that has been demonstrated, the safest avenue is to stick with what has been proven to work.

Behavior therapy for PTSD has as its centerpiece exposure to the traumatic events through imagery, initiated in the therapist's office. While the therapist guides you in imagining previous abusive episodes, you will be gradually desensitized to those events through: 1) training in muscle relaxation; 2) learning techniques for changing the thinking that surrounds those events; and 3) homework assignments that aid in the desensitization process. A prominent part of the treatment involves "stress inoculation," where you are taught to practice effective coping strategies while experiencing through imagery previous instances of abuse.

None of the research proving that behavior therapy works for PTSD has been applied specifically to formerly battered women. However, Foa's research has shown strong effects with similar types of trauma, such as sexual assault in women raped by strangers. Following in the footsteps of Foa's pioneering work, Dr. Mary Ann Dutton has applied behavior therapy to formerly battered women.[3] In addition to the strategies developed by Foa, Dutton's behavioral techniques are designed to

- help reduce any shame you might feel after the relationship is over;
- find effective ways of expressing whatever anger you continue to feel toward your former partner;
- cope with whatever sense of loss you may experience once

you have left. You may still feel somewhat attached to him despite the abuse. You may have lost your home. The escape may have thrown you into a state of financial insecurity. It may have cost you custody of your children. Some of your friends may not have remained loyal to you. Behavior therapy teaches techniques for coping with such losses.
- make sense out of your having been battered;
- build a new life.

The aspect of Dutton's therapy that involves making sense out of being battered warrants special attention, because you, like other formerly battered women, may come out of an abusive relationship with great confusion about the meaning of life, whether or not people can be trusted, and who you are now that you are no longer a victim but a survivor of battering. Many beliefs that most of us have about the world are shattered when battering occurs. For example, we assume that we can be safe and comfortable with those who claim to love us. Many of us also assume that the world is fair, and bad things only happen to those who deserve them. As a result, you may blame yourself for the abuse, even though in reality your former partner is to blame. In order to get your life back, you may have to reexamine these basic beliefs, and develop a new way of looking at the world that allows you to move on.

It was common in our sample for women to have trouble coping with life following the shattering of beliefs such as these. Part of the heroism in the women we studied was revealed in their struggle to overcome the loss of faith in oneself and the world. Dr. Dutton described one instance where a battered woman used a new community of battered women (a support group) to restore her faith in the existence of trustworthy people. Another woman reported that she felt a sense of solidarity with other mistreated and oppressed women, and this solidarity helped her feel connected to the world again. In other words, there are various ways that you might find meaning in experiences that follow escape from an abusive relationship. Therapy can be helpful in this process, although many of the women in our sample came to new conclusions about the meaning of life without therapy.

Depression. In addition to being a part of PTSD, clinical depression can be viewed as a separate problem, and at times exists in formerly battered women even though the other symptoms of PTSD are absent. Often, the depression is a rational, natural, and perhaps even inevitable response to the practical obstacles formerly battered women face, and sometimes the depression will subside as these practical problems are successfully resolved—with or without professional help. At other times, additional therapy is indicated. Antidepressant medications have been found to be effective for a majority of moderately depressed adults:[4] the classes of drugs where the evidence is strongest are the tricyclic antidepressants (e.g., imipramine, desipramine) and the selective serotonin reuptake inhibitors (Prozac, Zoloft, or Paxil). All physicians are capable of prescribing these medications, although psychiatrists are likely to be more aware of the appropriate therapeutic dose, the diagnostic indicators, and the possible side effects for a given individual. Various psychotherapies also have been shown to be effective in treating major depression:

• *Cognitive therapy.* This form of therapy was developed by Dr. Aaron T. Beck,[5] and is described in a self-help regimen in a book by Dr. David Burns, *Feeling Good.*[6] Its focus is on changing the way depressed people think: it includes strategies which help depressed people examine the reality of their negative thinking. Cognitive therapy also helps depressed people cope with negative thinking about themselves, the world, and the future. It directly counters the hopelessness experienced by so many battered women after getting out of an abusive relationship.

• *Behavior therapy.* Behavior therapy for depression helps

people get back out into the world again, and find the types of gratification that have been lacking in the person's life.[7] It is brief, action-oriented, and assumes that the depression resulted from unpleasant events in the person's life. For example, one common behavioral technique is to help clients identify pleasurable or formerly pleasurable activities, and work out a plan for engaging in these pleasant activities. Behavior therapy also helps people with interpersonal problems, for example, by fostering the development of interpersonal skills that might be lacking at the time the person seeks therapy. Finally, behavior therapy tries to relieve specific symptoms of depression, such as sleep disturbances, loss of energy, and difficulties in concentrating. When indicated, the therapist helps the client learn strategies for coping with and eventually eliminating these specific symptoms.

• *Interpersonal therapy.* Although many psychotherapies for depression focus on "interpersonal problems," Interpersonal Therapy (IPT) refers to a specific set of techniques developed by Drs. Gerald Klerman, Myrna Weissman, and associates.[8] IPT is also a brief therapy and targets what the creators of the treatment believe to be the most common interpersonal problems faced by depressed people: disruptions in close relationships and unresolved grief, for example. Through a combination of tasks created in the therapy session, analyses of the interpersonal problems, and explorations of the pros and cons of various actions, the therapist and the client work out solutions to the problems most relevant to a particular individual.

Again, when seeking psychotherapy for depression, ask the therapist for evidence to support the effectiveness of that therapy. It is important *not* to assume that a therapist is competent simply because he or she is certified or licensed. What matters is not the degree the therapist has, but the comfort level you feel with a particular therapist, and the experience the therapist has had treating formerly battered women. Both the comfort level and the experience level of the therapist will be enhanced if you are confident that the therapist is using an approach which has been shown to be effective. By questioning therapists on their familiarity with various approaches, you can get their opinion on and familiarity with those treatments which have been proven effective in treating depression.

More generally, the Association for the Advancement of Behavior Therapy (AABT), located in New York City, is an excellent resource for referrals in the areas of PTSD and depression. AABT can refer interested consumers to therapists specializing in these areas across the United States. Although AABT does not certify the competence of the therapist, at the very least a referral from AABT suggests that the therapist is using treatments for PTSD and depression that have been tested and found to be effective. Nevertheless, it is important to remember that techniques in and of themselves can be performed competently or incompetently, depending on the individual. You have the right to check out prospective therapists and determine your comfort level with them.

The Practical Life Problems Faced by Formerly Battered Women

The euphoria of finally being free of an abusive partner does not last forever. You may not even experience the euphoria. Although it may appear to others that your struggle has ended successfully once you are safe, you may find that your own personal struggle has just begun. There are a number of practical problems that you may face once you are out of the abusive relationship.

Economic Survival. Leaving your abusive partner may often send you into poverty. If you were not working outside the home during the relationship, you will have to find a way of supporting yourself financially. It is not uncommon for battered women to have to apply for welfare and food stamps. If you have been out of the workforce for a lengthy period of time, you may need job training or advice on how to find gainful employment. If you have already been working, the income may no longer suffice. The problem is compounded if you have children, since working requires day care, and your partner may be an unreliable source of child support. He is legally obligated to pay child support, and with the help of your support system, you may be able to bring the law to bear and obtain the support you need. But batterers are notoriously elusive when it comes to paying child support, even when they are legally obligated to do so.

Finding a place to live is difficult when the economic situation is dire, and you may have been so isolated during your marriage that you have severed ties with potential roommates, including family members.

Adjusting to Being Single. You may experience continued attachment to your partner for a period of time, despite the fact that he abused you. This is a very common reaction, and it is perfectly normal. For this and a host of other reasons, single life may be a difficult adjustment. This may seem surprising to some of your friends and family since they might believe that anything would be "nirvana" compared to being with the man who abused you. However, recovering from an abusive relationship is often more complicated than such a perception would suggest. Not all of the battered women in our sample were "over" their partners. The lingering attachment, combined with the attempts your former partner might make to coax you back, may make life confusing after you have escaped. Learning to live with loneliness is not easy for any of us.

In our culture, when couples separate or divorce, single life is usually viewed as a transition period between the old and new relationship, rather than as a viable lifestyle in its own right. This is even more true for men than it is for women: the vast majority of divorced men remarry within five years; with women, a high percentage remarry, but the percentage is not as high as it is for men. There are various ways in which our culture does not support single women, with or without children. The pressure to be part of a couple can seem overwhelming, and if not resisted, can easily lead you prematurely into a new relationship.

Learning to feel happy and whole without a romantic partner is difficult, but not impossible. Many of the brief treatments for depression described earlier would identify this as an issue worth working on if you wanted to. The goal would be to define yourself as a person who can be happy with or without a partner, and to learn to prefer your own company or that of friends to a relationship that doesn't meet your standards. We noticed that many of the women in our sample were worried about finding someone else even before leaving their battering partner: in fact, this worry deterred some from leaving sooner, almost as if even an abusive relationship is better than no relationship. You not only don't deserve to be beaten, you deserve a good relationship. In our clinical experience, one of the great ironies is that people are more likely to get what they want if they can let go of their need for it: in other words, your chances of finding a man who really meets your needs are greater if you become convinced that you can be happy without a man than they are if you feel desperate for a relationship.

After getting out of an abusive relationship, you need time to figure out what *you* want out of life. Chances are you've been living your life on automatic pilot for months or years according to your abusive partner's directions. Perhaps you've never had time to get to know yourself apart from the relationships you're in. After escaping from a batterer, you have an opportunity that you may never have had before. We recommend taking advantage of that opportunity by embracing your single status, and not rushing to entangle yourself romantically. Before even thinking about recoupling, live life according to your rules, decide what your goals and dreams are, and explore as many alternatives as you can. You may have an ideal opportunity for such exploration if you have joined a battered women's support group. Psychotherapy can also help you explore the state of being single as a lifestyle in and of itself, rather than simply as a transition state between relationships. But you can do it without therapy. Learning how to embrace single life is well within your reach, provided you can solve the sometimes overwhelming economic burdens involved. It's certainly no harder than ending an abusive relationship.

Forming New Romantic Relationships. You may have trouble trusting your judgment when new relationship opportunities arise. You made at least one bad choice: who's to say the next man will prove to be different? It may be reassuring for you to get guidance from a therapist in making the next choice. For starters, we can suggest some characteristics in men that you should avoid at all costs:

• The man has admitted to hitting his previous wife, but claimed that she deserved it. In fact, he may be convincing. Until you are back on your feet, you may need a reality check. No woman deserves to be beaten. Any man who tells you that he was a "battered husband," as O. J. Simpson described himself, is lying. Any man with a history of battering is a bad risk; he is likely to batter again, no matter how he seems during the courtship.

Our red flags include:

• a history of battering in previous relationships;
• sexist attitudes toward women;
• drug or alcohol abuse; and
• the expressed opinion that the man should be the head of the household.

Again, you may benefit from professional help in making the transition to a new life. But therapy is not the only source of support for formerly battered women. There is an excellent book for battered women by Ginny NiCarthy called *Getting*

Free: You Can End Abuse and Take Back Your Life. We highly recommend this book for women getting out of abusive relationships.[9]

One must never underestimate the risks of getting out of abusive relationships. For most women, though, being out of an abusive relationship and being safe is better by far than being in one.

10

Ending Domestic Violence Against Women

For the past eight years, we have been studying violence between batterers and battered women using the methods of science. As a result, we have confirmed some of what experts have long believed to be true, and discovered some things that no one knew. This knowledge is valuable in its own right, just like any scientific findings. However, because battered women are beaten, murdered, and stalked every day in this country, research on this population will inevitably be judged on its relevance: how can it contribute to ending violence against women? Acquiring scientific knowledge and applying it to social problems takes time. And only time will determine how useful our research into the relationships of batterers and battered women will be.

The beating of wives by their husbands has been legal for most of our history.[1] The first formal protest against the absolute authority of male patriarchy in the United States was the women's suffrage movement in the early part of the twentieth century;[2] theirs was the first organized voice of outrage against battering. The feminist movement of the 1970s created a more focused advocacy campaign on behalf of battered women. The battered women's movement has now been active for over twenty years, and we owe virtually all of the considerable improvements in the institutional options available to battered women to these advocacy efforts. We mentioned some results of the battered women's movement in chapters 8 and 9: providing resources and information for battered women; changing laws so that men who batter are more likely to be arrested and prosecuted; contributing to the Coordinated Community Response (CCR) movement—perhaps the most promising development thus far for protecting battered women; and providing public education in order to break down stereotypes and raise public consciousness about domestic violence.

But battering remains a problem of epidemic proportions. Public education is expensive, and until recently, a majority of battered women in this country were not even aware that battering was against the law. In fact, the one positive outcome of the O. J. Simpson trials has been that, despite all the tabloid sensationalism surrounding the case, a great deal of information about domestic violence has been disseminated to the public. But it is a tragic commentary on our society that we have to rely on celebrity murder cases to educate the public about domestic violence. An even more frustrating problem has been that advocacy networks have been chronically and grossly underfunded. Because of this, despite the best efforts of state and national coalitions, there are simply not enough shelters, not enough services, and not enough advocates to serve the needs of battered women. This point was driven home in dramatic fashion by an article in *The New York Times*.[3] In New York City, despite Mayor Giuliani's pledge to tackle domestic violence and the existence of hot lines, shelters, and services, often there is no help for battered women when they need it— which is usually immediately. The shelters are full. Hot lines are so busy and understaffed that there is often no answer when women call. Not nearly enough money is being spent on services for battered women. All the good intentions in the world can't overcome this grim reality.

Patriarchy Continues

It wasn't until 1871 that two states—Alabama and Massachusetts—made wife beating illegal. The courts gradually frowned upon the authority of husbands to beat their wives until by 1910 most states regarded wife beating as grounds for divorce. This reform coincided with the women's suffrage campaign.

Now the laws have changed, but the beatings continue. Perhaps husbands are less inclined to beat their wives now that it is illegal, but we believe the continued high rates of battering are directly related to our cultural heritage. Many men still see it as their right to batter women who oppose their authority. Many law enforcement officials who are supposed to enforce the law agree with that point of view. Perhaps most importantly, marriage as an institution is still structured in such a way as to institutionalize male dominance, and such dominance makes high rates of battering inevitable.

In other words, battering, and the values supporting it, cannot be understood apart from other aspects of the culture that sanction male superiority. Once male privilege is granted, the right to enforce it directly follows. The dominance of men in marriages is seen everywhere, not just in couples where men batter. It is reflected in the various ways in which marriage continues to function as an institution that was created by and for men.[4] Male dominance explains why women are much more likely than men to seek marital therapy, why the rates of depression in married women are much higher than the rates of depression in married men, and why working women do as much housework, relative to their husbands, as women who do not work outside the home. These gender-based power differentials in marriage lead one to the conclusion that battering is simply an exaggerated version of the power and control that remain the norm in American marriages, the "politics" of intimacy.

Meanwhile, battering continues to occur in epidemic proportions. Although social scientists and other experts of violence have been slow to realize it, violent crime against women is largely a matter of husbands assaulting wives.[5] Women are virtually as likely to be killed by husbands, ex-husbands, boyfriends, and ex-boyfriends as by strangers. In contrast, men are much more likely to be killed by strangers than by their intimate partners. When women kill their intimate partners, they are usually battered women who fear for their lives.[6] When men kill their intimate partners, it is the ultimate act of control. If society could significantly reduce battering, we would be cutting violent crime against women by more than half.

The Battered Women's Movement

The first modern movement to stop wife battering came in the early seventies. The battered women's movement has gradually expanded the scope of the aid they provide from short- to long-term goals. Survival must come first. So the domestic violence community begins with crisis intervention and immediate survival; then provides resources that battered women will need once long-term survival has been ensured; and finally, focuses attention on stopping the violence and protecting battered women through sanctions and rehabilitation for batterers.

Shelters. Shelters serve the most immediate need of battered women: survival. Battered women in danger of assault or murder need a place where their partner cannot find them. The shelters are not intended to be permanent solutions to problems for either individual battered women or for the societal problem of battering. From the beginning shelters were safe houses, and they still are. As long as battered women stay in the shelters, they are protected. Despite a new disturbing trend for shelters in some locales to publicly reveal their addresses, for the most part their partners do not know where they are and cannot gain access to them.

Resources for Battered Women. Resources for battered women emanate from the shelter movement. Shelters began to offer legal services, practical tips on how to get welfare and food stamps, support groups, and services for children. Also emanating from the shelters were the initial efforts to bring about changes in the law and the criminal justice system. Gradually, the initiative for these changes and for public education efforts began to shift to groups organized specifically to change public policy and enhance public awareness of domestic violence.

For example, advocacy organizations taught doctors in emergency rooms and family practice clinics methods for detecting battering: this involved not only instructing doctors in evaluating whether or not battering has occurred, but counteracting stereotypes that tended to blame battered women in subtle and not so subtle ways. The education and training of physicians is an ongoing process: many doctors still don't appreciate the importance of external validation and knowing where the appropriate referral agencies are.

In chapter 9, we provided a national hot line where anyone can call to find out about basic resources for battered women. Such hot lines did not exist before 1972, when telephone counseling became available in Minnesota. A similar hot line was created in New York City in 1975, and the same group of women who started the hot line created a shelter in 1976. This was, to our knowledge, the first coordinated effort to link shelters with other services for battered women. It was a forerunner to coordinated community response (CCR). At the same time, the National Organization for Women (NOW) began to provide materials for battered women and to establish networks for national coordination. NOW, as well as other organizations, led a flurry of organized efforts in the late seventies, and for the first time we began to have a national social movement focused on battering.

Public Policy and Education. In 1992, the first Federal Domestic Violence Protection Act was passed, making it a federal offense for a batterer to cross state lines to pursue a battered woman, and today batterers are being prosecuted under this act. The National Coalition Against Domestic Violence was formed in 1978, originally as a result of a conference on policy issues commissioned by the United States Commission on Civil Rights. The hot line we reported in chapter 9 is run by the national coalition. Additionally, each state has its own separate coalition, which is directly responsible for advocacy at the statutory level, and also works hard at public education and in the training of officials within the criminal justice system.

The federal government began to support domestic violence research around 1980, but even prior to that the first of two national surveys that were to have a major impact on both the academic and advocacy communities were released. Sociologists Murray Straus and Richard Gelles gave us the most accurate information we now have on the widespread practice of domestic violence.[7] These findings served as a wake-up call for the National Institute of Justice and the National Institute of Health, which shortly thereafter began to fund research on domestic violence. Dr. Lenore Walker wrote two books which exposed the problem of battering to a wider audience, describing the cycle of violence and coining the term "battered women's syndrome," a forerunner to the post-traumatic stress disorder diagnosis commonly applied to battered women today.[8] Straus created a Family Violence Research Center that not only became a mecca for research on domestic violence, but also sponsored semiannual conferences where scientists, therapists, and advocates could come together and discuss their findings.

By the mid-1980s there were numerous scientific and professional journals devoted to the topic of domestic violence, most of which included members of at least the following disciplines: social work, psychiatry, psychology, sociology, law, criminal justice, and family studies. We know of no topic which spans such a wide range of disciplines. A great many workers in the field have no advanced degrees and are considered specialists in advocacy. The divergence in specializations characterizing the field of domestic violence has hindered the process of working together to solve the problem of violence against women. But the attempts to remedy the problem—conferences, clearinghouses for information, and interdisciplinary journals—have helped considerably in the dissemination of knowledge within the professional disciplines.

Continued Challenges to the Battered Women's Movement. All of these reforms and initiatives are to be applauded. Yet battering continues to be a serious social problem. Why?

• *It is one thing to pass laws; it is quite another to enforce them.* As we have discussed, not all law enforcement officials have changed their practices, despite the existence of training programs, and despite changes in the laws. According to statistics provided by the Department of Justice, two-thirds of arrested batterers are charged with simple assault, the least serious category of assault—a misdemeanor rather than a felony. However, half of these assaults cause at least as much injury as rapes, robberies, and aggravated assaults, all of which are felonies.

• *Mandatory arrest is not universal.* It is also true that mandatory arrest is still not in place everywhere, and it is not consistently enforced even when it is in place. Police officers often go to the scene of a battering episode and don't arrest anyone. The great majority of battering episodes still go unpunished. Dr. Daniel Saunders has found that arrest practices are directly related to the beliefs of police officers regarding domestic violence:[9] The more sexist the policeman's stated beliefs and the less disapproving he or she is of battering, the less likely an arrest.

• *Too many judges and prosecutors still see domestic violence as a family matter: this results in not enough prosecutions and not enough accountability.* Judges often don't take domestic disputes as seriously as violence against strangers. All too often, the judge dismisses the complaint and admonishes the couple to work out their problems. Prosecutors themselves often decide not to prosecute or attempt to persuade battered women to drop the charges. If prosecution does occur, it is often made a low priority, resulting in long delays. These delays can produce repeated episodes of violence, or threats that are scary enough to get the battered woman to drop the charges.

• *Agencies for battered women are short of money.* As we discussed at the beginning of the chapter, there remains the constant problem of agencies for battered women being underfunded. Shelters are often full, and despite their existence, women in danger can be turned away. A recent American Psychological Association task force on domestic violence reported that more than half of all counties in the United States still lack resources of any kind for battered women. Even when shelters are available, the transition into permanent housing is often difficult, since battered women are often indigent and financially dependent on their husbands. Some battered women return to their partners for this reason; some become homeless. Some lose custody of their children because life circumstances create the false impression that they are neglecting their children.

All of these problems can inhibit a battered woman from relying on the criminal justice system or even agencies run by members of the advocacy community. A bad experience in the past—whether it has been with a judge, a police officer, a shelter, or a prosecutor—can contribute to the sense of entrapment suffered by many battered women and a feeling of futility.

In short, the battered women's movement has brought about

some dramatic changes in this country, changes which have improved the chances that battered women will get the help they need and that batterers will be held accountable. The remaining challenges are formidable, but the determination of the advocacy community should not be underestimated. As we look to the future, let us place our research in the context of the plight of battered women in America and explore the implications.

Where Does Our Research Fit in?

We have reported our research findings throughout this book. We have also shared opinions from our research findings when the personal dramas of particular couples spoke loudly to us, but we had no way of quantifying them. Let us examine what we know, what we suspect, and how all of this fits into the heroic struggle of battered women.

Not All Batterers Are Alike. We are quite confident that our distinction between Cobras and Pit Bulls will stand the test of time. There is a growing consensus in the field that there are at least two very different types of batterers, and that these types correspond quite closely to our Pit Bulls and Cobras. This research on different types of batterers is analyzed in depth by Dr. Amy Holtzworth-Munroe and Gregory Stuart,[10] and types similar to ours have emerged consistently, using a variety of classification schemes and measurement techniques. However, our ability to uncover two distinct subtypes based on physiology suggests a relatively objective method for distinguishing among Cobras and Pit Bulls. We have confirmed what others have long suspected: One type of batterer, the Cobra, resembles the common criminal, commits crimes without experiencing or expressing a great deal of emotion, and is quite impulsive and hedonistic. In contrast, the other type is if anything, overly emotional and tremendously dependent on women.

Perhaps the most important long-term consequence of the

discovery that not all batterers are alike concerns their potential for treatment. As we mentioned in chapter 8, there is little evidence to support the effectiveness of any currently existing intervention for batterers. But it could be that if Pit Bulls and Cobras were examined separately, the effects of various treatments would emerge—if only for one subtype. For example, we would expect Pit Bulls to be better candidates than Cobras for virtually all currently existing sanctions and rehabilitation efforts. Yet since Cobras help clog the system of treatment delivery, we have not yet seen what can be accomplished by concentrating rehabilitation and education efforts on Pit Bulls.

What makes us so pessimistic about Cobras and at least somewhat optimistic about Pit Bulls? For one thing, Cobras seem particularly unmotivated to change. Their histories of abuse during their own childhoods, their long personal history of antisocial behavior, and their complete absorption in themselves and their own needs makes rehabilitation seem unproductive. In contrast, Pit Bulls have many reasons to change. First, they tend to experience a great deal of emotional discomfort. In other words, they don't generally experience their lives as going well. Second, they seem to be quite attached to their partners, and therefore would seem, under the right circumstances, motivated to keep the relationships intact. It would certainly be worthwhile to study the effectiveness of currently existing interventions for batterers with Pit Bulls separated from Cobras. Rehabilitation might be possible with Pit Bulls. Only careful scientific research could prove this definitively, and we recommend that such research be conducted.

One study, recently completed by Dr. Daniel Saunders at the University of Michigan,[11] suggests that a particular type of group therapy may have promise with Pit Bulls. Saunders compared a group therapy that was focused on insight into the origins of the battering as well as interpersonal problems to a more traditional anger-management group. There were no overall differences in effectiveness between the groups, but some interesting results emerged when Saunders divided the batterers into "dependent" and "antisocial" subtypes. For the dependent types, those whom we suspect are much like our Pit Bulls, the insight-oriented group therapy was quite successful (it was unsuccessful with the antisocial types). In contrast, the antisocial types had a positive response to a more standard anger-management program. The insight-oriented group therapy has not been widely advocated or tested as a treatment for batterers. But it may work with Pit Bulls. We are less confident that Cobras would be responsive to a standard anger-management program, despite Saunders's findings. As far as we can tell, even though the batterers in Saunders's study who responded well to anger management were *more* antisocial than the dependent batterers, they do not seem nearly as antisocial as the Cobras in our sample. In fact, we suspect that the great majority of batterers in Saunders's study are Pit Bulls. Nevertheless, it may be that within the Pit Bull population the more antisocial types may do better with skills training in managing anger, while the more classic Pit Bulls would be more responsive to a group therapy that resembles traditional psychotherapy: insight oriented and focused on early interpersonal relationships with members of their family of origin. Only time will tell if Saunders's findings can be confirmed and extended. But they offer a ray of hope in what has up until now been a rather dismal prognosis for psychotherapy.

Perhaps the most intriguing difference between Pit Bulls and Cobras involves the different long-term trajectories of the relationships. The wives of Pit Bulls were highly likely to end the relationship, whereas the wives of Cobras were not—at least over a two-year period. In addition to everything we learned about the kinds of Pit Bulls who drive women away and the kinds of women who leave Pit Bulls, we heard many stories during our exit interviews that could be used to offer guidance in how to expedite this seemingly inevitable departure.

Direct advice and verbal persuasion seemed to have little

effect on battered women. They did, however, listen to their own experience. When they realized that their dream of a normal nonabusive relationship would never come to pass with their current partner, they immediately made the decision to leave. "Giving up the dream" seemed to result in a shifting from fear to contempt and a determination to leave. If battered women could be helped to "give up their dream" sooner, and this process could occur in conjunction with a careful safety plan and the support of an experienced helper, women might be induced to get out sooner and more safely.

We found time after time that persuasion was ineffective at getting battered women out of relationships before they were ready to leave. However, those of you who are battered women may be able to come to your own conclusions more efficiently if you take the time to:

- Identify your dream.
- Compare your dream with the current reality of your relationship.
- Examine the likelihood of various scenarios. One scenario is that the situation will stay the same as it is now; a second is that the man will change; and a third is that the abuse will get even worse and end up with one or both of you getting killed, or your children being seriously harmed. To evaluate the likelihood of these various scenarios there are questions you can ask yourself: Does your husband minimize, deny, and distort the abuse? Is he interested in treatment oriented toward stopping the violence—not just saying so, but following through? Has he been held accountable for the violence by the criminal justice system? Is he an alcohol or drug abuser who refuses treatment for substance abuse, or worse yet, denies that he has a problem with drugs or alcohol? Has the severity of the violence been escalating over time? How severe is the emotional abuse, based on your responses to the tables in

chapter 6? Often an honest examination of these and similar questions will lead to the conclusion that the dream is
an illusion.

A counselor or advocate is there for you regardless of
whether or not you give up the dream. But the information in
this book should help you evaluate the likelihood that the
dream is eventually going to come true:

- In the absence of punishment or completion of a rehabilitation program, violence is highly unlikely to stop.
- Batterers who are unwilling to enter rehabilitation or education programs, insist upon couples therapy when they
  do agree to treatment, or drop out of a program before the
  counselor believes that it has been completed are unlikely
  to stop.
- Batterers who minimize, deny, and distort the violence (in
  other words, blame the wife) are unlikely to stop.
- Batterers who have problems with drugs or alcohol are
  unlikely to stop, at least until the drug and alcohol problems have been solved.
- Batterers who express beliefs that the man should be the
  head of the household and that his wife should obey him
  even if she disagrees are less likely to stop the violence.
- Batterers who are not punished by the courts (fines or
  imprisonment) are unlikely to stop. Arrest is not enough:
  being held accountable means prosecuted and punished.
- Batterers who are extremely emotionally abusive, especially when the emotional abuse includes insulting and
  humiliating the wife or attempting to isolate her from the
  rest of the world, are unlikely to stop the violence.

When you examine your dream in light of these sobering
realities, you may let go of it. Once you recognize that you are
holding onto a dream, you may come to the conclusion that

the dream was unrealistic. Just participation in our study was enough for some battered women. You may recall that both Martha and Vicky cited participation in our study as the first step in realizing that their dream was unrealistic.

Cobras May Be More Difficult to Leave in the Short Run, but Pit Bulls May Require Long-Term Safety Planning. We focus our safety plans on the immediate risks when it comes to leaving Cobras, whereas the battered woman's safety is often at risk for a greater period of time with Pit Bulls. This is because Cobras react impulsively and therefore are dangerous in the short run, but are less likely to make a long-term investment in keeping the battered woman in the relationship. He may feel outraged that he has lost control of his partner and deprived of the gratification that she has provided him, but Cobras tend to get distracted by new pursuits. If a woman can survive the immediate bursts of fury, she is more likely to be home free. For the wife of a Cobra, the safety plan should involve extreme precautions to keep the woman safe for a period of time, and then gradual testing of the waters to make sure the coast is clear. With Pit Bulls, there will seldom be an explosive outburst immediately upon separation because the Pit Bull believes at the time of separation that she will return. As it becomes apparent that she will not, he begins to threaten, stalk, and escalate the abuse—anything to get her back. His desperation may be such that an order of protection will mean nothing to him, not worth the paper it is printed on. Women married to Pit Bulls would often be wise to have safety plans that last two years or more following separation.

The Importance of Drugs and Alcohol. We have become so convinced of the importance of drug and alcohol abuse that we plan research that will allow us to document just how powerful this variable is. We believe that state-of-the-art treatments for drug and alcohol abuse have to be integrated into rehabilitation programs in a more systematic way if these programs are to have any chance of helping Pit Bulls. This effort is complicated by the difficulties in treating drug and alcohol problems, which are among the most difficult of all mental-health problems to treat. But up until now, drug and alcohol experts have been working apart from domestic-violence experts, and their efforts need to be brought together if we expect rehabilitation to have an impact on abuse.

Gender Differences in Physical and Emotional Abuse. We have found that in all couples where there is battering, the husband is in control in every way. The wife is afraid of him. She is the one who is getting injured, even when she fights back. Why would a battered woman fight back, knowing that she is placing herself at risk? In part, battered women fight back because they are defending themselves while they are being beaten. At other times, they fight back out of anger and frustration, because the control and powerlessness is so aversive that women are often desperate to retain some semblance of control—even if it means that they will pay for it later. Finally, at times when acts are examined out of context, it looks as if the women are actually starting the violent altercations. Although women are on occasion the perpetrators of violence, these isolated acts of initiation must be considered within a long history of battering and emotional abuse. Women react in different ways to this chronic abuse. Some develop revenge fantasies; in fact, we consider this to be quite understandable and natural, to the point where we wondered why it wasn't even more common than it was. But the revenge fantasies lead to plans, and at times men are hurt, wounded, and even humiliated by calculated acts of revenge on the part of battered women. Although some of these acts indicate that the women are partners in crime, the vast majority are simply part of their victimization.

The Slippery Slope of Fighting Back. Battered women who fought back were more likely to leave their partners within a two-year period. Women who defended their positions and held their ground during verbal arguments were also more likely to leave the relationship. From the exit interviews, resistance to control seemed to be associated with escape from the relationship, and also with a gradual reduction in control efforts for those couples where the relationships continued. In other words, our results suggested that women's efforts to counter their battering husbands' control efforts served them well: either these efforts led to getting out of the relationship, or they led to decreased violence.

Take Derek and Karen as an example. Karen seemed impervious to Derek's beatings. She continued to chastise him verbally, and she came and went as she pleased, despite the beatings. Eventually, Derek stopped the violence, and the relationship actually improved to the point where both described themselves as happy and content.

However, despite the fact that fighting back seemed to be associated with good things, we would not advise battered women to fight back. First, such advice is risky. Even if it were good advice, in the short run it might lead to further beatings. Second, we can not assume from our research that fighting back caused the men to stop the beatings. It may be that the kinds of women who naturally fight back naturally *choose* the kinds of men who respond to fighting back by decreasing the abuse. Or it may be that the kinds of women who naturally fight back are the kinds of women who are least likely to tolerate abuse, and therefore are most likely to get out; if they don't get out of the relationships, the husbands may sense that the wives will leave if they don't stop.

Moving from research findings to clinical practice is hazardous. But armed with the information that assertive self-defense and even physical retaliation tend to be associated with better outcomes than submission at least in the long run, battered women can work *with trained and experienced professionals,* and in collaboration with the trained professionals, design a safety plan that is appropriate to the situation. The risks of defending oneself—either verbally or physically—

vary from case to case. Professionals can help battered women try the waters. Tests can be conducted to see if in the short run, resistance prior to an abusive episode is successful. If steps are taken—one at a time—it may be possible to minimize the risks.

Prevention. At the level of public policy, many experts have concluded that battering may not be treatable, but it may be preventable. Prevention of battering can take many forms: the least ambitious programs are the ones that are most likely to pay off in the short run. They assume that once a batterer, always a batterer. The goal is then to protect the woman from him by punishing him as much as the law allows, and when the punishment allowed by the law is insufficient, changing the law to make the penalties worse.

A more ambitious form of prevention involves identifying people at risk for becoming batterers and trying to change them before they become batterers. If we know the kinds of boys or men that are likely to become batterers then we can attempt to work with them before they use violence against their own partners.

The most ambitious prevention programs are the ones with the greatest potential payoff, but the least short-term return. They attempt to create a culture and a society that produces more civilized men, and marriages where the partners are equal. The blueprint for creating such a culture is far from clear, but battering is unlikely to stop being a serious social problem until peer marriages are the norm rather than the exception.[12] As long as our culture remains dominated by patriarchy, peer marriages seem destined to be rare and exceptional.

In the meantime, the development and testing of interventions for batterers can and should continue. It is interesting that even though none of the currently existing models has been shown to be effective, a husband's willingness to enter treatment and complete it does appear to provide valuable information about his motivation to stop.[13] The programs must be available for that reason, even if for no other. We think that treatments should be certified as effective by the state only if they have been proven to be safe and effective, just as drugs are approved by the FDA. Political lobbying does not constitute a sound basis for recommending treatments for a problem as serious as battering. We need proof before considering them anything but experimental.

Because all currently existing treatments for batterers are untested, we oppose judges mandating rehabilitation and education programs as an alternative to punishment through incarceration. On the other hand, we do believe that batterers should be offered such programs on a voluntary basis, and we would not be averse to their parole being affected by their voluntary participation in rehabilitation and education. Of course, any such programs would have to be coordinated with the criminal justice system, as is typical of a CCR.

We also strongly believe that the laws need to be more punitive than they currently are. One excellent reform, now operative in some states, requires prosecution even if the battered woman drops the charges. Mandatory prosecution after an arrest is a step in the right direction. Furthermore, we would recommend that all instances of arrests for battering be classified as felonies rather than misdemeanors. We think that such a change in the laws would result in more prosecutions, more convictions, and stiffer sentencing—all of which would further the cause of holding the batterer accountable.

A major gap in the accountability of the batterer is the lenient or suspended sentence a convicted batterer often gets. Rarely do batterers serve time in jail, and the fines would pose a financial hardship only to the indigent. Often the batterer is given probation contingent upon entering a treatment program. We have already seen the problems with this kind of sentence. For now, simply reflect back on Derek and Karen, where after Derek's first two arrests, he was "sentenced" to therapy and kept on hitting Karen. After his third arrest, he actually did some time, and he stopped battering Karen. When he was finally held accountable, the battering stopped.

If more consistent prosecution and stiffer sentencing were combined with mandatory arrest, the criminal justice system would be doing its job as long as the laws are enforced. But laws do no one any good if they are not enforced. At the very least, prosecution and punishment keep the batterer away for a period of time, thus buying time for the woman so that she can form a safety plan.

Preventing the Creation of Batterers. By the time batterers enter an anger-management group, or face the criminal justice system for the first time, they have been subjected to years of socialization. Although some may believe that batterers are born, we think that in general batterers are produced by a culture that trains certain men to batter as a means of establishing power and control over their intimate partners. For example, one study sponsored by the National Institute of Mental Health has been following a group of children into adulthood for over twenty years. It has helped determine which boys grow up to be batterers. Up to now, every boy who has grown up to be a batterer was a delinquent teenager, and in most cases a violent teenager.[14] Therefore, programs that successfully prevent boys from becoming violent delinquents should help prevent them from becoming batterers.

Currently, there is a major effort at the federal level to evaluate programs designed to prevent delinquency in teenagers. One such project, called FASTRACK, has invested millions of dollars in identifying high-risk children and intervening in the schools as well as in the families to prevent the high-risk boys from becoming delinquents. Through working with the schools and with the families of these boys, the hope is that, if we start early enough in their lives, we can socialize children in ways that prevent them from becoming antisocial teenagers.[15] The results of these programs are unclear at present. But the theory behind them seems sound.

It strikes us that Cobras come from such chaotic and traumatic family backgrounds that the only way to prevent their turning into hard-core batterers is to work with them at a very early age. There is hope for future generations if we can start early enough.

Other federally funded prevention programs include one study at the University of South Carolina that is currently attempting to modify the behavior of young men in college,[16] since the rates of battering are even higher among dating couples than they are among those who eventually marry. Another program funded at the State University of New York at Stony Brook involves intervening with teenagers before their dating habits become established to teach different ways of relating to the opposite sex in order to establish alternatives to violence.[17] Again, it is too early to tell whether these programs will be successful. But we favor the approach of prevention programs. Although we have more confidence in programs that begin when boys are very young, any attempt to train boys before they become batterers is more likely to succeed than an intervention after the battering has become an established part of the man's way of treating women.

It is not that we lack sympathy for the perpetrators of domestic violence, because their lives have often been plagued by difficulties unfathomable to most of us. By labeling them as Pit Bulls and Cobras, we do not mean to imply that they are subhuman, simply that—as far as battered women are concerned—they are best thought of as predators. As scientists such as Dutton have pointed out, they are, in many ways, victims themselves. They were often abused, and Pit Bulls may often suffer from their own version of post-traumatic stress disorder. However, their own traumatic histories do not render them any less responsible for the battering. Whereas these histories may help explain the battering, they do not justify it.

Social Change. If we examine our patriarchal roots, and recognize battering as a phenomenon that has existed throughout the world for at least two thousand years, we must conclude that the elimination of violence against women—especially intimate partners—seems like a daunting task indeed. We leave the reader back where we started at the beginning of this chapter, with our belief that change will, by necessity, occur from the bottom up or not at all. Until our society is remade, the commitment of individual activists, professionals, criminal justice officials, and scientists is what we have to fall back on.

But, most of all, we can fall back on our greatest resource: the intelligence, the heroism, the wisdom, and the collective experiences of battered women. It is neither reasonable nor fair to expect battered women to solve the problem of domestic violence: that is up to the perpetrators, not the victims. But despite the failure of cultural and societal institutions to come to grips with this problem, we remain inspired by the victims of battering. We have learned that they *do* escape, despite grave personal risks, and that their means of doing so can inspire those who have not as yet left their abusive partners. We have also learned that those who have not escaped are no less heroic, but simply in life circumstances that have made their situations more difficult. We began this study with the goal of learning about the relationships between batterers and battered women, and we learned a great deal. We expected to focus on the men, especially when we came upon the distinction between Pit Bulls and Cobras. But as we followed the couples over time, we began to realize that our book was as much or more about the heroic struggle of battered women. These women start off with a dream that turns into a nightmare. They truly descend into hell, and for a period of time seem stuck there. But they do not give up. They continue to struggle. Our main cause for optimism is that many of them emerge from hell and live to love again.

Notes

Chapter 1

1. For example, see the groundbreaking national survey published by Murray A. Straus, Richard J. Gelles, and Suzanne K. Steinmetz, *Behind Closed Doors* (New York: Doubleday Press, 1980).
2. For example, see Robert E. Dobash and Russell P. Dobash, *Violence Against Wives: A Case Against Patriarchy* (New York: Free Press, 1979).
3. Lenore E. Walker, *The Battered Woman* (New York: Harper & Row, 1979); Lenore E. Walker, *The Battered Woman Syndrome* (New York: Springer Publishing Company, 1984).
4. Straus, Gelles, and Steinmetz, *Behind Closed Doors*.
5. Colleagues before us, most notably Dr. Gayla Margolin at the University of Southern California, had directly observed the interaction of couples where there was physical aggression. However, the couples they studied were not severely violent and would not have met criteria for inclusion into our study.
6. This work is nicely summarized in a book by Robyn Dawes, *House of Cards* (New York: Free Press, 1994).
7. See John M. Gottman, *Why Marriages Succeed or Fail* (New York: Simon & Schuster, 1994).
8. Ibid.
9. For example, see Mary P. Koss et al., *No Safe Haven* (Washington, D.C.: American Psychological Association Press, 1994).
10. Gottman has recently collected a substantial amount of data on a sample of newlywed couples, data which have not as yet been published. Dr. Thomas Bradbury at UCLA has collected similar data, as yet unpublished, which corroborate the high rate of physical aggression among newlyweds.
11. Two recent studies of couples prior to marriage and in the early

287

years following marriage have greatly increased our knowledge of the frequency of physical aggression during the early years of marriage. One study, conducted by Dr. K. Daniel O'Leary at the State University of New York at Stony Brook, is summarized in a chapter entitled "Physical Aggression Between Spouses" in *Handbook of Family Violence*, edited by V. B. Van Hasselt et al. (New York: Plenum Press, 1988). The other research program was conducted by Dr. Kenneth E. Leonard from the Research Institute on Addictions in Buffalo. This work is starting to be published. See, for example, Kenneth E. Leonard and Marilyn Senchak, "Prospective Prediction of Husband Marital Aggression within Newlywed Couples," *Journal of Abnormal Psychology* 105 (1996): 369–380.

12. Koss et al., *No Safe Haven*.
13. See Martin Daly and Margo Wilson, *Homicide* (New York: Aldine de Gruyter, 1988).

Chapter 2

1. Murray A. Straus, Richard J. Gelles, and Suzanne K. Steinmetz, *Behind Closed Doors* (New York: Doubleday Press, 1980).
2. See, for example, Janice E. Stets and Murray A. Straus, "Gender Differences in Reporting of Marital Violence and Its Medical and Psychological Consequences," in *Physical Violence in American Families*, edited by Murray A. Straus and Richard J. Gelles (New Brunswick, NJ: Transaction Publishers, 1990), pp. 151–165.
3. For example, see Dina Vivian and Jennifer Langhinrichsen-Rohling, "Are Bi-directionality Violent Couples Mutually Victimized? A Gender-sensitive Comparison," *Violence and Victims* 9 (1994): 107–123.
4. Angela Browne and Kirk R. Williams, "Exploring the Effect of Resource Availability and the Likelihood of Female-perpetrated Homicides," *Law and Society Review* 23 (1989): 75–94.
5. Amy Holtzworth-Munroe and Gregory L. Stuart, "Typologies of Male Batterers," *Psychological Bulletin* 116 (1994): 476–497.
6. Robert D. Hare, *Without Conscience* (New York: Pocket Books, 1993).
7. Kenneth E. Leonard, "Drinking Patterns and Intoxication in Marital Violence," in *Alcohol and Interpersonal Violence*, edited by S. E. Martin (National Institute of Alcohol and Alcohol Abuse Monograph No. 24, National Institute of Health Pub. No. 93-3496). (Rockville, MD: National Institutes of Health, 1993).
8. Kenneth E. Leonard and Marilyn Senchak, "Prospective Prediction of Husband Marital Aggression within Newlywed Couples," *Journal of Abnormal Psychology* 105 (1996): 369–380.

9. Donald G. Dutton, *The Batterer* (New York: Basic Books, 1995).
10. For example, see Amy Holtzworth-Munroe et al., "The Assessment and Treatment of Marital Violence," in *Clinical Handbook of Couple Therapy*, edited by Neil S. Jacobson and Alan S. Gurman (New York: Guilford Press, 1995), pp. 317–339.
11. Ibid.
12. Koss et al., *No Safe Haven* (Washington, D.C.: American Psychological Association Press, 1994).
13. Lenore E. Walker, *The Battered Woman Syndrome* (New York: Springer Publishing Company, 1984); Dutton, *The Batterer*.
14. John M. Gottman, *Why Marriages Succeed or Fail* (New York: Simon & Schuster, 1994).
15. Michael J. Strube and Linda S. Barbour, "The Decision to Leave an Abusive Relationship," *Journal of Marriage and the Family* 45 (1983): 785–793.
16. Margo Wilson and Martin Daly, "Spousal Homicide Risk and Estrangement," *Violence and Victims* 8 (1993): 3–16.
17. Koss et al., *No Safe Haven*.

Chapter 3

1. John M. Gottman, *Why Marriages Succeed or Fail* (New York: Simon & Schuster, 1994).
2. Robert E. Dobash and Russell P. Dobash, *Violence Against Wives: A Case Against Patriarchy* (New York: Free Press, 1979).
3. Neil S. Jacobson, "The Politics of Intimacy," *The Behavior Therapist* 11 (1989): 1–4.
4. Andrew Christensen and Christopher L. Heavey, "Gender Differences in Marital Conflict: The Demand-withdraw Interaction Pattern," in *Gender Issues in Contemporary Society*, edited by Stuart Oskamp and Mark Costanzo (Newbury Park, CA: Sage, 1993).

Chapter 6

1. John M. Gottman, *Why Marriages Succeed or Fail* (New York: Simon & Schuster, 1994).
2. Mary P. Koss et al., *No Safe Haven* (Washington, D.C.: American Psychological Association Press, 1994).
3. Amy Holtzworth-Munroe et al., "The Assessment and Treatment of Marital Violence," in *Clinical Handbook of Couple Therapy*, edited by Neil S. Jacobson and Alan S. Gurman (New York: Guilford Press, 1995), pp. 317–339.
4. Donald G. Dutton, *The Batterer* (New York: Basic Books, 1995).

Chapter 7

1. Brian M. Quigley, Kenneth E. Leonard, and Marilyn Senchak, "Desistance from Marital Violence in the Early Years of Marriage," *Violence and Victims* 11 (1996): 355–370. See also Scott L. Feld and Murray A. Straus, "Escalation and Desistance from Wife Assault," in *Physical Violence in American Families*, edited by Murray A. Straus and Richard J. Gelles (New Brunswick, NJ: Transaction Publishers, 1995).
2. Murray A. Straus, "Measuring Intrafamily Conflict: The Conflict Tactics Scale," *Journal of Marriage and the Family* 41 (1979): 75–88.
3. Etiony Aldarondo, "Cessation and Persistence of Wife Assault," *American Journal of Orthopsychiatry* 66 (1996): 141–151.
4. Ibid.; Koss et al., *No Safe Haven* (Washington, D.C.: American Psychological Association Press, 1994).
5. Donald G. Dutton, *The Batterer* (New York: Basic Books, 1995).
6. Diane R. Follingstad et al., "Effects of Battered Women's Early Responses on Later Abuse Patterns," *Violence and Victims* 7 (1992): 109–128.

Chapter 8

1. Margo Wilson and Martin Daly, "Spousal Homicide Risk and Estrangement," *Violence and Victims* 8 (1993): 3–16.
2. This story has been widely reported in the media, and our version condenses many sources. In particular, we relied on a report of the case which appeared on the television show *20/20* on September 17, 1991.
3. Donald G. Dutton, *The Domestic Assault of Women* (Boston: Allyn and Bacon, Inc., 1988).
4. Donald G. Dutton, *The Batterer* (New York: Basic Books, 1995).
5. Mary P. Koss et al., *No Safe Haven* (Washington, D.C.: American Psychological Association Press, 1994).
6. Dutton, *The Batterer*.
7. Dutton, *The Batterer*.
8. Amy Holtzworth-Munroe et al., "The Assessment and Treatment of Marital Violence," in *Clinical Handbook of Couple Therapy*, edited by Neil S. Jacobson and Alan S. Gurman (New York: Guilford Press, 1995), pp. 317–339.
9. Cited in Dutton, *The Batterer*.

10. *B.E.R.T.H.A.: A Practical Guide to Working at a Domestic Violence Program in Washington State* (Olympia, WA: Washington State Coalition Against Domestic Violence, 1996).

11. Ibid.

12. Holtzworth-Munroe et al., "Assessment and Treatment."

13. Ibid.

14. "Mental Health: Does Therapy Help?" *Consumer Reports* (November 1995): 734–739.

15. See Barry D. Rosenfeld, "Court-ordered Treatment of Spouse Abuse," *Clinical Psychology Review* 12 (1992): 205–226.

16. Dr. Christopher Murphy recently reported some findings at the 1996 meeting of the American Psychological Association suggesting that batterers are less likely to be arrested again for the first year and a half after being referred by a judge to court-mandated treatment. However, since only a small proportion of battering episodes lead to arrest, and since emotional abuse was not measured in Murphy's study, these findings do not contradict the point we are making.

17. For example, see Neil S. Jacobson and Gayla Margolin, *Marital Therapy* (New York: Brunner/Mazel, 1979). See also Neil S. Jacobson and Andrew Christensen, *Integrative Couple Therapy* (New York: W. W. Norton, 1996).

18. See John M. Gottman et al., *Couples' Guide to Communication* (Champaign, IL: Research Press, 1976).

19. John M. Gottman, *Why Marriages Succeed or Fail* (New York: Simon & Schuster, 1994).

20. Jacobson and Christensen, *Integrative Couple Therapy*.

21. For example, see K. Daniel O'Leary, Dina Vivian, and Jean Malone, "Assessment of Physical Aggression in Marriage," *Behavioral Assessment* 14 (1992): 5–14.

22. Holtzworth-Munroe et al., "Assessment and Treatment."

23. Ellen Pence and Michael Paymar, *Education Groups for Men Who Batter* (New York: Springer, 1993).

24. L. Kevin Hamberger and J. M. Lohr, "Proximal Causes of Spouse Violence"; and D. G. Saunders, "Cognitive and Behavioral Interventions with Men Who Batter," in *Treating Men Who Batter*, edited by P. Lynn Caesar and L. Kevin Hamberger (New York: Springer, 1989).

25. Ibid.

26. For example, at Harborview Medical Center in the Department of Psychiatry, University of Washington, Dr. Steven Avery, in collaboration with Dr. Roland Maiuro, have been collecting preliminary data on batterers who are court-mandated for treatment.

27. For example, see Collins E. Lewis, "Neurochemical Mechanisms of Chronic Antisocial Behavior," *Journal of Nervous and Mental Disease* 179 (1991): 720–727.
28. Ibid.
29. Wilson and Daly, "Spousal Homicide."
30. Susan A. Wilt, Jeffrey Fagan, and Garth Davies, "Spatial and Structural Predictors of Domestic and Nondomestic Homicides of Women" (paper presented at the Fifth International Family Violence Research Conference, Durham, New Hampshire, June 29–July 2, 1997).

Chapter 9

1. Lenore E. Walker, *The Battered Woman Syndrome* (New York: Springer Publishing Company, 1984).
2. For example, see Edna Foa et al., "Behavioral/Cognitive Conceptualization of Post-traumatic Stress Disorder," *Behavior Therapy* 20 (1989): 155–176.
3. Mary A. Dutton, *Empowering and Healing the Battered Woman* (New York: Springer, 1992).
4. Donald F. Klein and Paul H. Wender, *Do You Have a Depressive Illness?* (New York: New American Library Trade, 1990).
5. Aaron T. Beck, A. John Rush, Brian F. Shaw, and Gary Emery, *Cognitive Therapy of Depression* (New York: Guilford Press, 1979).
6. David Burns, *Feeling Good* (New York: Bantam, 1982).
7. Peter M. Lewinsohn, *Control Your Depression* (Englewood Cliffs, NJ: Spectrum Companies/Macmillan General Reference, 1978).
8. Gerald L. Klerman, Myrna M. Weissman, Bruce J. Rounsaville, and Eve Chevron, *Interpersonal Psychotherapy of Depression* (New York: Basic Books, 1984).
9. Ginny NiCarthy, *Getting Free: You Can End Abuse and Take Back Your Life* (Seattle: Seal Press, 1986).

Chapter 10

1. Robert E. Dobash and Russell P. Dobash, *Violence Against Wives* (New York: Free Press, 1979).
2. Gerald Tierney, "The History of Domestic Violence as a Social Problem," *Social Problems* 160 (1984): 1–16.
3. Deborah Sontag, "For Some Battered Women, Aid Is Only a Promise," *New York Times*, February 14, 1997.
4. Dobash and Dobash, *Violence Against Wives*. See also Neil S. Jacob-

son and Andrew Christensen, *Integrative Couple Therapy* (New York: W. W. Norton, 1996).

5. *New York Times*, March 31, 1997. For a more complete report of homicide against women by their partners, see Federal Bureau of Investigation, *Crime in the United States 1995* (Washington, D.C.: U.S. Government Printing Office, 1996).

6. Angela Browne, *When Battered Women Kill* (New York: Free Press, 1987).

7. Murray A. Straus, Richard J. Gelles, and Suzanne K. Steinmetz, *Behind Closed Doors* (New York: Doubleday Press, 1980).

8. Lenore E. Walker, *The Battered Woman* (New York: Harper & Row, 1979); Lenore E. Walker, *The Battered Woman Syndrome* (New York: Springer Publishing Company, 1984); Mary P. Koss et al., *No Safe Haven* (Washington, D.C.: American Psychological Association Press, 1994).

9. Daniel G. Saunders, "Feminist-Cognitive-Behavioral and Process-Psychodynamic Treatments for Men Who Batter: Interaction of Abuser Traits and Treatment Models," *Violence and Victims* 11 (1996): 393–414.

10. Amy Holtzworth-Munroe and Gregory L. Stuart, "Typologies of Male Batterers: Three Subtypes and the Differences between Them," *Psychological Bulletin* 116 (1994): 476–477.

11. Saunders, "Feminist-Cognitive-Behavioral."

12. Pepper Schwartz, *Peer Marriage: How Love between Equals Really Works* (New York: Free Press, 1994).

13. Christopher Murphy, "The Effects of Coordinated Community Response on Recidivism." Paper presented at the meeting of the American Psychological Association, 1996.

14. Delbert S. Elliott, "Serious Violent Offenders: Onset, Developmental Course, and Termination—The American Society of Criminology 1993 Presidential Address," *Criminology* 32 (1994): 1–21. And Sharon Wofford-Mihalic, Delbert S. Elliott, and Scott Menard, "Continuities in Marital Violence," *Journal of Family Violence* 9 (1994): 195–225.

15. Conduct Problems Prevention Research Group, "A Developmental and Clinical Model for the Prevention of Conduct Disorder: The FAST Track Program," *Development and Psychopathology* 4 (1992): 509–527.

16. This research is being carried out by Diane Follingstad, Professor of Psychology, University of South Carolina.

17. This research is being conducted by K. Daniel O'Leary, Ph.D., Professor of Psychology at State University of New York at Stony Brook.

Index

295